HARD CHOICES:
FINANCIAL EXCLUSION
AND POVERTY IN URBAN CANADA

When low-income city dwellers lack access to mainstream banking services, many end up turning to 'fringe banks,' such as cheque-cashers and pawnshops, for some or all of their financial transactions. *Hard Choices* examines this predicament of 'financial exclusion' faced by those underserved by conventional financial institutions.

In this book Jerry Buckland thoroughly integrates economic and social data on consumer choice, bank behaviour, and government policy to determine the nature and causes of financial exclusion. He demonstrates why the current two-tier system of banking is becoming increasingly dysfunctional, especially in the context of new credit products that exacerbate financial inequality and stifle local economic growth. The first study of its kind in Canada, *Hard Choices* also presents policy recommendations on both the public and private levels to promote financial inclusion for all.

JERRY BUCKLAND is a professor at Menno Simons College at the Canadian Mennonite University, and is affiliated with the University of Winnipeg.

JERRY BUCKLAND

Hard Choices

Financial Exclusion, Fringe Banks, and Poverty in Urban Canada

UNIVERSITY OF TORONTO PRESS
Toronto Buffalo London

© University of Toronto Press 2012
Toronto   Buffalo   London
www.utppublishing.com
Printed in Canada

ISBN 978-1-4426-4033-7 (cloth)
ISBN 978-1-4426-1252-5 (paper)

Printed on acid-free, 100% post-consumer recycled paper with vegetable-based inks.

Library and Archives Canada Cataloguing in Publication

Buckland, Jerry, 1961–
Hard choices : financial exclusion, fringe banks, and poverty in urban
Canada / Jerry Buckland.

Includes bibliographical references and index.
ISBN 978-1-4426-4033-7 (bound).   ISBN 978-1-4426-1252-5 (pbk.)

1. Discrimination in banking – Canada.   2. Urban poor – Canada.
3. Urban poor – Canada – Finance, Personal.   4. Banks and banking –
Canada.   5. Poverty – Canada.   I. Title.

HG2704.B83 2011   332.1′750869420971   C2011-906301-8

University of Toronto Press acknowledges the financial assistance to its
publishing program of the Canada Council for the Arts and the Ontario
Arts Council.

   Canada Council   Conseil des Arts
   for the Arts   du Canada   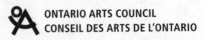 ONTARIO ARTS COUNCIL
   CONSEIL DES ARTS DE L'ONTARIO

University of Toronto Press acknowledges the financial support of the
Government of Canada through the Canada Book Fund for its publishing
activities.

To Elizabeth and Daniel

As the big door swung behind me I caught the echo of a roar of laughter that went up to the ceiling of the bank. Since then I bank no more. I keep my money in cash in my trousers pocket and my savings in silver dollars in my sock.

Stephen Leacock, My Financial Career

Contents

x   Contents

Illustrations

Tables

Figures

Foreword

Many low-income urban residents in Canada obtain basic financial services from cheque-cashing outlets, payday lenders, and pawnshops. Yet the payment services and loans offered by these 'fringe banks' are much more expensive than comparable services offered by banks and credit unions. Why do the poor pay more? Are they economically irrational? Are there barriers excluding them from mainstream banks? Furthermore, are there policy measures that the federal and provincial governments or banks might take that would improve the financial service options for those who use fringe banks?

Exploration of these questions is at the heart of this engaging, well-informed book. Jerry Buckland's approach is to frame the issues and draw on a broad range of research conducted in Canada, the United States, Great Britain, and other countries that yields essential insights. In the case of the research focusing on Canada, Buckland himself conducted or participated in the majority of the projects. In fact, over the past decade he has undoubtedly been the most prolific scholar focusing on financial exclusion in Canada, and *Hard Choices* provides a comprehensive account of what he has learned about the reasons people turn to fringe banks and what policies he thinks might improve financial services for many marginalized members of society. As someone who has conducted research for over twenty years on these issues as they relate to the United States, I have often turned to Buckland's writings to understand the Canadian context and to challenge my thinking about the subject.

The research that Buckland draws on in *Hard Choices* ranges from classics in the field, such as David Caplovitz's 1967 book, *The Poor Pay More*, to articles published as recently as 2010. The work also varies by methodology. Much of it is quantitative. Buckland, for example, reviews what we know from formal household surveys addressing the use of financial services by various demographic groups. He provides data on the relevant financial services offered by banks and fringe banks in Canada and the associated fees and regulations. He documents changes over time in the numbers of fringe banks and mainstream bank branches. In addition to this quantitative analysis, *Hard Choices* includes an overview of what Buckland learned from field research that he and others conducted in low-income communities in Toronto, Vancouver, and Winnipeg. In this research they talked with about a hundred socially and economically marginalized individuals about the financial services they use, their rationales for their choices to use banks or fringe banks, and their related experiences and perceptions. While such intensive, small-scale field research does not provide statistically reliable results, it does yield insights into the thinking behind people's financial choices and enriches the portrait provided by the numerical data alone.

In tackling these topics, Buckland takes a balanced and nuanced perspective. Banks and fringe banks are not villains or saints, and their lower-income customers are not ignorant pawns. Many individuals clearly make rational choices to use fringe banks because they face a variety of barriers to using mainstream banks, such as transportation costs or inadequate identification. And Buckland certainly does not romanticize the situation of the people he interviews. As he reports from his field work, 'Substance abuse took a huge toll on the lives of several respondents.'

In analysing possible policy measures that might improve financial service options for the urban poor, Buckland is clear about his fundamental perspective: 'Financial inclusion is a must for all Canadians. . . . And the state has a responsibility to ensure that this can happen.' Specifically, Buckland argues for increasing the pressures on banks to offer financial services that meet the needs of the poor in terms of location, operating hours, and cheque-hold policies, among other things. The fees for basic banking services should be simple, low, and, whenever possible, levied up front. Buckland proposes that the costs associated with this outreach effort might be covered by a 'basic banking' tax on banks. Buckland also analyses four recent innovative initiatives in various Canadian cities to bring marginalized individuals into the banking system. Three of these initiatives involved partnerships between banks or credit unions and community groups. Buckland argues that these pilot programs suggest a direction that public policy could support if financial inclusion is to become the priority he argues it should be.

Hard Choices should be read widely by Canadians interested in poverty issues or the structure of the financial system. One does not need to agree with the author's public policy prescriptions to recognize that the book provides the most comprehensive existing account of what Buckland calls a 'two-tiered' Canadian banking system and why many low-income urban households turn to fringe banks. The book should also greatly interest scholars and policymakers outside of Canada who focus on financial services for the poor in high-income countries, for it frames the issues clearly, provides an excellent overview of the relevant literature, and is a first-rate case study of the Canadian situation.

John P. Caskey
Professor and Chair, Department of Economics, Swarthmore College
Author of *Fringe Banking: Check-Cashing Outlets, Pawnshops, and the Poor*

Acknowledgments

I am grateful to many people for sharing with me their insights and enthusiasm on the topic of financial exclusion. I am particularly thankful to Rick Eagan, Antonia Fikkert, and Marilyn Brennan for the assistance and leadership in a research project that informed portions of this book.

Some of the research on which I drew for this book comes from a project funded by the Social Sciences and Humanities Research Council (SSHRC), to which I am grateful. The research project involved many people in three cities – Toronto, Vancouver, and Winnipeg – and included many residents who participated in the field research, gave their time, and shared with us parts of their lives. I would like to thank some of the many research assistants on the project: Daniel Liadsky, Marni Lifshan, and Jennifer Mussell in Toronto; Barbara Caldwell and Stacy Clark in Vancouver; and Coralee Buckley, Jennifer Braun, Jessica Leigh, Teresa Chernecki, Angela Slater, and Erin Vosters in Winnipeg. The project was facilitated by people within several organizations, including Marcia Nozick (Embers); Kersten Stuerzbecher and Dan Small (PHS Community Services Society); Andrew Douglas (SEED Winnipeg); and Lynne Woolcott, Miryam Zerballos, and Maureen Fair (St Christopher House).

I am grateful for the collaborative research on financial exclusion with which I have been involved over the last ten years with people from a variety of backgrounds, including Priscilla Boucher, David Clarke, Xiao-Yuan Dong, Françoise Gosselin, Charles Klingman, Thibault Martin, Brian McGregor, Barry Nolan, Chris Robinson, Jennifer Robson, Wayne Simpson, and Byron Williams.

I would like to thank John P. Caskey, who read the entire draft manuscript and provided me with timely and helpful comments and support. I would also like to thank the two anonymous reviewers of the draft manuscript for their helpful comments. I would like to thank the many people with whom I worked at the University of Toronto Press including Virgil Duff, Doug Hildebrand, and Anne Laughlin. I am most grateful for the careful editing of the manuscript by Angela Wingfield and the extensive index created by Judy Dunlop.

I am grateful to Menno Simons College (a part of Canadian Mennonite University and affiliated with the University of Winnipeg), Dean Peachey, and Earl Davey for support during the research and writing process. I would also like to thank Jino Distasio, Tom Carter, and the staff at the Institute of Urban Studies at the University of Winnipeg for logistical support.

I am most grateful to my wife, Elizabeth Buckland, who has supported and encouraged me throughout the research and writing process.

HARD CHOICES:
FINANCIAL EXCLUSION, FRINGE BANKS,
AND POVERTY IN URBAN CANADA

Introduction

Hard Choices: Financial Exclusion, Fringe Banks, and Poverty in Urban Canada examines financial exclusion among low-income people in inner cities and the resulting hard choices they need to make about their banking. This book seeks to understand why some urban, often inner city, citizens do not have a bank account or access to other banking services. This introduction and chapters 1 through 4 analyse the nature, causes, and consequences of not having access to sufficient banking while living on a low income. In chapter 5 the book takes a prescriptive approach by examining how the policy and practice of banking might be changed to build financial inclusion.

Financial exclusion is the situation faced by people who have no relationship, or an insufficient relationship, with a mainstream financial institution, such as a bank or credit union, to meet all their financial service needs. As a consequence, many people rely for all or a portion of their financial services on fringe banks such cheque cashers and pawnshops. Some argue that financial exclusion is the result of a voluntary decision on the part of the poor consumer. Mainstream bank branches, their services, and their staff are readily available so that consumers can freely choose to use these services, or not. Others argue that it is difficult to make voluntary decisions when they are faced by profound structural obstacles. This group argues that the determinants of financial exclusion lie in structural obstacles created by mainstream banks and, indirectly, by government policy.

Rather than arguing that financial exclusion is caused by one particular reason, this book argues that there are three important elements to financial exclusion: banking operations, citizen's choice, and government policy. Bank operations, including account offerings and branch placement, are guided by the profit goals of the bank's shareholders. Citizens use banking services to facilitate their financial lives, and choose those services based on what is available to them. Finally, through government policy, various levels of government establish the parameters within which banks can operate and consumers are or are not protected.

By *mainstream* financial institution (FI) or bank is meant a bank, trust, credit union, or *caisse populaire* that accepts deposits and is regulated by the federal or provincial governments. Financially excluded people rely for some of their financial services on fringe banks, such as cheque cashers, payday lenders, and pawnshops, or informal financial services through, for example, the corner store, a family member, or a friend. *Fringe banks*, defined as companies that are primarily or exclusively in the business of financial service provision but do not accept deposits or face federal regulations, have been around in the form of pawnshops for centuries. Today they are better known thanks to the rapid and recent growth in the number of payday lender outlets in urban Canada. *Informal financial services* have also been around for centuries and are defined as those financial services that are offered through family, friends, and local retailers, but are not their principal business.

This book is concerned with the situation of financial exclusion for low-income people living in Canadian inner cities. This is not to say that financial exclusion is faced only by these people. The data suggest that some better-off people are, for various reasons, financially excluded. For instance, some who use payday loans are middle-income people who do not get all their banking services from mainstream financial institutions. These people are not the focus of this study. Also, there are, no doubt, poor people in urban suburbs and rural areas who do not have sufficient bank access. This book does not examine these groups, although some of its analysis may be relevant for suburban poor. The financial exclusion situation of the rural poor is not addressed here, and likely their situation is qualitatively different.

Why focus on urban, specifically *inner-city*, financial exclusion? Inner cities (and depressed suburbs) face multiple challenges, including residents with high rates of poverty and an impoverished community economy. These urban neighbourhoods struggle with high rates of unemployment, incidence of low income, and low rates of social indicators such as mean years of schooling and incidence of home ownership. An interesting analysis of a struggling community economy is David

Caplovitz's (1967) *The Poor Pay More*, which studied the spending experiences of residents of a New York City neighbourhood. It found that they often relied on small-sized local retailers and consequently paid more for their goods than if they had gone to larger retailers. The community economic development literature has expanded on this notion of a struggling local economy to add characteristics such as few and poorly paid local jobs, lack of infrastructure, and an unsafe local environment (Loxley, Silver, and Sexsmith 2007; Shragge 1993). Exclusion is more than financial, as it includes exclusion from other retail services, and it is more than consumer related, as it includes exclusion from well-paying jobs and safe and well-constructed neighbourhoods.

The focus on *Canadian* inner cities was justified by the relatively limited amount of analysis available on the topic for Canada. The literature on financial exclusion in the United States has been around for some time (Caskey 1994; Squires 2004; Squires and O'Connor 2001). The British (for example, Leyshon 2004; Kempson and Whyley 1999b) and European (Anderloni et al. 2008; Carbo 2007) literature on the topic is also better developed than that in Canada. Important Canadian studies, discussed in more detail in chapter 2, include both analytical and empirical work by Ramsay (2001, 2003) and Robinson (2006).

Hard Choices is meant to highlight the fact that low-income urban people face difficult decisions about financial services. There has been a growth in the number of fringe bank outlets in many inner cities, while available evidence points to a reduction in the number of mainstream bank branches. As we shall see, fringe bank services often have certain benefits such as convenience and possibly friendlier service than that of mainstream banks. However, in comparison with equivalent mainstream bank services, they are expensive and often unregulated or under-regulated, leading to variable service quality. So where does one bank? At the fringe bank that offers convenience, higher fees, less rigid rules, possibly friendlier and/or shakier service quality? Or does one travel further, to a mainstream bank, in order to pay less but face more rigid rules and staff who are less interested in your business? It is a hard decision because none of the options is good, particularly in comparison with the type of banking that many non-poor people utilize. Banking operations and government policy create a context in which urban residents have limited options, and the banking services they use may reinforce their poverty.

While the book focuses on the relationship between the consumer and the firm, it pays some attention to the structure of financial services markets. Portions of the book, particularly chapter 4, draw on basic concepts from the economics industrial organization (IO) literature to understand financial exclusion, but it is certainly not an in-depth IO study of banking in Canada.

Argument

The argument presented in this book is that financial exclusion has a lot to do with the social and economic context in which people live. That is not to say that individuals have no agency to make choices. Clearly they do. This is no doubt important, but *Hard Choices* is not an examination of the psychological behaviour of a group of people with regard to their financial service choices. That would be an interesting study, and the growing work in the field of behavioural economics is one way in which this might be done. This particular study, however, is one that finds the social and economic context to be important in determining bank choice. Some of the more salient factors affecting financial exclusion are the income and consumption levels of the bottom quintiles of the population; bank policy regarding such things as branch placement and fees and rules for basic banking services; and government policy regarding social entitlements and bank responsibilities. The context of the choice matters. That is the argument in this book and the focus of this study. Getting the context right does not completely resolve financial exclusion, but it is an important factor.

Theory

There is a variety of theories and methods that are used to analyse financial exclusion. They range from neoclassical economic theory to poverty-community analysis to political economy. Owing to the variety of theories and their importance in the examination process, an entire chapter of the book, chapter 2, is dedicated to looking at them. The study gets its theoretical direction from two main sources: poverty-community analysis and institutional theory. *Poverty-community analysis* is an approach that begins with the experiences of low-income people and includes an understanding of the structures that reinforce inequality and poverty. This approach pays particular attention to class, gender, ethnicity, and urban locale as causes of poverty. Here, *institutional theory* refers to analyses that seek to understand the broad context and key institutions involved in the social reality being studied, with particular reference to economic and social issues such as the demand side and the supply side of financial services.

Some key components of the theory used in this book include the geographic locus, the key actors, the relationship between financial exclusion and poverty, and financial service needs. Let us examine each of these in turn.

Geographic Locus and Actors

The approach taken in this study is, in part, rooted in poverty and community studies. The literature is concerned to understand local places and people that struggle with poverty. The primary geographic locus of this book is Canadian low-income inner-city and suburban neighbourhoods. It is understood that these neighbourhoods are located within a wider national and international space. Since banking is regulated at the national level, this book will also be concerned with certain national-level issues. Found in many Canadian cities, the inner city is a region sandwiched between the downtown and the suburbs. It is also a concept that is linked to geographic poverty and marginalization. Of course, inner cities are not static places; over time, some witness improved economic position, and some experience deteriorating position. Some of the neighbourhoods in this study have experienced economic improvement via gentrification. Moreover, some inner city neighbourhoods are better off, and some are worse off. Conversely, as in the case of Toronto, some suburban neighbourhoods are worse off than other suburban and inner-city neighbourhoods.

THE KEY ACTORS

With a root in institutional theory, this study identifies and examines the key actors involved in financial exclusion. The actors that are considered central to the study of financial exclusion in this book are the financially excluded, banks, and government. Chapter 1 and, in particular, chapter 3 examine financially excluded people. Chapter 1 and, in particular, chapter 4, examine banks. Chapters 1 and 5 explore government actors and their policies.

FINANCIAL EXCLUSION AND POVERTY

Urban financial exclusion is closely tied to poverty. That is to say, inner cities in Canada have high rates of unemployment and reliance on social assistance; low incomes and assets; and a low level of education.

Along with low incomes and high unemployment, one finds higher rates of financial exclusion in inner cities. This will be discussed more below. The poverty and financial exclusion relationship is complex, but generally those who are poor are more likely to be those who are without a mainstream bank account and who rely on fringe banks. We do not offer a view on whether one factor – financial exclusion or poverty – causes the other factor, but these factors do move together to a certain extent. If income poverty were overcome in Canada, it would not mean that financial exclusion would be wiped out. Conversely, if there were adequate mainstream bank services in inner cities, it would not mean that poverty would be overcome. However, if income poverty were overcome and mainstream bank provision improved in inner cities, significant strides would have been made to overcome financial exclusion.

FINANCIAL SERVICE NEEDS: TRANSACTION AND DEVELOPMENTAL

An important distinction is drawn in this book with regard to transactions and developmental financial services. Individuals require financial services to meet daily and weekly needs, and they require financial services to meet longer-term needs. Short-term needs are for cash and bill payment services, and these are referred to as *transaction services*. Long-term needs are obtaining lump sums through savings or credit, and these are referred to as *developmental services*. Of course, financial services can sometime fall between or encompass both of these categories. For instance, a credit card – a lending system – can be used as a means of payment. Conversely, cashing a cheque at a fringe bank that does not require a hold period could be considered a short-term loan.

Nevertheless, it is understood that individuals and households need both types of financial services, transaction and developmental. Generally speaking, fringe banks specialize in transaction services: cheque cashing and bill payments. However, they also engage in lending – through rent-to-own agreements, payday loans, and pawn loans – and, by the definition above, these are a form of developmental service, albeit a very basic one. This is where the categories become muddied because fringe bank loans are small loans that are often for short periods and not tied with the mainstream bank system of credit reporting. Thus these types of loans might be seen more as an elaborate form of transaction service. The small size and short term of the loan makes it not too unlike cheque cashing; a payday loan is for twelve days, while cheque cashing might be considered a five-to-seven-day loan, depending on the hold period at a mainstream bank. On the other hand, repaying a payday loan in a timely fashion is not included in a mainstream bank–related credit report. Therefore, it does not matter how many payday loans are repaid in a timely fashion; the client's credit report will not improve to allow him or her access to cheaper sources of credit.

In addition to offering basic banking services, mainstream banks offer a variety of developmental financial services. Timely repayment of one's credit card, line of credit, loan, or mortgage can improve one's credit rating and allow one to obtain cheaper credit. Thus, using a mainstream financial institution presents scope for developing a relationship that works to the mutual advantage of the borrower (who gets cheaper credit) and the lender (who is better able to identify the credit-worthy customers).

Perspective

This book is rooted primarily in a reformist perspective. What this means is that it has identified a problem – financial exclusion – and it sees the solution coming from reforms to government and bank policy and practice. The problem is that the banking services available to certain urban residents are inferior to those available to other citizens. This problem is most clearly documented in poverty-and-community studies (chapter 3), but other data (for example, income distribution and low-income head count), discussed in chapter 1, reinforce the difficult economic situation facing certain people.

Change is needed to address the gaps in banking for these people. Reforms are understood to be qualitatively important to building financial inclusion, but they do require the dismantling of the financial services industry. What is required to combat the problem is ongoing attention, participation, and resources from banks and government. This is not to say that radical restructuring is not useful. Indeed, chapter 5 considers some radical restructuring of banking that might address financial exclusion. Some might argue that financial exclusion in Canada can only be addressed through radical restructuring. Some might argue for other reasons, such as the environment, that radical restructuring is necessary. These are legitimate arguments, but this book does not examine them in detail. Rather, it considers reforms that might improve things, on the edges, for people who have been marginalized by financial exclusion.

Approach

Analysis of the problem will be combined with possible solutions. As noted above, the book is primarily rooted in a reformist approach. Chapters 1 through 4 are largely analytical in their approach, and chapter 5 presents prescriptions for improved bank practice and policy with regard to financial inclusion. By combining analysis and prescription, the study seeks to participate in both the critiquing and the 'fixing' of the system. The risk is that the prescriptions are too removed from the reality of the people who are financially excluded or from the challenges of banking. However, it is felt that the risk is acceptable, particularly when it is understood that the prescriptions are put forward here with, I hope, humility and that implementation on a trial-and-error or learning approach is advisable.

The Sub-prime Mortgage Crisis

The U.S. sub-prime mortgage crisis affected economies around the world, including the economy of Canada. The impact was felt by financial institutions, their investors, and their consumers and, through an international recession, by states, workers, and citizens who were well removed from the banks and borrowers involved in the sub-prime mortgages. For many countries of the global North, this has meant higher unemployment, lower economic growth, and worsening poverty rates. The crisis has caused regulators in the United States, and elsewhere, to reconsider the orthodox view that financial sector liberalization is helpful for the economy and not dangerous. In the United States, liberalization is now making room for greater regulation of the financial sector.

Although Canada was affected by the sub-prime mortgage crisis, it was more insulated than some other countries, such as the United Kingdom and Iceland. Canada was affected directly in that the sub-prime mortgage product was used here, though not as extensively as in the United States, and Canadian banks were invested in U.S. bank holdings, though not as invested as other banks were. The indirect impact, through the U.S. recession, is another story. The United States is such a huge trade and investment partner that, indirectly, the Canadian economy was hit hard by its recession.

Canadian banks and the federal government took Canada's relative insulation from the sub-prime mortgage crisis as a vindication of our financial system. Instead of using the crisis as an opportunity to consider the state of its financial system, the federal government used the crisis as an occasion to trumpet its soundness. But what about the fact that there are sub-prime mortgages, sub-prime credit cards, payday loans, buy-back schemes, and other fringe financial services? These financial services may not be as large as the sub-prime mortgages in the United States, but they are similar devices: the suppliers are not well regulated, the services and fees lack transparency for the consumer, and they are high priced. Moreover, it is the most vulnerable consumers who often use these services. The U.S. sub-prime mortgage crisis was a powerful example of how an unhealthy relationship between banks and vulnerable consumers can ultimately cripple an economy. It has also led to a major rethink about economic theory and policy.

Data Sources and Purposes

The primary data for the book come from two sources: national surveys and field methods. The assumption of this study is that the different data offer useful insights for understanding financial exclusion. It is important to understand the purpose and limitations of these different types of data, which relate to the methods used to collect them. The purpose of quantitative methods such as national surveys is to provide data, for predetermined questions, that are representative of a population. The purposes of qualitative methods are quite different; they are intended to shape theory, diagnose problems, or simply ensure that the measurement is made for things that matter to the people being studied.

The few national surveys that have relevance to the study of financial exclusion are primarily referred to in this introduction. One source is the Statistics Canada Survey of Financial Security that was implemented in 1999 and 2005. It asked respondents about their banking and (in 2005) if they used payday loans; it also offers some insight into household finances. There are weaknesses with the survey, which will be discussed. There is a new relevant survey, the Statistics Canada Canadian Financial Capability Survey, which was implemented in 2009, but the data set was not publicly available at the time of writing.

Field research methods are also used, and these are drawn on particularly in chapter 2. These methods include small-sample neighbourhood surveys (which are actually described as a mixed method, having both quantitative and qualitative components) and life histories.

Quantitative methods, such as national surveys, have roots in a positivist approach to understanding; the researcher can separate himself or herself from the issue at hand and therefore objectively examine it. Qualitative methods, such as small-sample neighbourhood surveys and life histories, have roots in a 'post-positivist' tradition that starts from the premise that the researcher cannot be completely removed from the subject because he or she tends to take his or her own biases and assumptions into the research.

One way to think about quantitative and qualitative methods is to consider the concepts of *data reliability* and *data validity*. Data are reliable, in the research sense, when a method, as it is applied over and over again to different samples, leads to the same result. However, for a result to be valid, it must be a true statement about the population. It is possible to imagine data that are reliable (same results again and again) but not valid. So the result, when repeated, leads to the same results again and again but does not provide a valid (truthful) result.

For instance, imagine a group of academics who want to study financial exclusion. Their study may begin by defining financial exclusion and identifying some indicators of it. From the perspective of this group, it might be assumed that financial exclusion is largely the result of limited education, particularly financial education, on the part of the financially excluded. This might lead them to undertake a national survey about financial literacy, as a means to understand financial exclusion. But the resulting survey questions embed basic assumptions about the relationship between financial illiteracy and financial exclusion. These assumptions can create biases in the generated data. In fact, in some cases the questions can lead to results that confirm the relationship, when the relationship may be actually reverse or non-existent.

All dollar figures are in Canadian dollars unless otherwise noted. U.S. dollars have not been converted into Canadian dollars because, at the time of writing, the dollar values were roughly equivalent.

Outline of the Book

As mentioned above, this introduction and chapters 2 through 4 are largely analytical, while chapter 5 is prescriptive. The topics for each chapter are, respectively, the context of financial exclusion (chapter 1), theories of financial exclusion (chapter 2), an explanation of household-

level financial exclusion (chapter 3), the business of inner-city banking (chapter 4), and the options for improving financial inclusion
(chapter 5).

Chapter 1 examines the context of financial exclusion by presenting
available data on financial exclusion and its correlates. These correlates
are factors that seem to work in tandem with financial exclusion and
relate to indicators of low income or income poverty. The chapter provides data for Canada and compares these data with data from other
countries. It also examines salient elements of the policy and practice
of banking as they relate to financial exclusion. The chapter introduces
the main actors involved in banking policy and provision and considers their relationship to financial exclusion. Mainstream and fringe financial institutions are discussed, as are relevant federal government
policies such as the Access to Basic Banking Services Regulations and
provincial government-based consumer protection.

Chapter 2 considers theories of particular relevance to the study of
financial exclusion. Since financial exclusion is a complex problem, it
has been examined from a number of theoretical perspectives including neoclassical economic theory, behavioural economic theory, institutional theory, and political economy theory. This chapter describes key
elements of the theories with reference to financial exclusion and then
evaluates each approach. The chapter argues that a careful institutional
theoretical perspective that includes insight from a poverty-community
perspective provides a useful approach to understanding financial
exclusion.

Chapter 3 examines the reasons that people choose to be unbanked
and/or underbanked. It does this by drawing on field research that
examined financial service choice among inner-city residents in three
cities, Toronto, Vancouver, and Winnipeg. The chapter begins with a
description of the study neighbourhoods, the research methods, and
the background on the participating households. The next section examines the reasons that people choose certain types of financial services and describes respondents' recommendations for improving
mainstream banking services. The final section of chapter 3 seeks to
understand how poverty more generally affects peoples' lives and their
capabilities.

While chapter 3 explores the 'citizen side' of the financial exclusion
relationship, chapter 4 explores the 'business side' of inner-city banking. This chapter examines the financial services that are provided
in inner cities and seeks to understand the costs and returns of the

different types of banks that provide these services. It also presents data on bank branch numbers and considers evidence about changing bank locations. Finally, it presents data on mystery shopping completed in the three cities.

Chapter 5 examines options for improving financial inclusion. It begins by describing contrasting visions of what banking could be: radical, reformed, or the status quo. Then, picking up from the discussion of government policy in this introduction, it considers ways in which relevant government policy in Canada might be reformed to promote financial inclusion. Most notably, this could be achieved by expanding the basic banking regulations, extending government services, and unifying financial consumer protection. Drawing in part on lessons from chapter 2, the chapter then considers changes to banking that could make it more accessible, and services more useful for low-income people. Finally, it examines some currently available projects that address financial inclusion to a certain extent. These include community banking projects, asset-building projects, and financial literacy projects.

Chapter 6 presents some concluding thoughts about the nature of financial exclusion, particularly its relationship to poverty and the role of institutions. It also presents some prescriptive suggestions to advance our knowledge and response to financial exclusion.

1 The Context of Financial Exclusion in Canada

This chapter provides a contextual foundation for understanding financial exclusion in Canada. First, it seeks to measure financial exclusion by using national-level indicators. The results from these analyses will be summarized and compared with those of financial exclusion in other countries. This will include an examination of the evidence for the relationship between financial exclusion and poverty. Second, there will be an examination of the principal actors shaping the basic financial services sector, including banks, government agencies, and civil society organizations. Finally, the chapter reviews the government policies and regulations that shape basic financial services.

National Indicators of Household Finances, Financial Exclusion, and Financial Literacy

This section investigates various aspects of financial exclusion and literacy with particular regard to low-income Canadians. Before investigating specific issues, we first examine some important contextual features of Canadian society, such as trends in income, consumption, and debt. In some cases these data are available by income level, but not always. Moreover, even when data are available by income group, there is reason to believe that at least some variables for low-income Canadians are not entirely accurate. This point will be discussed below.

Household Finances

By analysing trends in household income, consumption, and debt, this section presents important insights into the reasons that some people are financial excluded.

Table 1.1
Annual after-tax income in constant 2007 dollars for all
units, 1976–2007

Year	After-tax income
1976	$58,600
1980	58,900
1985	56,400
1990	57,000
1995	54,100
2000	61,800
2005	65,800
2007	69,500

Source: Statistics Canada, n.d., *Table 2020706*

Canada is among the richest countries in the world and has had a good record with respect to social outcomes. According to the United Nations, in 2007 Canada had the seventh highest average national income – US$36,687. Its recent economic growth record has been strong. Between 1990 and 2005 Canada's real per capita income grew annually by 2.2%, reaching US$33,375 in 2005 (United Nations Development Program 2007–8, 277). This is higher than the Organisation for Economic Co-operation and Development (OECD) average of 1.8% during that same period. The Human Development Index (HDI) is a measure of human welfare and does so by equally weighing average national income, life expectancy, and educational attainment. With its good performance in all three of these measures, Canada had the fourth highest level of human development among 179 nations in 2007–8.

These data, however, do not directly address the distribution of economic and social outcomes. To explore this issue, we will consider economic performance in more detail. In the thirty-one-year period from 1976 to 2007, annual income for economic families and unattached individuals[1] changed only marginally (table 1.1). Real income sat at $58,600 in 1976 and dipped to $54,100 in 1995, rising to $69,500 in 2007 (Statistics Canada, n.d., *Table 2020706*). In thirty-one years the average income rose by just under $11,000, representing a 19% increase.

There is considerable discussion in the literature about the trend in income and asset distribution in Canada over the last twenty years.

Table 1.2
Gini coefficient for income distribution in Canada,
1976–2006

Year	Gini coefficient
1976	0.364
1981	0.348
1986	0.358
1991	0.364
1996	0.377
2001	0.392
2006	0.392

Source: Statistics Canada, n.d., *Table 2020705*

There seems to be a growing consensus that, overall, income distribution remained stable through the 1980s but started to become more unequal in the mid to late 1990s: 'In short, inequality of income and earnings increased significantly in the 1990s and particularly in the last half of that decade, a period that also displayed reduced buffering of inequalities in market incomes by the tax and transfer system' (Green and Kesselman 2006, 29).

One way to measure income distribution is with the Gini coefficient.[2] Over the fourteen-year period from 1996 to 2000, the Gini coefficient rose from 0.377 to 0.392, representing a 4% increase towards greater inequality (table 1.2). With a Gini coefficient of 0.392, inequality in Canada was higher than that of any of the other top twenty countries on the Human Development Index list, with the exception of the United States. This point is important in an analysis of financial exclusion as it may be a factor in explaining persistent low income, itself a factor that leads some people to rely less on mainstream banks.

Perhaps the worsening income distribution partly explains the subjective measures of happiness. According to the General Social Survey of Canada in 1986, 50% of respondents were very happy and 43% were happy. By 2005 those figure had reversed: 43% were very happy and 50% were happy (Statistics Canada 1986 and 2005). A declining share of Canadians claimed to be 'very happy.' Studies on happiness have found that happiness is more positively affected as one's relative position in society improves and not significantly affected if everyone's position improves (Anielski 2007, 28). If relative position is the deter-mining factor, then as income distribution worsens, subjective happi-ness will rise for the people whose income is rising and drop for the people whose income is declining. As a side point, one wonders if worsening income distribution and declining subjective evaluation of happiness might be a factor in explaining growing consumer debt, an issue dealt with below.

Incidence of low income is another factor to consider when examin-ing financial exclusion. As with income inequality, there is evidence that the incidence of low income rose through the 1990s. However, the data find that the low-income incidence stabilized in the 2000s. Using Statistics Canada's low-income cut-off (LICO) as the measure, there were just over 1.4 million families with low income in 1976, and this number jumped to almost 2.4 million in 1996; it dropped to just under 2.0 million in 2006 (table 1.3) (Statistics Canada, n.d., *Table 2020803*). The relevance of the incidence of low income is that, as we shall see below, it is negatively correlated with the probability of being banked. Thus, a rise in the incidence of low income will likely lead to a rise in financial exclusion.

Consumer debt-led growth is a term coined to describe an economic strategy, pursued particularly by Anglo-American states, that encour-ages consumer-debt accumulation in order to stimulate the macroecon-omy (Montgomerie 2007). The strategy is driven by the simultaneous goals of economic growth and low inflation. Low inflation is achieved by keeping wage demands, and therefore income, down. Since eco-nomic growth relies on consumption growth, expanding credit allows the economy to be stimulated through debt accumulation. Since subjec-tive measures of happiness are affected by one's relative position, it is understandable that some people facing stagnant wages and accessible credit will be pressured to maintain a living standard by engaging in debt accumulation.

Consumption is a major driver of the Canadian economy. Over the past forty-five years or so, personal expenditure has represented around 60% of the Canadian national income, with the largest remain-ing expenditure being government spending and business investment (each running at close to 20% of national income in 2007).[3] In per capita terms, personal spending grew slightly from 1986 through the 1990s and grew faster in the 2000s (Statistics Canada, n.d., *Table 3800009*). Gov-ernment spending as a share of national income dropped slightly from around 23% in the 1960s to approximately 20% in the 2000s. Meanwhile business investment has risen from 10% in the 1960s to close to 20% in

Table 1.3
Incidence of low income in Canada, 1976–2006

Year	Number of people with low income
1976	1,438,000
1981	1,481,000
1986	1,635,000
1991	1,976,000
1996	2,384,000
2001	1,963,000
2006	1,996,000

Source: Statistics Canada, n.d., *Table 2020803*

the 2000s. This shows the macroeconomy has a persistent reliance on consumption. Disposable income per capita showed a similar trend to that of personal spending, rising slower in the 1990s than in the 2000s (Statistics Canada, n.d., *Table 384).*[4] Spending made up a growing share of disposable income from 1986 (83.0%) to 2001 (96.3%).

Canadian consumer debt has risen to historic levels. And this has attracted attention in the popular press. Of course, consumer debt per se is not a problem; it can be used to raise productivity and increase a household's ability to service debt. But debt can become unwieldy or unsustainable. One way to measure the sustainability of debt is with the debt-to-income ratio, that is the ratio of the average household's stock of debt to its annual income. This ratio is high and has been rising steadily through the 1990s, to 142% by 2009 (second quarter) (Bank of Canada 2009, 24). As compared with a group of fifteen OECD countries, Canada ranked in the middle of the group in 2005, just below other, sometimes referred to as Anglo-American countries (United States, United Kingdom, Australia, and New Zealand) and the Netherlands and Denmark. In terms of the share of the population holding non-mortgage debt in 2006, among twelve OECD nations Canada ranked third, with just over one-half holding non-mortgage debt, after New Zealand and the United States (OECD 2006). The proportion of households holding this debt in France and Germany was much lower, at 30% and 15% respectively.

Other indicators of debt sustainability are not as troubling. When debt is considered in relation to household assets or net worth, then the figures have not risen so steeply, owing to the rising value – in 2007 – of home and equity holdings. Average household debt-to-assets (household debt as a ratio to household assets) rose slightly from 14.9% in 1990 to 16.2% in 2006 (Bank of Canada 2008, 29) and reached 17.8% in 2008, the highest since 1991 (21). The direction of asset prices is critical in this analysis because the sustainability of debt moves in concert with asset prices. In its review of asset values the Bank of Canada commented, 'In the near term, asset values are unlikely to provide much support to the financial situation of Canadian households' (2008, 21).

A final indicator of debt sustainability considered here is debt servicing. Household debt servicing (debt servicing costs as a percentage of income) stood at 7.7% in the second quarter of 2010 owing to low interest rates. Examining the host of debt indicators, even the Bank of Canada is beginning to be concerned about household debt levels:'While these simulation results are purely illustrative, based on simplifying assumptions, they remain qualitatively informative. They suggest that, over the medium term, more households would have a reduced ability to weather adverse shocks with further growth in the debt-to-income ratio in an environment of rising interest rates' (Bank of Canada 2009, 26).

What is more concerning is how the debt is distributed through the population. In a recent analysis of Canadian consumer debt, one study found that 30% of households have no debt, but it also found that the least wealthy quintile had the second-fastest rate of debt growth between 1999 and 2005 (4.4% per annum), and it was the only group to experience a decline in median net worth, by 2.3% (Certified General Accountants Association of Canada 2007). The authors note, 'What is possibly more perplexing is that those with the least amount of net worth had been able to increase their access to credit at a much steeper pace than that of other families' (37). The numbers of people with debt in the lowest quintile tripled between 1999 and 2005, and in the 1999–2005 comparison the people with annual incomes between $20,000 and $29,000 had the highest increase in debt-to-asset ratios, from 10% to 14%.

Finally, Canadians, on average, are spending a larger amount of money on financial service fees. Since 1997, these fees have increased from $238 in 1997 to $333 in 2007. This represents a 40% increase (Statistics Canada, n.d., *Table 2030015*).[5]

The Canadian economy has grown in the last twenty years, but that growth has benefited some more than others, and it has not effectively translated into subjective well-being. Moreover, consumer-led growth in the face of low inflation targets has fostered growing debt that may be unsustainable for the average person and is more likely unsustainable for the low-income debtor. Commenting on the economic growth strategy of the United States, the United Kingdom, and Canada, Montgomerie notes, 'Thus, economic growth in the 1990s has heavily relied on consumer debt-led spending. Therefore, despite the claims made by the advocates of neoliberalism, policies of non-inflationary growth have not led to enduring prosperity. Instead, the over dependence on private individuals to continue consuming to drive the system forward [has] led to new prospects for instability and crisis' (2007, 170).

Financial Exclusion

The proportion of people who do not have a bank account is the common measure for *unbanked*, one of two forms of financial exclusion. The second measure, the *underbanked*, is less well defined but has to do with people who are unable to access the full range of banking services that they need. Since unbanked is a relatively straightforward concept, there are more data available for it. Data to examine the underbanked concept are less available.

Measuring financial exclusion is complicated by the fact that the quality of national survey data may not be as strong for low-income people as it is for the non-poor. This is due to the under-coverage problem for low income and affects some types of surveys (for example, telephone-based) more than others (in-person). The reason for this is that low-income people are more likely to not have a long-term residence, to be transient (the homeless), and to not have a telephone. The first two points act as a factor in under-coverage of low-income people through in-person surveys, while the last factor acts as an obstacle for adequate coverage in telephone-based surveys.[6]

INTERNATIONALLY

In terms of people without a bank account, Canada ranks near the top of Northern nations. Unbanked proportions in the global North range from very low levels in some northern European countries (Netherlands, 0.5%; Denmark, 0.7%; Sweden, 1.6%) through low levels in France (2.8%) and Germany (2.9%) to higher levels in the United Kingdom (8%) and the United States (9%). The highest levels in the North are found in, among others, Ireland (16.7%) and Italy (22.4%).

Unbanked rates are much higher in the global South, ranging from 54% in South Africa through 65% in Mexico to 80% in India.

Financial exclusion in the global South has been the subject of a number of studies recently (World Bank 2009; Fernando 2007; Beck, Demirguc-Kunt, and Peria 2006, 2005; Commonwealth Business Council and Visa 2004). Factors explaining the substantially larger shares of unbanked populations in the South relate to lower levels of infrastructure (such as roads and communications), poorer levels of governance in the formal economy, and the tradition and experience of people with informal financial services. Interestingly, the rapid increase in microcredit is changing the complexion of financial services in some Southern nations, notably Cambodia, Afghanistan, Nicaragua, Democratic Republic of Congo, Ethiopia, and Bangladesh. For most countries in the South, banks serve the bulk of the banked population. One study of forty-six Southern nations concluded that in twenty-five of those nations 90% of the banked population was served by banks (World Bank 2009, 66). However, for some Southern nations, microfinance institutions (for example, non-governmental organizations and microcredit banks) have raised the banked portion of the population substantially, in some cases from 40% to 70% (World Bank 2009, 66). Consider, for instance, Bangladesh, an important original site of microcredit and where Mohammad Yunus famously began the Grameen Bank. It is estimated that approximately 50% of the adult population is banked (World Bank 2009, 7). However, roughly one-half of these banked persons receive their financial services through banks, and the other half receive their financial services through microcredit institutions (World Bank 2009, 66). In 2005, microcredit institutions were serving 13.6 million Bangladeshis (Fernando 2007, 18).

Studies that examine the socio-economic characteristics of the unbanked generally find that the probability of being unbanked rises with lower incomes. For instance, for the United States in 2001 where approximately 9% of adults are unbanked, the proportion of unbanked rises to 36.7% of households at the bottom decile (Hogarth, Anguelov, and Lee 2005, 14). Moreover, based on a logistic regression, Hogarth, Anguelov, and Lee found that banked household members had higher income and net worth, were married without children, had higher levels of education, were white and employed, and owned a vehicle (2005, 8). A recent study drawing on a large sample of unbanked residents of Detroit noted that many people are not permanently unbanked, but are temporarily so. People may move in to, and out of, a relationship with a bank over the course of their life (Blank and Barr 2009). Moreover, many people use both fringe and mainstream bank services simultaneously.

Studies in the United Kingdom come to similar conclusions where approximately 8% of adults are unbanked. One study estimated that a further 20% of adults are 'on the margins of financial services.' Once again, using a logistic model based on a survey of almost 16,000 respondents, this study found that the likelihood of being unbanked rose with unemployment, lower income, and more insecure housing tenure and that marital status, age, and educational attainment were also related (Devlin 2005, 96).

CANADA

The benchmark measure for unbanked in Canada is found in the MacKay Report (Task Force on the Future of the Canadian Financial Services Sector 1998b), which found that 3% of adult Canadians were unbanked. This places the Canadian unbanked share close to Germany and France, below the United States and the United Kingdom, but above the northern European level. The MacKay Report drew its unbanked number from a survey conducted in 1996 by Options Consommateurs, a non-profit consumer organization based in Quebec. Other surveys measuring the unbanked include EKOS Research Associates (2001) (1.3%), Ipsos-Reid Corporation (2005) (2.9%), and the Canadian Financial Capability Survey (0.5%). The only unbanked indicator in the Surveys of Financial Security (1999 and 2005) came from a question asking respondents whether or not they had a bank account with a positive balance. The resulting unbanked variable lumped together those with no bank accounts and those with bank accounts having zero balances. This figure rose from 12% in 1999 to 13% in 2005 (Buckland and Simpson 2008).

All of these national survey results should be treated cautiously because of the tendency of these surveys to under-represent low-income people.[7] Given the relationship between unbanked and low income, under-surveying low-income people could lead to underestimation problems. The Options Consommateurs survey sought to address the under-representation problem by selecting respondents on the basis of location. The two surveys (EKOS and Ipsos-Reid) sponsored by the Financial Consumer Agency of Canada (FCAC) did not; they derived their sample through telephone calls. The major limitation of telephone surveys is that their samples are limited to

Table 1.4
Minimum number of unbanked in Canada, 1996–2005

Year	Population	Adult population*	3% Unbanked
1996	28,846,761	25,096,682	752,900
2001	31,021,300	26,988,531	809,656
2005	32,270,500	28,075,335	842,260

Source: Buckland 2007
*Assuming a constant adult share of the population for all three years, at 87%.

people who have a telephone. The Options Consommateurs survey sought to address possible under-representation of new immigrants and homeless people. If we assume that 3% of Canadian adults are unbanked, then the number of unbanked adults has increased from 752,900 in 1996 to 842,260 in 2005 (table 1.4).

There have been some efforts to use national-level data to examine the determinants of financial exclusion in Canada (Buckland and Dong 2008; Simpson and Buckland 2009). The evidence is that financial exclusion is correlated with poverty, but the causation question has not been addressed head-on. One study that used 1999 Survey of Financial Security data found that financial exclusion – indicated by bank account holding,[8] being denied a credit card, or using a pawnshop – was commoner among people who had low income, held low assets, and were single parents (Buckland and Dong 2008). Moreover, 'the financially excluded are more likely to have lower incomes and net worth and no registered savings, to not own a home, to have more children, rely more on government transfer payments, be sole parents, be less educated, and have fewer people to turn to for financial support' (Buckland and Dong 2008, 261).

A study that used both the 1999 and the 2005 Surveys of Financial Security to examine financial exclusion and credit constraint found similar results (Simpson and Buckland 2009). It found a modest increase in people without a non-zero bank account, from 12% to 13%. It found a larger share of people with no credit card, 21.1%, in 1999, dropping to 16.5% in 2005. The proportion of people using pawnshops[9] dropped slightly from 2.2% to 2.1%. The proportion of respondents using payday loans[10] in 2005, the only year that this topic was raised, was 2.6%. In terms of correlates with financial exclusion, the following were all significant independent variables for one or more financial exclusion variables: income, assets, age (through life-cycle changes), education, larger families with fewer earners, lone parents and families with children aged five to seventeen years, and home ownership (particularly mortgage-free). When the two samples were combined, Simpson and Buckland found a 'statistically significant evidence of growth in the incidence of each indicator of financial exclusion when other factors are held constant' (2009, 966).

Looking at measurements of the underbanked, the indicators presented above were not as straightforward as those for the unbanked. Devlin uses the UK Financial Services Authority definition of underbanked as people operating on the 'margins of financial services,' and he operationalizes this as people with only a few financial services (Devlin 2005, 78). He reports on the share of the British population that has no access to bank credit, no pension, no home insurance, and no life insurance, which ranges from 25% to 40%. For Canada, the share of people without a credit card was 16.5% (2005) (Buckland and Simpson 2008); the share without a registered retirement pension plan was 34.8% (1999) (Buckland and Dong 2008). One FCAC survey found that the share of respondents without insurance was 8.5% (EKOS Research Associates 2001). Of course, the underestimation problem affects all of these measurements, particularly the insurance measurement.

Financial Crises: The U.S. Sub-prime Mortgage Crisis and Beyond

The boom-and-bust cycles of growth and decline that characterize capitalist economies are driven sometimes by factors from the real economy and sometimes by factors from the financial economy. The international debt crisis of the 1980s, the Asian, Russian, and Argentinian financial crises of the late 1990s, the U.S. sub-prime mortgage crisis from 2007, and the Greek financial crisis of 2010 are examples of crises with financial roots.

Financial crises are driven by banking changes rooted in policy, practice, and/or technological change. The 1970s international debt crisis was rooted in the hasty lending practices of Northern banks to Southern states and businesses. The origin of the Asian financial crisis was the misguided financial sector liberalization that was driven by structural adjustment of the International Monetary Fund and the World Bank. Financial crises may spill over onto the rest of the economy (and global economy), but they often involve big economic actors such as banks, governments, and big business. The U.S. sub-prime mortgage crisis is an interesting case in that it involved big banks *and* low- and modest-income borrowers.

For our purposes, the U.S. sub-prime mortgage crisis involves two important components: securitization and sub-prime mortgages. Securitization is the bank process of bundling sub-prime mortgages into securities and then offering these 'asset-backed' securities to other borrowers. By doing so, the banks were able to offload the risky mortgages onto other investors in the United States and elsewhere. The interesting connection to the study of financial exclusion, and discussed in the introduction, is the sub-prime mortgage device. These mortgages were targeted towards people who were either highly indebted or poor. Borrower found the mortgages attractive because of such things as 'teaser' interest rates. Teaser rates are rates that are close to prime rate for a short term, say three years, after which the rates rise substantially. The convergence of declining housing prices, over-leveraged homeowners, and ignorant institutional investors conspired to create a financial and economic crisis.

The sub-prime mortgage crisis crippled the economy of the United States and, through investment channels, several others in Europe, notably Iceland, Ireland, and the United Kingdom. Canada was affected through Canadian banks' holdings of U.S. asset-backed securities. More significantly, however, Canada was affected because of our intertwined economies: as the U.S. economy went down, so did our exports. But Canada has its own sub-prime mortgage industry. It is estimated that the sub-prime mortgage industry in Canada is rapidly growing, representing 7% of all mortgages (compared with 22% in the United States), and was associated with a flurry of foreclosures in 2009 (McArthur and McNish 2009).

The innovation of the sub-prime mortgage device was to get credit out to marginal borrowers (poor or over-indebted), but at a price (higher interest rates). The impetus of sub-prime mortgages rings a similar note to that of fringe financial products. One author noted the similarity in sub-prime mortgages and payday loans with regard to low-income people in the United States: 'These new credit markets inverted the previous lending situation in minority areas. Before, banks would be reluctant to make any loans in these areas and residents were credit-starved. Now, banks rushed in, directly or through intermediaries, to make and securitise subprime (and payday) loans' (Dymski 2010, 247).

These new financing devices are used more extensively in the United States, but they are certainly available in Canada. That Canada has avoided its own sub-prime crisis is partly related to the smaller size of the sub-prime mortgage and fringe bank market and to a stronger real estate market, compared to those of the United States. But is this by luck or design? The Bank of Canada claims that Canada's relative insulation from the crisis is due to a principles-based system of careful supervision (Murray 2010).

The sub-prime mortgage crisis has altered the balance of power in the thinking and policymaking about financial services that favoured neoclassical economics, to favour other approaches such as behavioural economics and political economy (discussed in chapter 2).

Financial Literacy

It is sometimes argued that financial exclusion is the result of low financial literacy. People choose to use fringe banks because they simply do not understand the benefits of using mainstream banks. This argument – a version of 'blaming the victim'– is troublesome for two reasons. First, it assumes that poverty is explained by personal choice, and it dismisses the role of institutions and family history in influencing poverty. Second, it implies that, if poor people are poor because of poor decisions, then rich people must be rich because of good decisions.

The argument that financially excluded people are financially illiterate often comes from national-level surveys that do not identify the fact that people from different socio-economic backgrounds face different literacy requirements. A middle-class person who is saving for retirement through a defined contribution plan needs to understand the yield and risk levels of different types of investment products. A low-income person who has no plan to save does not need this knowledge. Therefore, to conclude that low-income people are less financially literate because they cannot compare different investment products is problematic. This type of conclusion was reached from national survey data for the United Kingdom (Atkinson et al. 2007) and for the United States (Hilgert, Hogarth, and Beverly 2003). Studies that have sought a more nuanced understanding of financial literacy across income levels are rare.

For Canada, data are more limited, being confined to a few questions in certain national surveys and small-scale surveys (for example, Buckland 2010).[11] The Canadian Financial Capability Survey was implemented in 2009, but, at the time of writing, only preliminary analysis was available (Arrowsmith and Pignal 2010). Other national surveys that contain some data on financial literacy include surveys sponsored by FCAC (2001, 2005, and 2006), and Statistics Canada's Survey of Financial Security (SFS) (1999 and 2006). The data are limited to questions about use of household budget. These surveys found that between one-third and two-thirds of respondents used a budget for household planning. One survey found that only one-third of respondents followed the budget closely (Les Études de Marché Createc 2006). However, in this same survey, 92% of respondents felt confident that they were making effective financial decisions. In their examination of a relationship between budgeting and income level, using SFS 1999 data, Buckland and Dong (2008) concluded that low-income respondents were just as likely as others to undertake budgeting. Drawing on a qualitative survey of residents in three Canadian inner cities, one study concluded:

> Contrary to results from some quantitative national surveys the results from this research found evidence of financial literacy among low-income respondents. Many participants were able to survive with very meager income and some found [creative] ways to diversify their income. Participants were knowledgeable about relative (not necessarily absolute) market prices and had some conception of relevant government programs and banking services. Given their limited credit and savings options most participants engaged in limited borrowing and savings. Where constraints were noted in financial literacy they related more to attitudes about finances and life goals and to detailed knowledge about institutional policies. Given these results come from a qualitative survey, in order to test the financial literacy question further a next step would be to develop a quantitative survey shaped by these results to administer to low-income people. (Buckland 2010)

Institutions of Relevance to Financial Exclusion

Banks: Sizes, Networks, Products, and Fees

MAINSTREAM BANKS AND CREDIT UNIONS

Mainstream banks and trust companies operate nationally and are regulated at the federal level. Credit unions and caisses populaires operate at the provincial level and are regulated provincially.[12] The current legislation dates from 1999, which was informed by the *Task Force Report on the Future of the Canadian Financial Services Sector* (the MacKay Report). The task force addressed several issues including foreign competition and financial consumer protection. The next review of the banking system is slated for 2012.

These regulations place banks into three groups, with *Schedule 1 banks* referring to Canadian banks. Regulations allow foreign banks that are seeking to establish operations in Canada to follow one of two routes. These banks – referred to as *Schedule 3 banks* – can operate branches in Canada, but the branches are subject to stricter regulations (for example, capital equivalency requirement) than are those of Schedule 1 banks.[13] *Schedule 2 banks*, foreign banks that establish Canadian subsidiaries, can accept deposits and may receive deposit insurance from the Canada Deposit Insurance Corporation. Canadian banks are large by global standards: in 2007, based on assets, the Royal Bank of Canada (RBC) was the thirty-eighth largest bank in the world, and all five of the Canadian big-five banks fell within the top fifty-five banks (Canadian Bankers Association 2009b). The largest six Canadian banks hold a large share of the financial services market, including more than 90% of total bank assets and about 76% of the total assets.[14] The top eight banks[15] in Canada had assets of just over $2.7 trillion at the end of 2008 (Canadian Bankers Association 2009b).

Canadian domestic banks are a major economic force in terms of providing liquidity services, contributing to national income and employment, and generating profit for shareholders. Canadian banks weathered the United States–based sub-prime financial crisis more effectively than did banks elsewhere. There are 6,000 bank branches in Canada, over 16,000 bank-owned automated teller machines (ATMs), 39,000 non-bank ATMs, 603,000 Interac direct-payment terminals, plus access to accounts via the Internet and telephone (Canadian Bankers Association 2009a). The big five banks had a total of 5,320 branches and 15,453 ATMs in Canada (table 1.5). Data on customer numbers are harder to find: RBC states that it had approximately 10 million clients in 2008. Banks operating in Canada contribute 3% to Canada's gross domestic product (GDP), paid $8.7 billion in 2007 taxes, and directly employ a quarter of a million people (Canadian Bankers Association 2009b). The finance and insurance sector combined had just over 700,000 full-time employees in 2008, which represented 5% of the full-time workforce in Canada (Statistics Canada, n.d., *Table 282*).[16]

Domestic banks and foreign-owned subsidiaries have generated profit for many years, topping out in 2007 with over $20 billion in net

Table 1.5
The big-five banks' branches, ABMs, and clients

	Bank branches	Bank ABMs	Clients
BMO	983	2,026	
RBC	1,174	4,149	~10 million
Scotiabank	1,016	2,943	
TD	1,097	2,635	~10 million (Canada and international)
CIBC	1,050	3,700	
Subtotal	5,320	15,453	

Source: 2008 annual reports and accountability statements

Table 1.6
Domestic and foreign bank net income, 2004–2008

	2004	2005	2006	2007	2008
Domestic bank net income	$13,559,250	$12,176,561	$19,348,206	$19,833,476	$12,583,124
Foreign bank subsidiary net income	$807,061	$929,762	$1,012,470	$923,161	$1,012,004
Domestic and foreign bank subsidiary total net income	$14,366,311	$13,106,323	$20,360,676	$20,756,637	$13,595,128
Domestic bank net income as % of total net income	94.4%	92.9%	95.0%	95.6%	92.6%

Source: Office of the Superintendent of Financial Institutions (n.d.)

income (table 1.6). Profitability declined in 2008 to $13.5 billion. Domestic banks earned the lion's share of total banks' profits. From 2004 to 2008 the share of profits going to domestic banks ranged from 92% to 96%. This left somewhere between 4% and 8% of profits accruing to foreign-owned subsidiaries.

Generally, banks in Canada are considered a good investment with rates of return that are higher than those in other major sectors of the economy (Ernst and Young LLP 2004). In fact, return on equity percentage

Table 1.7
Return on equity (%) for the big six domestic banks, 2004–2008

	2004	2005	2006	2007	2008	Average (2–5 years)
RBC			23.5	24.6	18.0	22.0
CIBC	18.7	−1.6	27.9	28.7	−19.4	10.9
Scotiabank	19.9	20.9	22.1	22.0	16.7	20.3
TD Bank Financial Group*			15.6	17.1	12.4	15.0
Bank of Montreal	19.4	18.8	19.2	14.4	13.0	17.0
National Bank of Canada				11.5	16.4	14.0

Source: Bank 2008 annual reports
*Return on invested capital

through the mid 2000s largely ranged from the mid-teens to the mid-twenties (table 1.7). With the exception of CIBC, the rates for each bank were consistent through this period. From the available data, RBC averaged the highest rate of return (for three years) at 22.0%, followed by Scotiabank (for five years) at 20.3% and Bank of Montreal at 17.0%. CIBC rates of return were the most volatile during this period, ranging from the highest, 27.9%, in 2007 to the lowest, −19.4%, in 2008.

Financial institutions in Canada are required to submit annual public accountability statements. These statements report on the bank's contributions to the Canadian economy and are required to include reporting on activities intended to improve access to banking services on the part of low-income, disabled, and senior citizens; involvement in support of community development, small business, and microcredit; branch closures; and charitable contributions. Specific data are not required for each of these issues. In reviewing the 2008 reports for the largest five domestic banks – BMO, CIBC, RBC, TD, and Scotiabank – one finds documents ranging in detail and topics and from a total size of 24 pages to 184 pages. Some credit unions, such as Vancity and Assiniboine Credit Unions, have followed suit. Some of these financial institutions have mission statements, or general statements about their underlying motives, that suggest a serious commitment to 'double- or multiple-bottom' lines including profitability, consumer satisfaction, and broader social and environmental commitments (box 1.1). Whether these financial institutions in fact deliver on these statements is beyond the scope of this study.

Box 1.1 Mainstream-Bank Statements about Goals and Missions

TD Bank Financial Group's 'Approach': 'We want to be the better bank – that includes being a sustainable, responsible, caring business. We simply can't do that by focusing only on the bottom line. We do it by having strategies to invest in our people, by becoming more diverse, by contributing to causes that matter to the community and by reducing the impact we have on the environment. We strive to do the right thing for our stakeholders and, in serving them, operate with integrity and respect on the job and in the community' (TD Bank Financial Group 2008, 19).

Bank of Montreal: 'As a responsible corporate citizen, BMO focuses on succeeding as a business, an outcome that best serves our shareholders and enables us to contribute to the wellbeing of our communities as well as society. At the same time, we operate our business ethically and transparently, endeavour every day to exceed our customers' expectations and strive always to be an employer of choice' (Bank of Montreal 2008, 3).

Vancity Credit Union's 'Mission': 'To be a democratic, ethical and innovative provider of financial services to our members. Through strong financial performance, we serve as a catalyst for the self-reliance and economic well-being of our membership and community' (Vancity Credit Union 2007, 16).

Caisses Desjardins du Québec's 'Mission': 'To contribute to improving the economic and social well-being of people and communities within the compatible limits of its field of activity:

• by continually developing an integrated cooperative network of secure and profitable financial services, owned and administered by the members, as well as a network of complementary financial organizations with competitive returns, controlled by the members;
• by educating people, particularly members, officers and employees, about democracy, economics, solidarity, and individual and collective responsibility' (Caisses Desjardins du Québec 2010.

With respect to improved banking access, several bank public accountability reports refer to low-fee accounts and improved access to ATMs for physically disabled people. Regarding the low-fee account, for instance, RBC refers to its low-fee account that allows fifteen transactions per month for a low fee; TD offers the Value Account, described as a low-fee basic account. These low-fee accounts are a part of a voluntary agreement that banks made with the FCAC: to offer an account with up to fifteen debit transactions for a monthly fee of around $4. The existence of these accounts says little about how these accounts are promoted and how many of these accounts were opened and closed for the year. Moreover, the banks do not report on how other factors – such as branch closures – might affect accessibility of these accounts. Several banks reported on the efforts they have made to make ATMs more accessible to physically disabled; for example, RBC and TD refer to the height of the ATM and the availability of audio jacks.

There was very little reporting in the bank accountability documents, however, about community development efforts. Two of the five reports (by CIBC and Scotiabank) had no reference to 'community development' (or 'community economic development'), and BMO's report had all of ninety-one words devoted to the topic including two projects, one of which was the funding of a large mural in Quebec City (Bank of Montreal 2008, 23). RBC's report for Canada was somewhat more detailed, describing its support for several financial literacy programs (Royal Bank of Canada 2009b, 22). TD referred to support of a few community initiatives including a neighbourhood engagement centre, Habitat for Humanity, and the United Way (TD Bank Financial Group 2009b, 131).

In terms of details on these community development initiatives, three of five banks had little or nothing to report, and one pointed to education programs that were largely directed to improve individual finances. The projects supported by TD had perhaps the closest fit to a typical community development approach. However, in this case – and the others – it is not clear how the bank supported these initiatives. In some cases there is reference to a grant (for example, TD's support for the neighbourhood education initiative was $1 million; RBC's support for a teacher-training program on financial literacy was $110,000), but in many cases there were no data provided.

While these reports may have their use, a general problem with them is a lack of standardized reporting, including an absence of data that would allow one to understand the significance of the points that are raised. In their present state one wonders if they provide 'window dressing' rather than deliberate goals and requirements to be good corporate citizens.

Credit unions and caisses populaires are an important element of Canada's banking sector. The credit union system in North America has its origins in Quebec with the leadership of Alfonse Desjardins. Inspired by models in Germany and Britain, Desjardins established the first credit union in Canada, La Caisse Populaire de Lévis in Levis, Quebec, in 1901 (McGuiness and Young 1976). Later the model spread to the United States in Boston as Desjardins assisted Edward Filene, and to Nova Scotia through working with Moses Coady and James Tompkins (24). Mainstream banks closed branches during the Great Depression of the 1930s, and this stimulated the credit union movement in the Prairies.

Credit unions are smaller than the large Canadian banks, often with roots in one particular locale and, in some cases, one particular civic (for example, transit workers) or ethno-religious group (for example, Mennonite). In all provinces but Quebec there are usually several separately incorporated credit unions, with the Credit Union Central playing a coordination function. In Quebec the system is more centralized with the Desjardins Federation coordinating activities and engaging in federated programs such as contributing to the social economy. Credit unions are currently regulated at the provincial level. All combined, the credit union and caisse populaire assets in 2009 were approximately $227 billion (8.4% of the top eight banks' assets) and were made up of just under 1,000 credit unions and caisses populaires, with approximately 3,300 branches and just under 11 million members (Credit Union Central of Canada 2009, 6).

Credit unions prove to be important financial institution actors – on the basis of their size in comparison to that of banks and in terms of addressing financial inclusion. This will be examined in chapter 5.

FRINGE BANKS

When examining banking services for low-income Canadians, particularly those living in inner cities, it is important to consider 'non-mainstream' sources of financial services, meaning fringe and informal financial services. There is a plethora of these financial services to be found in inner cities, but often a scarcity of mainstream bank branches. Whereas one of the big five banks may be the banker of choice for many middle-income Canadians, many low-income Canadians rely as much on fringe and informal financial services. This section presents background information on fringe banking in Canada, a difficult sector for which to collect information because of its quasi-formal status.

This means that there is no official register of, let alone data on, service volumes and fees. This discussion does not examine informal financial services. Informal financial services such as cheque cashing at a small grocery store and borrowing money from a friend are even more difficult to examine than fringe banking in that the services are not regulated and are widely dispersed through many types and numbers of retail outlets.

By *fringe banks*, we refer to firms that offer financial services either as their principal good or service (for example, cheque cashing) or in order to provide their principal good or service (for example, renting to own). Pawnshops are the longest-standing fringe banks, with roots into early history and prehistory. They offer small short-term loans secured with a household item. Since some borrowers default on their loans, they naturally collect some of these items, so they are also second-hand good retailers. Some second-hand stores offer something akin to pawn loans through a 'buy-back' option. Other fringe banks are a more recent invention: cheque cashers, payday lenders, rent-to-own furniture stores, and tax-refund advancers. *Cheque cashers*, as the name suggests, will give you immediate cash for your employment cheque but at a significant fee. They generally also offer a number of other services such as money wiring and bill payment, and many offer payday loans. Cheque cashers grew in numbers in the United States from the 1970s (Caskey, 1994, 34). Historic data are not available for Canada, but in Winnipeg their numbers rose rapidly through the 1980s (Buckland et al. 2003). While employers may have provided something akin to payday loans for many years, it has only been in the 1990s in the United States and in the 2000s in Canada that payday lenders have been established and have rapidly grown in their number of outlets. A *payday loan* is a short-term small-sum loan that is 'secured' with a post-dated cheque left by the borrower with the lender. *Rent-to-own retailers* offer household goods within an agreement that converts from a rental arrangement to a purchase arrangement if the payments are completed. *Tax advancers* charge for completing an individual's income tax return and then provide the cash value of the refund up front, less their fees.

The scale of different types of fringe bank services varies significantly. Informal financial services are usually the smallest in scale. They can be obtained at a corner store, from a family member, or from a friend and might include cashing a cheque, supplying a $20 loan, or arranging for $200 to be sent to one's family overseas. The dollar value of these financial services is generally small, the organization providing the service is small, and there is often some type of familial-style relationship between the client and the supplier (even if the relationship is fictive). The principal operations of fringe banks are financial services, or, at least with rent-to-own, financial services are a central part of the business model. Commonly, fringe bank operations are bigger than those of informal financial service providers. In some cases, this is apparent in the number of the larger chains' outlets, for example, Money Mart. In other cases, it is less apparent, for example in the concentration of ownership of pawnbrokers in Winnipeg (Buckland et al. 2003). There is a range in size for fringe banks, from single outlets to several hundred outlets. Mainstream banks dwarf the other two types of banks in terms of assets, revenue, and number of branches – large banks in Canada have multi-millions of assets and many hundreds of branches – but in many inner cities, fringe banks are more commonly found.

The established definition of *a bank* is that it accepts deposits and then uses them to finance its lending facilities. Banks and trust companies are able to accept deposits. One way in which a bank generates a profit is by charging its borrowers a higher interest rate than it pays to its depositors. Fringe and informal banks, however, are not able to accept deposits and so are not banks in this sense.[17] They provide financial services, and in this sense they compete with certain banking services. This is akin to the relationship between a bank and a loan or mortgage company. Like a payday lender, the loan company provides a loan and does not accept deposits. The result is that fringe and informal financial service providers and loan companies must raise their loan capital either personally or from capital markets, but not from depositors. So instead of paying to savers the market rate for their deposits, they must pay to banks the market rate for their loans.

The final difference between the types of banks deals with the services that they provide. Mainstream banks offer the largest variety of services, which include transactional and development services. *Transactional financial services* are services that allow for making payments or obtaining cash, for example, cashing a cheque, withdrawing cash from an account, and paying a bill. *Developmental services* support longer-term needs including savings, investments, access to credit for loans and mortgages, and advice on finances. Fringe banks rely exclusively on transactions service fees for their income. In this sense, fringe banks and their clients who rely solely on them face a similar barrier. Doing all one's banking at fringe banks means that one cannot develop a credit rating, borrow at close to prime interest rates, and save through lucrative investments. Fringe banks place a brake on the financial development process, as these services are simply not offered. Moreover, the higher fees of fringe banks (discussed below) and weak regulations make fringe banking more expensive and potentially harmful to consumers. Similarly, relying on transactions services places a brake on the income growth of the fringe bank. The growth of its income is limited to the number of new clients it can attract for its limited services and the amount it can charge in fees. This places heavy pressure to expand the clientele, encourage repeat clientele, and charge high fees.

Currently in Canada the most visible, and likely the largest, fringe banks are National Money Mart Company and Cash Store Financial Inc. These firms provide payday loans, cheque cashing, and a variety of other financial services (for example, money transfers and credit cards). As these are publicly traded companies, some data are available for their operations. Data for other fringe banks are limited. Money Mart is owned by Dollar Financial Corporation (DFC), a United States–based transnational with operations also in the United Kingdom and Poland.

One important source of publicly available data about payday lending has come from provincial regulation processes. New provincial regulations are the result of an exemption for payday lenders from the criminal rate of interest. This exemption applied if provinces enacted regulations (for example, to cap fees and disclose fees fairly, among other things). Several provinces either have enacted regulations or are in the process of doing so. The Manitoba regulation process, which began with the Public Utilities Board, was particularly helpful in gaining insight into the industry.[18] Ultimately, this process led to a cap on the fees for payday lending at $17 per $100 loaned (tiered). One analysis found that the industry is oligopolistic and that some firms are earning profits in excess of what is normally expected:

> Another source on industry profit is the Ernst and Young LLP (2004) report. It did not disclose profit levels for firms it interviewed but did comment on average data on the payday loan sample and found that as a group, payday lenders are 'earning returns on equity that are comparable in other segments of the financial industry[;] a significant proportion of the industry is not making adequate returns' (Ernst and Young LLP 2004, 44). In addition Ernst and Young LLP found that 7 of the 19 respondents had an overall business loss for the reporting period (Ernst and Young

LLP 2004, 44). It was noted that, 'given the return on equity reported in the mainstream financial services sector (Ernst and Young LLP 2004, 26) was reported as 18.97%, this suggests that while the average return for the group of pay-day lenders is near 20%, since several firms are losing money, other firms must be making much higher than 20%. This is evidence of some very high profit rates among the most profitable firms.' (Buckland 2006b, 29)

National Money Mart Company. Dollar Financial Corporation is the parent company of National Money Mart Company and describes itself as 'a leading international financial services company serving underbanked consumers' (DFC 2008, 1). It claims to be the second-largest such network in the United States and the largest in Canada and the United Kingdom. DFC claims that customers use its services for various reasons, including having inadequate assets, a need for immediate cash, a dislike or distrust of banks, and no mainstream bank in the neighbourhood. It maintains that the industry has growth potential because of the growth of the service sector and 'failure of commercial banks and other traditional financial service providers to adequately address the needs of service sector and other working-class individuals.' It also asserts that the industry is characterized by economies of scale that favour larger firms such as DFC (DFC2008, 2–4). DFC describes its typical Canadian customers as follows:

The average age of our Canadian check cashing customer is 34. Our typical check casher is more likely to be male and never married. He graduated from high school and is employed full time with an income of US$23,000 a year. He does not own a car or a home. He has a cell phone, internet access, bank account but not a credit card. We believe he is very satisfied with his experience at Money Mart and lists convenient hours, simple process, teller attitudes, fast service and convenient locations as his favorite attributes. The average Canadian short-term consumer [payday] loan customer is 41. Our typical loan customer is more likely to be female and is or has been married. She graduated from high school and has taken some college/technical course work. She is employed full time and earns over US$34,000 a year. She owns her car but not her house. She has a cell phone, internet access, bank account, credit card and bank debit card. She is very satisfied with her experience at Money Mart and lists teller attitude, friendliness, convenient hours, and simple process as her favorite attributes. (2008, 6–7)

Table 1.8
Dollar Financial Corporation's revenue and net income

	2004	2005	2006	2007	2008
Revenue	$270,596,000	$320,991,000	$358,888,000	$455,732,000	$572,184,000
Net income	-28,033,000	-357,000	6,965,000	-32,203,000	51,173,000

Source: DFC 2008

Table 1.9
Money Mart's outlets

	2004	2005	2006	2007	2008
Company operated	194	214	242	360	419
Franchised locations	117	129	128	54	61
Total	311	343	370	414	480

Source: DFC 2008

Table 1.10
Money Mart's contributions to DFC revenue

	2006	2007	2008
Cheque cashing	14.5%	14.6%	14.4%
Consumer loans	19.5	24.1	25.7
Money transfer	2.3	2.6	2.8
Other	5.4	5.3	5.9

Source: DFC 2008

DFC's revenues have steadily grown in the 2000s, rising to over $500 million in 2008 (table 1.8). However, its net income over time has been more mixed – in the red in 2004, 2005, and 2007 and in the black in 2006 and 2008. In comparison, Dollar Financial Group, a subsidiary of DFC, experienced positive net income from 2002 through 2006.[19] DFC reported that a large and rising share of its revenues came from the Canadian subsidiary, whose contributions for 2006, 2007, and 2008 were 41.7%, 46.6%, and 48.8%, respectively (DFC 2008, 41).

Money Mart has grown rapidly from 2004, when there were 311 outlets, to 2008, when there were 480 outlets (table 1.9). In addition, during this period a rising share of the outlets were owned by Money Mart, as opposed to being franchises. In 2004, 62.4% of the outlets were owned by Money Mart, and in 2008 this had risen to 87.3% of the outlets.

Since cheque cashers and payday lenders do not declare net income by type of service, we cannot comment on the profitability of the different services they offer. DFC does report on each service's contribution to its revenues. The largest, and rising, share of its revenue comes from payday lending; it represented 19.5% of DFC's revenues in 2006, and this rose to just over 25.7% of its revenues in 2008 (table 1.10). To gain a sense of the significance of Money Mart's cheque-cashing operation, note that in 2008 it cashed a total of just over 4.3 million cheques, worth just over US$1.93 billion (DFG 2008, 8). According to the Canadian Payments Association, in 2007 the number of cheques cleared through CPA was 1.05 billion, worth $1.15 trillion (Canadian Bankers' Association 2009b). Money Mart's share of the total number of cheques cashed was 0.41%; its share of the face value of cheques was 0.17%.

Cash Store Financial Inc. Cash Store Financial Inc., formerly Rentcash Inc., is the other large publicly traded payday lender in Canada, headquartered in Edmonton. Cash Store Financial operates the Cash Store, Instaloans, and until 2007 a rent-to-own division, Insta-rent. In 2001 it had only five 'brokerage' (payday lending) and three rental stores (Buckland 2006b, 27), but by 2007 there were 358 brokerage and 65 rental stores (table 1.11). Revenue has risen steadily through this period but dropped a little in 2007. In 2008 Cash Store Financial had 384 outlets. Its net income rose from a loss of $58,000 in 2001 to a profit of $10.8 million in 2008.

Government Actors

Banks and trust companies operate nationally and are regulated by the federal government. The Department of Finance is the chief architect of these regulations. Credit unions operate within provinces and are regulated provincially. Their regulations are often lodged in provincial finance departments. These regulations are long-standing except that now the federal government is establishing federal credit union regulations that will allow credit unions to operate nationally.

Fringe banks are another matter. The Criminal Rate of Interest, section 347 of the Criminal Code of Canada, prohibits charging interest in excess of 60%, but this regulation has not been widely used to regulate fringe banks. Otherwise, the principal regulation of fringe banks falls within consumer protection, relating to provincial consumer affairs. Pawnshops are regulated to stop the sale of stolen goods. These regulations are lodged at the provincial and municipal levels. Other regulations regarding fringe banks are limited and include federal caps on what an income tax advancer can charge for an advance on a tax return, as well as provincial regulation of payday lenders. Both of these regulations stem from an exemption to the Criminal Rate of Interest.

FEDERAL DEPARTMENTS AND AGENCIES

While the Department of Finance is the chief architect of bank regulations, through the Bank Act, several other agencies are involved. One of the Department of Finance's responsibilities is to develop regulations to govern financial institutions, thereby ensuring their financial soundness and safety and the satisfaction of consumers' needs. To meet its objectives the department works in conjunction with, among others, the Bank of Canada, the Financial Consumer Agency of Canada, Canada Deposit Insurance Corporation, and the Office of the Superintendent of Financial Institutions. Representatives from these five departments or agencies are linked though the Financial Institutions Supervisory Committee (FISC).

The Office of the Superintendent of Financial Institutions. The purpose of the Office of the Superintendent of Financial Institutions (OSFI) is to promote the financial soundness of financial and insurance institutions. It does this by monitoring financial institutions and the macroeconomy and administering financial soundness regulations. OSFI regulates mainstream banks, trust companies, loan companies, and credit union centrals. It is an arm's-length agency that reports to Parliament through the Minister of Finance (OSFI, n.d.).

Financial Consumer Agency of Canada. An important agency with respect to consumer protection is the Financial Consumer Agency of Canada (FCAC). It was created in 2001 as part of the government's response to the MacKay Report. FCAC's purpose is to 'strengthen oversight of consumer issues and expand consumer education in the financial sector' (FCAC, n.d., website). Its work involves monitoring banks' compliance with consumer-related regulations and agreements and providing information and tools to consumers to assist them with financial services. Regulations and agreements that are of particular

Table 1.11
Cash Store Financial's operations

	2005	2006	2007	2008
	Brokerage and rental	Brokerage and rental	Brokerage and rental	Brokerage alone
Revenue	$76,772,000	$154,169,000	$123,562,000	$130,799,000
Net income	$6,796,000	$13,960,000	$5,882,000	$10,806,000
Branches				
Brokerage	277	338	358	384
Rental	84	92	65	0
Total	361	430	423	384

Source: Cash Store Financial Corporation's annual reports

relevance to the agency include Access to Basic Banking Regulations, voluntary codes, and public commitments, for example, regarding low-fee accounts and cheque-holds (both of which are discussed below).

FCAC also ensures that banks have an internal complaint-handling mechanism. If the consumer is dissatisfied with the results of the internal processing, he or she can lodge a complaint with the Ombudsman for Banking Services and Investments (OBSI).

PROVINCIAL DEPARTMENTS AND AGENCIES
Provinces, through their finance departments, are responsible for regulating credit unions. Provinces and municipalities also have legislation regarding pawnbroking, and recently they have been required to establish regulations for payday lenders. Additionally the provinces are responsible for consumer protection, often directed by departments of consumer affairs.[20] The Office of Consumer Affairs, within the federal government department Industry Canada, also works to promote consumer protection. The Consumer Measures Committee is a federal, provincial, and territorial committee that seeks to promote consumer protection by harmonizing laws and regulations relating to consumer protection. Consumer protection legislation, discussed below, is designed to protect consumers from bad and misleading business practices.

MUNICIPAL REGULATION OF PAWNBROKING
Pawnshops and second-hand stores are ordinarily regulated via laws at the provincial and/or municipal level, often enforced by the police.

The regulations usually require the pawnbroker to have a licence and to submit reports on the pawn merchandise received. Pawn monitoring, if it is undertaken, is concerned not with consumer protection (for example, by capping fees) but with monitoring the pawned goods to ensure that they have not been stolen. Pawnbrokers are required to regularly submit lists of items received with their serial numbers to the police. The police then check these lists against lists of stolen goods. Of course, this system can only work if consumers report the serial number of the stolen good.

Civil Society Actors

Governments and banks are key actors in framing and delivering financial services, but civil society actors have an important role, particularly with reference to low-income people. Low-income people may find themselves more marginalized than others – on the basis of location, income level, and ethnicity – from government and bank decision making. This may lead to their having weaker access to financial services and a greater sense of alienation from these providers. Civil society organizations can offer services, supports, and advocacy to enable low-income people to access and engage with banks and government.

SERVICES

Asset-Building Projects. Generally, asset building is a strategy that encourages people to save financial assets to build financial, physical, natural, and/or social assets. Common goals of asset building include house purchase, education, and retirement. In Canada the federal government spends or forgoes tax revenue to the tune of $22 billion annually through various programs to support asset building, such as registered retirement savings plans (RRSPs) and registered pensions (Robson and Nares 2006, 30–1). This support largely benefits middle- and upper-income people. Government support in the United States is around $300 billion annually (Robson and Nares 2006).

Only in the last ten to fifteen years has the question arisen about creating asset building options for low-income people. However, the situation for low-income people, especially those relying on social assistance, is complicated by what some refer to as the 'welfare wall.' The welfare wall is a series of barriers faced by welfare recipients that create disincentives to their becoming independent of welfare. In order to clear away these obstacles, new opportunities (or 'pathways') must be created for those people who rely on social assistance and are able to move from welfare to employment. Asset building programs, proponents claim, are one way to achieve this.

The individual development account (IDA) is a device that is typically designed for lower-income people, delivered or implemented by a community or non-profit organization, and funded by government and private funders. It provides a means for individuals to save over a short-time frame for a particular asset such as a home, education, or a small business; it matches savings, often at a two-to-one or three-to-one ratio; and it is often delivered in a group-support context, including financial management training.

The impact of asset-building programs has been documented in the case of the American Dream demonstration project in the United States the Savings Gateway program in the United Kingdom, and the Learn$ave program in Canada. In the United States there is evidence that IDAs induce low-income people to save and to use that savings for education; they also boosted the confidence of the participants and made them less vulnerable to shocks (Leckie, Dowie, and Gyorfi-Dyke 2008, 60). In the United Kingdom, evidence found that the program was able to boost participants' savings and somewhat improve future savings and financial management. However, in some cases, total household savings did not increase, for instance through the Learn$ave program. Other results from Learn$ave include the following: participants had engaged in new savings, the increased savings did not generate economic hardship, participants were more likely to have a budget through the program, and participants had improved attitudes about education.

The cost-effectiveness of IDAs has not been clearly documented yet, because they are in the early stages. As there has been little (or no) evaluation of other asset-building programs such as RRSP deduction plans, to require extensive evaluation of the one and not the other is something of a double standard. No doubt, evaluation of both types of programs is necessary. Effective evaluation of IDAs can assist in the improvement of implementation.

Social and Enterprise Development Innovations (SEDI) has been an important organization at the national level in promoting individual development accounts. Often there are local organizations, such as SEED Winnipeg Inc., that implement the asset-building programs.

Household Financial Management. Some civil society organizations offer financial management or financial literacy courses for low-income people. Sometimes these are stand-alone programs, and sometimes they are offered through programs such as asset building, financial counselling, and/or microcredit. These programs include basic financial education about household budgeting, investing, and planning, and in the case of microcredit the education is related to business finances. In some cases, these courses include information about financial service choice, through examining the benefits and costs of mainstream and fringe bank services.

The Canadian Task Force on Financial Literacy has recommended more consumer-focused financial literacy, so these types of programs will likely be better funded in the future.

Credit Counselling and Consolidation Services. Another role that non-profit organizations play is in providing credit counselling and consolidation services, a role that is shared with for-profit businesses. It involves counselling debt-strapped individuals about their debt and working with them to develop a strategy to overcome the problem. In some cases this may involve their declaring bankruptcy, and in other cases debt may be consolidated to bring the debt servicing to a manageable level. These agencies work with the client's creditors including, in some cases, identifying one creditor who is willing to consolidate the debt.

Producer Services: Microcredit and Microenterprise. Another means by which financial inclusion might be fostered, albeit indirectly, is producer-oriented programs such as microcredit and microenterprise. Here, clients receive supports such as business planning education and access to credit in order to start their own business. There are microcredit and microenterprise programs throughout the country, often provided by community organizations and government agencies and with support from banks. Banks and credit unions might provide the capital (sometimes with loan guarantees from government) and offer transactions accounts for businesses.

RESEARCH AND ADVOCACY

A second general activity in which civil society organizations engage is research and advocacy. Advocacy is understood as an action undertaken – such as research, publicity, protest, and direct dialogue – by one actor to affect the policy of another actor (usually, but not always, government). Advocacy may take a more reformist approach. It can also take a more radical tone, and this may be based less on an evaluation of current policy than on an alternative vision or ideology to that policy. Important advocates in the area of financial exclusion include the Canadian Community Reinvestment Coalition, ACORN Canada, and Public Interest Advocacy Centre.

Government Regulations Relating to Financial Exclusion

The 1980s ushered in a period of neoliberal economic policies influenced by the work of Milton Friedman and the neoclassical economic school.[21] Margaret Thatcher's Conservatives in the United Kingdom, Ronald Regan's Republicans in the United States, and Brian Mulroney's Progressive Conservatives in Canada represented this new version of the market-centred means to society betterment. Neoliberalism influences all sectors of the economy, in particular the financial sector, calling for liberalized markets and reduced barriers to trade. The World Trade Organization (WTO), taking over from the General Agreement on Tariffs and Trade in 1995, included an agreement to liberalize services: the General Agreement on Trade in Services. By requiring member states of the WTO to reduce non-tariff and tariff barriers on services such as financial services, some hoped that financial services, like agriculture via the Agreement on Agriculture, would be liberalized in the way that manufacturing had been.

In Canada the government implemented a process of examining and then reforming regulations of the financial services sector. The Task Force on the Future of the Canadian Financial Services Sector was established in 1996 to examine and make recommendations on the financial services sector in the light of liberalization and consumer protection. The MacKay Report stated, 'The current framework for consumer protection is not as effective as it should be in reducing the information and power imbalance between institutions and consumers' (Task Force on the Future of the Canadian Financial Services Sector 1998b, 15). The government response to the MacKay Report called for, among other things, improved access to basic banking for the financially excluded, and the establishment of a financial consumer agency; it also laid the foundation for Bill C-8.[22] This bill included the Access to Basic Banking Services Regulations and led to the creation of the Financial Consumer Agency of Canada in 2001.

Access to Basic Banking Services Regulations

The Access to Basic Banking Services Regulations require that banks open deposit accounts for all persons, including unemployed persons, as long as they have appropriate personal identification and that banks cash federal government cheques to a maximum of $1,500 for no charge for non-customers with similarly appropriate identification.[23] In addition to these regulations, banks have agreed to certain codes and made certain public commitments with respect to financial inclusion, including the cheque-hold commitment (Canadian Bankers Association members reduced cheque holds from ten business days to seven business days) and low-fee account provision (banks have agreed to provide a low-fee account for $4–$5 monthly for a basic set of transactions – approximately ten to fifteeen per month). Bank compliance with these regulations is monitored via the FCAC through mystery shopping and its consumer-complaint telephone line. The FCAC commissioner has sanction powers that range from issuing a letter of reprimand to imposing monetary penalties.

The regulations and monitoring of compliance are important steps in addressing financial inclusion. However, the telephone-based complaint system assumes that people are neither reluctant to use the complaint system nor unaware of it. This may not always be the case, particularly for low-income people with less access to information about government policy. In addition, following the letter of these laws may not promote financial inclusion, because exclusion is the result of several factors (as will be discussed in chapter 3); addressing account opening alone is insufficient. For instance, a bank may offer a low-fee account but may not promote it, it may close branches in the inner city, and it may not train its staff about the particular financial needs and realities of low-income people.

Another regulation faced by banks is that they are required to organize a public meeting for residents who are affected by a branch closure if people in the area call for it. If there is a call for a meeting, then the FCAC must ensure that the bank holds the public meeting. The precise purpose of these meetings is not clear. In 2003 when CIBC announced that it would close its branch in Winnipeg's north end, at Main Street just down from Selkirk Avenue, the residents called for a meeting, and it was well attended by area residents and bank staff. In short, the outcome of the meeting was that the bank restated its plan to shut the branch, and the residents voiced their concerns about this. That was it. The branch shut down soon afterwards.[24]

There are also voluntary commitments that banks have made regarding a number of issues (for example, debit cards and electronic transactions), some relating to basic banking.[25] For instance, Canadian banks voluntarily committed to offering a basic bank account for a low fee. In addition, in 2007, banks committed to keeping the hold period for cashing cheques to seven business days. More recently, the federal government budget of March 2010 included new rules for banks regarding hold periods: 'The government is committed to ensuring affordable access to basic banking services. As consumers need timelier access to funds, the government will make regulations to reduce the maximum cheque hold period to 4 days from the current 7 days and provide consumers access to the first $100 within 24 hours' (Flaherty 2010, 116).

Income Tax Advances

Income tax refunds can be an important source of lump-sum savings for low-income people. Obtaining one's refund immediately is popular with some people, but, like other forms of small-sum, short-term loans, it is relatively expensive.

In the 1980s the federal government created an exemption to the Criminal Code, section 347, that allowed income-tax-preparation companies to charge what amounted to an interest rate beyond the criminal rate of interest. This exemption to the Criminal Code allowed the 1985 Tax Rebate Discounting Act[26] which places a ceiling, set by the Governor-in-Council, on the fees charged for income tax advances. Currently, for a refund equal to or less than $300, the cap amounts to a maximum fee of 15% of the estimated refund; for a refund estimated to be greater than $300, it amounts to a maximum fee of $45 plus 5% of the amount over $300.[27] Calculating the total fee and converting it into an annual percentage rate (APR),[28] assuming a fourteen-day period, leads to the following: for a loan of $250, the maximum fee can be $37.50, for an APR of 391.1%; for a loan of $500, the maximum fee can be $55.00, for an APR of 286.8%.

Pawnshops

Pawnshops are generally regulated at the municipal level through either municipal by-laws or provincial legislation. However, pawnshop regulations have to do more with stemming the trade of stolen property and less to do with regulating pawnshop fees.

In Ontario the Pawnbrokers Act[29] outlines the licensing, redemption, and data collection requirements of the pawnbroker. Enforcement is done at the municipal level through licensing officials and police. In some cases in Ontario, municipal by-laws are also enacted to regulate pawnshops (for example, the City of Toronto[30]). The act also outlines the maximum fees chargeable by a pawnbroker: interest on the loan at no more than the lawful rate; a charge of $0.20 for the pawn ticket; and a charge of $0.10 per month per cubic foot for storage of the pawned item. These regulations also require the pawnbroker to hold on to the good for at least one year, after which time he or she must inform the customer before it becomes the pawnbroker's item. One informant claimed that the one-year hold period had led some dealers in second-hand goods to offer a buy-back option for the goods brought in, rather than get into the pawn trade. The dealer holds onto the item for a period of time, say one month, and if it is not redeemed, then it is sold. Redeeming the item requires the patron to repay the principal plus substantial fees.

In other provinces, such as Manitoba, pawnshops are regulated entirely at the municipal level. In Winnipeg, pawnshop regulations are municipal by-laws[31] that are enforced through the Pawn Unit[32] of the Winnipeg Police Services. These by-laws specify the licensing and data collection requirements of the broker but do not place a maximum charge for pawning. It is unclear how effective the monitoring of pawning is in stemming the flow of stolen goods. Data from the Winnipeg Police Service's 2007 annual report show that in this year there were 106,313 items pawned (57,757 items with a serial number), but only 119 items (0.1% of all items pawned) were 'connected to crimes of break and enter, theft, robbery, and fraud' (Winnipeg Police Service 2007, 9).

Consumer Protection

The purpose of consumer protection regulation is to shield consumers from harmful business practices. In Canada, consumer protection is primarily a provincial responsibility. For instance in Manitoba, the Consumers' Bureau is responsible for consumer protection. In the case of federally regulated banks, the FCAC is responsible to deal with consumer complaints.

In the case of financial services some salient consumer-protection issues include unfair price disclosure, tied selling schemes, unfair collection of debt, and salary garnishment. Unfair price disclosure occurs when service fees are not clearly disclosed or are too complicated to make comparison shopping possible. This is the case with some fringe banking services. Fair price disclosure requires that fees be simply and clearly disclosed, for example, using an annual percentage rate[33] for a credit product. Some jurisdictions in Canada have fair disclosure requirements for fringe banks as a result of work undertaken by the Consumer Measures Committee.

Tied selling takes place when a firm requires a consumer to purchase a second good or service when he or she is purchasing the first good or service. This is considered a form of consumer manipulation, and it is illegal. An example would be a payday lender's requiring a borrower to use its cheque-cashing service to repay the loan. The Bank Act also prohibits banks from engaging in tied selling. Unfair collection of debt occurs when the lender aggressively pursues the borrower for repayment of a loan. In the case of salary garnishment, which is not lawful, the lender has the borrower sign an agreement that allows the lender to garnish wages if the loan is defaulted.

While consumer protection laws are useful, they have limitations. They seek to protect consumers from outlier or 'rogue' firms that are gouging the consumer. They are based on the premise that, aside from a few rogue firms, the market operates in such a way as to benefit most people. Consumer protection itself is based on the concept that in most cases markets meet consumer needs through competition and that no particular group experiences a disadvantage from these markets. However, this is not always the case with regard to market competition (discussed below) and with regard to social exclusion (discussed in chapter 3). If markets are not competitive or if particular groups are disadvantaged, then consumer protection laws may be ineffective. If consumers do not know about the complaint process, if they do not have good access to a telephone or the Internet, and if they do not trust large government and business institutions, then the complaint mechanism might not be trusted. If consumer protection were to identify particular vulnerable consumers (see Ramsay 2001), then the regulations might be more effective.

REGULATING CHEQUE-CASHING AND PAYDAY-LENDING FEES

The number of payday lenders has risen rapidly in Canada since the early 2000s. The government chose to frame payday lending as a consumer-protection issue as opposed to a small-loans issue (in which case the federal Small Loans Act of the past might have served as a model). As a consumer-protection issue the responsibility was given to the provinces. The obstacle to regulation was that section 347 of the Criminal Code of Canada outlaws the charging of a criminal rate of interest, which it defines as an interest rate – including all fees – in excess of 60%. Since payday loans universally exceed this rate, often at a 400% APR or higher, they were technically illegal. Thus, the provinces could not legitimately regulate a service that was illegal. The decision was made to create an exemption to the criminal rate of interest in the case of payday loans and to have provinces regulate them. The federal government passed Bill C-26, which included an exemption to the criminal rate of interest for payday lenders in provinces that have regulations to protect consumers and to cap the lending fees.[34]

At the time of writing, six provinces had enacted these regulations: Alberta,[35] British Columbia,[36] Manitoba, Nova Scotia,[37] Ontario,[38] and Saskatchewan.[39] The regulations generally require the licensing of the lender and address issues such as disclosure and rate caps. The provincial rate caps range from $17 per $100 borrowed (639% APR) to $31 per $100 borrowed (943% APR). The Manitoba regulations cap the fees to $17 per $100 for loans up to $250 (517% APR), and tiered thereafter.[40] Quebec has its own usury law that does not allow payday lenders to operate in the province.

Two provinces, Ontario and Manitoba, have also recently established legislation regarding cashing of government cheques.[41] These regulations cap the fees that can be charged for cashing government cheques. They do not change the federal regulation under the Access to Basic Banking Services Regulations whereby banks are not allowed to charge a fee for federal government cheques written for less than $1,500. The free cashing by banks of these federal government cheques is supported through an indemnification agreement between the government and the banks.

Competitiveness of Financial Markets

Consumer protection regulations can be helpful if particular groups are not excluded from markets and if markets are operating competitively. In neoclassical economic theory, perfect competition is the ideal market state in which no one firm or one consumer can influence the outcome; instead, prices and output are determined through firm-consumer interaction, and equilibrium is reached. In this situation, firms are said to be 'price takers' in that they are told by the market the price at which they can sell their goods or services. The firms' only choice relates to the amount of good or service to produce at the given price. The neoclassical theory is able to show that when perfect competition exists (and other assumptions are met, including perfect information, for example), then the outcome is most beneficial for society. However, for most markets in Canada perfect competition does not exist. Rather, most markets are characterized by some state of imperfect competition. Variations of imperfect competition include monopoly (one seller, for example De Beers and the diamond market), oligopoly (a few large sellers), and monopolistic competitors (many sellers, but heterogeneous products). In addition, market structure may vary by location; markets may be competitive at the national level but imperfectly competitive at a local level, for instance in an inner city or a rural locale. In such a spatial monopoly situation, a firm may have market power and be able to exploit local consumers.[42] The outcome of imperfect competition can be harmful to the environment and society.

The Competition Bureau is responsible to enforce the Competition Act, which has the purpose of promoting competitive markets associated with fair prices and quality products. When four major banks in Canada were seeking to merge their operations into two, the Competition Bureau investigated and disallowed the mergers.[43] This was based on the finding: 'the Commissioner determined that the proposed mergers, as they were presented, would likely lead to a substantial lessening or prevention of competition that would cause higher prices and lower levels of service and choice for several key banking services in Canada.'[44] Conacher (1998) argued that the Competition Bureau's analysis of the level of bank competition during the merger-review process was insufficient because of flawed geographic analysis and because the Competition Bureau did not consider bank profits (Buckland 2008b). While the Competition Bureau does respond to consumer complaints, it does not engage in ongoing investigations of the state of banking services nationally or the state of banking services in particular locales. It is also unclear whether financially excluded consumers are in a very good position to take advantage of the bureau's consumer-complaint mechanism. Moreover, there is no evidence that the bureau has investigated fringe banks. The reliance of low-income people on them, and the fact that two firms control a large share of the payday loan market, would suggest that this is an important issue.

Greater competition within and among types of banks nationally and locally is an important factor in addressing financial inclusion. The Competition Bureau must pay more attention to the existing structure of mainstream bank and fringe bank markets at national and local levels, particularly in inner cities and remote rural areas. Where there is evidence of excessive profit rates, advertising expenditure, and brand proliferation, further investigation and regulation may be warranted.

Foreign Investment Benefits to the Economy

New foreign investment in Canada is reviewed by Investment Canada, the successor to the Foreign Investment Review Agency (FIRA). The review process is intended to ensure that the investment is in the interests of the country. During the 1970s there was a greater concern about the impact of foreign investment than there is at the present time, and so foreign investment was more carefully reviewed under FIRA. With the rise of the market orientation of the 1980s, foreign investment, like trade, was seen less suspiciously by the state. In 1985 Investment Canada replaced FIRA, and its mandate shifted from controlling foreign ownership to promoting domestic and foreign investment.[45] Financial services were liberalized, giving foreign banks greater access to the Canadian economy and Canadian banks greater access to other economies. Foreign banks were allowed to open branches and be subjected to more stringent regulation[46] or to open a Canadian subsidiary and face less stringent regulations.

As with liberalized trade, liberalized investment is justified as a way of promoting more competition and raising the levels of investment in the economy, ultimately increasing living standards. Foreign investment, however, will not necessarily increase competition where a large foreign company comes to dominate the economy, nor raise investment where the incoming company diverts local savings for its purposes. While foreign investment in mainstream banks is limited, involvement in fringe and sub-prime lending is more significant. Although Canadian banks provide the majority of the country's financial services and control 90% of total bank assets,[47] National Money Mart Inc. is owned by United States–based Dollar Financial Corporation and controls a significant share of the payday lending and cheque-cashing markets.

Savings and Financial Inclusion in Welfare Programs

Approximately 1.7 million, or 5%, of Canada's population relied on welfare income in 2005 (National Council of Welfare 2006).[48] These programs are an important source of income for people facing personal and/or institutional challenges. However, for some recipients their support levels in 2005 were lower than the support levels in 1986 (National Council of Welfare 2006). This low, and possibly declining, level of income makes financial inclusion less desirable because lower income makes bank developmental services less useful.

As mentioned above, the design features of many welfare programs create what some have called a 'welfare wall,' preventing people from becoming independent of assistance. These features can stifle income earning and savings strategies, locking people into reliance on social assistance. The principal feature of social assistance that creates the welfare wall is the precipitous decline that occurs in current benefits or future benefits (in the case of the Guaranteed Income Supplement)[49] if additional income is earned. The marginal effective tax rate is an indicator of the welfare wall. It measures 'the sum of direct taxes and indirect taxes associated with the clawback of income-tested subsidies' (TD Bank Financial Group 2005, 9). What this implies is that for every additional dollar the person earns, for instance through a new job, seventy-five cents to one dollar is clawed back through higher taxes or forgone welfare income. So, financially speaking, a person is better off, in the short run, to stick with welfare than to become independent of it. Additionally, welfare programs often stifle personal savings. They frequently disallow or limit savings before a person enters or while a person is participating in welfare.[50] Some welfare programs now are able to deliver their benefits via direct deposit, which can facilitate financial inclusion, particularly if there are other benefits to the client's being banked.[51]

Provision of Government Services

FINANCIAL SERVICES
In some countries, notably the United Kingdom, the state is involved in direct provision of banking services. In this case, they are provided through the post office. The post office system in the United Kingdom has 19,000 outlets and a presence in many low-income communities.[52] The UK Financial Services Authority concluded, 'It is generally

accepted that expanding the role of the Post Office will help tackle both financial and social exclusion. Not only will it increase access to financial services, but it will safeguard local post offices, and the shops in which many are based, in communities that, otherwise, have very few services within them' (2000).

In Canada, from Confederation (1867) until the early 1900s, savings accounts were available through the Post Office (McGuinness and Young 1976, 13).[53] However, in the past twenty years many post office outlets in Canada have been franchised to private companies, and therefore this option may not work. The franchised outlets are not necessarily located in underserved inner city or isolated rural locations. In addition, the training of staff on the particular financial service needs of low-income people may be more difficult in the case of franchises.

EDUCATION ON FINANCIAL MANAGEMENT

The popular market-centred approach to economic organization today places heavy responsibility on individuals to look after their own best interests. In the case of financial services, as the government and employer participation in retirement schemes declines, individuals must independently manage their retirement savings. Private options for health care continue to grow, and if this trend continues, Canadians will have even greater responsibility for financial management (in this case, for health care). To undertake these responsibilities effectively, people need to be financially literate. The fact that non-mortgage consumer debt in Canada is high is another indicator that financial education should be enhanced. At present the federal government does not have a national plan for financial literacy, but in the 2007 federal budget it committed $3 million to the FCAC to promote financial literacy among youth and investors; its 2008 Economic Action Plan committed to establish a plan. In 2009 the Task Force on Financial Literacy was established with a mandate to recommend to the federal government ways to improve Canadians' financial literacy (see box 1.2). The recommendations call for a national strategy for financial literacy that includes promotion of financial education, and a new federal government official responsible to promote financial literacy. The recommendations do not address regulatory measures that could support financial literacy (for example, consumer protection, fair disclosure, fair business practices) or recommendations to ensure financial institutions address financial exclusion.

UNIVERSAL PERSONAL IDENTIFICATION

A major challenge for low-income people in using mainstream banks is their lack of adequate personal identification, particularly photo identification. For example, in Manitoba it costs $30–$50 annually to maintain a driver's licence, which may be prohibitive (or useless if he or she does not have a car) for a low-income person.

Box 1.2 Recommendations from Canada's Task Force on Financial Literacy

The Need for a Comprehensive Strategy to Improve Financial Literacy

Over an 18-month period, we conducted and commissioned a considerable volume of research, examined international best practices in the field, consulted widely with Canadians and met frequently to deliberate on our findings. The result of this work is the basis for the proposed National Strategy on Financial Literacy (the "National Strategy"), for consideration by Canada's Minister of Finance.

The National Strategy aims to strengthen the knowledge, skills and confidence of Canadians to make responsible financial decisions. Under a framework of shared responsibility, stakeholders will collaborate with a designated leader to ensure effective implementation, sustain momentum and leverage resources. As an essential skill, financial literacy requires lifelong learning at home, at school, at work, and in the community. The diverse needs of Canadians will be met by enhancing existing programs, improving access, communications and delivery, and building awareness. Ongoing evaluation of progress will ensure accountability.

Under this Strategy, we are proposing an integrated set of 30 recommendations, with a mission to strengthen the financial literacy of Canadians. Because this important issue touches all residents, our recommendations are multi-faceted and emphasize the need for a collaborative approach. Whether financial literacy initiatives are undertaken by schools, governments, financial institutions, employers, labour organizations or voluntary bodies, collaboration and coordination will be essential to success.

Five Priorities

Although our recommendations are wide-ranging, five priorities define the Strategy's overall objective of strengthening the knowledge, skills and confidence of Canadians to make responsible financial decisions. Our specific recommendations build on the topics identified in our consultation paper *Leveraging Excellence* (February 2010), such as education, borrowing, saving and communication. These topics were commented on by Canadians during our public consultations and are summarized in our report *What We Heard* (September 2010).

The five priorities of the proposed National Strategy are:

1 Shared Responsibility
2 Leadership and Collaboration
3 Lifelong Learning
4 Delivery and Promotion
5 Accountability'

Source: Task Force on Financial Literacy, n.d.

Some Key Conclusions

Although consumption has remained a major contributor to Canada's national income over the last thirty years, in the 1990s disposable income stagnated, a growing number of Canadians faced low-income levels, and income inequality rose. In their study (2006, 30) Green and Kesselman concluded that 'at least until the turn of the century, Canada experienced deteriorating inequality and social justice in many dimensions ... In the short run, though, the impact of the combination of changes in the economy and in public policy at least through 2000 has been to increase inequality markedly. It is hard to escape the conclusion that these developments have also made Canada a less just society.'

Consumer debt has increased rapidly, but as long as asset values hold, an economic crisis seems to be averted. However, the evidence is that the Canadian macroeconomy has relied, to some extent, on its consumers' accumulating debt. This might have benefited the economy as a whole, but it is not clear that unsustainable household debt will benefit individual consumers in the long run, particularly if their incomes are low. These processes, income inequality and debt-driven growth, may further compound financial exclusion.

The actors of particular note regarding financial exclusion are banks because of their large size; credit unions because of their particular interests in and efforts at addressing the issue; fringe banks because of their being the default option for many low-income Canadians; and various government agencies that frame the markets in which banking services are bought and sold. The federal government agencies are perhaps the most important, but since many low-income people do not use mainstream banks, the relatively ad hoc provincial regulations are important. Consumer protection and the Access to Basic Banking Services Regulations appear to be the most important regulations related to financial exclusion. A major challenge to federal government regulations is that they lack effective enforcement tools; monitoring of banks through FCAC's mystery shopping does not necessarily lead to action against the offending party; and calling for public meetings when banks are closing their branches does not keep the branches open. Also, banks can sidestep regulations pertinent to opening bank accounts and cashing cheques, by closing their branches and not being responsive to certain types of people.

2 Theories about Financial Exclusion

This chapter will explore the key theories that have been used to explain the phenomenon of financial exclusion. In some cases, analyses of financial exclusion will explicitly identify a core theory, and, in other cases, the theory may be inferred. While this chapter is important for relating financial exclusion to core social science theories, readers who are less interested in theory can move, without missing too much, to chapter 3. Concepts from the economics industrial organization literature will be discussed in chapter 4.

Financial exclusion is a complex problem and has been examined from a number of theoretical perspectives including neoclassical economic theory, behavioural economic theory, institutional theory, and political economy theory. This chapter will describe each of these theories, apply the theory to the explanation of financial exclusion, and then evaluate each approach. It will be argued that a carefully limited institutional theoretical perspective, informed by a poverty-and-community perspective, provides the best set of tools for understanding financial exclusion. However, the other theoretical approaches offer additional insights that must not be lost in examining financial exclusion.

The Complex Nature of Theories Examining Financial Exclusion

Financial exclusion is a complex social problem. It involves factors that range from psychological to sociocultural to economic. A common psychological issue is the questioning of the fringe bank customer's behaviour: is she or he rational? Sociocultural issues come into play when studies probe the effects of class, gender, ethnicity, and locale on participation in mainstream banking. Economic studies ponder the efficiency of bank operations and markets. Other factors considered include political issues (for example, how big banks influence markets) and geographic issues (for example, the spatial location of bank branches).

In addition to its complexity the study of financial exclusion is still relatively young, so that much of the relevant analysis comes from the study of other topics (such as asset-building literature). This is particularly true in Canada where the first analyses were published in the early 2000s (for example, Ramsay 2001), but the longer-term study in the United States and the United Kingdom dates only back to the 1990s (Caskey 1994; Leyshon and Thrift 1996; Dymski and Veitch 1996).

Finally, political philosophy shapes the theorizing about financial exclusion. Neoclassical economic and political theories, which are premised on rational individualism and perfectly competitive markets, have informed what are known as neoliberal policies. Very popular today, these policies accent the role of markets and minimize the role of the state in meeting the common good. By *common good* is meant policies and practices that enhance the 'good' to all individuals and groups in a society (Daly and Cobb 1989). These approaches are challenged by left-of-centre perspectives from a variety of sources including post-Keynesian theory, international political economy, and self-reflexive disciplines such as geography and anthropology.

Perspectives on the Principal Constraint

Different theoretical approaches, models, or frameworks have been applied to the study of financial exclusion. These approaches are built on various assumptions about the constraints that we face and the means that we use to achieve well-being. Some approaches assume that the principal constraint is inadequate markets, and some approaches find that other institutions are inadequate. Neoclassical economics, the most influential approach in terms of policymaking, finds that the absence or underdevelopment of markets and rational individualism is the principal constraint to well-being. Conversely, this school claims that advancing markets and rational individualism into new realms such as mortgage securities will generate economic growth that will automatically enhance well-being. While this view has significantly influenced policy and culture, it is not widely embraced by non-economist social scientists. For instance, the political economy perspective has typically found that the power imbalances, and not the markets, are the main obstacle to the well-being of those with less power. By extension, the solution involves policies that can reallocate power either immediately (for example, through asset redistribution) or in the medium term (for example, through universal education).

Disciplinary and Interdisciplinary Approaches and Method

Theoretical approaches use a range of focuses to examine the financial exclusion or related topics. In some cases the approach is more narrowly focused. With the narrow focus comes an accent on *quantitative* research methods. Other approaches use a broader or interdisciplinary scope that is generally associated with *qualitative* research methods. In its study of consumer financial behaviour, neoclassical economics is more narrowly focused on individual economic agents' behaviour, and quantitative methods are the method of choice for this approach. Political economy studies of financial exclusion consider a wider range of subjects, including states and fringe and mainstream banks, and use qualitative methods that are not concerned so much with statistical and econometric analyses.

The Topic

As studies of financial exclusion are new, relevant studies focus on different issues. Some studies examine financial exclusion directly. Others focus on issues such as savings behaviour or credit use. Theories that centrally address financial exclusion tend to be more interdisciplinary such as political economy theory. The life cycle–permanent income theory, consistent with neoclassical economics, examines an individual's personal financial behaviour over a lifetime. While not focused on financial exclusion, this theory is relevant to the study of it. Behavioural life-cycle theory, a version of life-cycle theory, is rooted in behavioural economics' assumptions about human behaviour. Recently this method has been used to study credit choice. For instance, why pay such high fees for a payday loan when alternatives such as credit cards are on the market?

The Object of Study

A critical aspect of the way in which a theory addresses financial exclusion is the principal object of its study. In most cases the object is the individual or the household. In some cases, groups such as a community, gender, ethnicity, or class act as the base group. Neoclassical economics takes the individual as the object of study; it does not consider group membership in a community or class as relevant. Poverty theories are generally concerned with groupings, particularly marginalized groups such as welfare recipients or single parents.

Types of Theories

There are a variety of theories that can be used to understand financial exclusion. This section seeks to explain the basic characteristics of the most relevant theories by placing the theories within different categories. The two broad categories chosen are economic and interdisciplinary. While this may appear to unduly privilege economics and overstate the interdisciplinarity of other theories, it is done for two reasons. First, one economics school – neoclassical economics – has dominated both the discipline and the policymaking for roughly the last twenty-five years. Thus, as students of financial exclusion, it is important to seriously examine these theories. Second, while the term *interdisciplinary* may somewhat overstate the breadth of some of the theories included in this category, they are from disciplines that, unlike economics, have broadened in their scope during the last two decades (Shaw 2003). Geography in particular but also political studies (excluding international relations) and sociology have sought to broaden their analysis to consider factors previously excluded. This is true for the interdisciplinary financial exclusion theories examined here.

One way to think about financial exclusion theories is to identify the key assumptions that they make. Two key assumptions relate to human rationality and the role of institutions. Some theories hold that human behaviour is rational while others claim that rationality is limited or 'bounded.' Some theories hold that society is best understood as operating within a series of frictionless markets while others find that society is made up of groups – such as rich and poor nations, classes, genders, and locales – with harmonious and conflicting interests. Thus, theories can be mapped onto this 'rationalist-institutional' space (see figure 2.1). Starting at the more populated north-west corner we find theories that assume that humans are rational and that institutions – be they rules, norms, classes, genders, or nations – play an important role

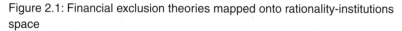

Figure 2.1: Financial exclusion theories mapped onto rationality-institutions space

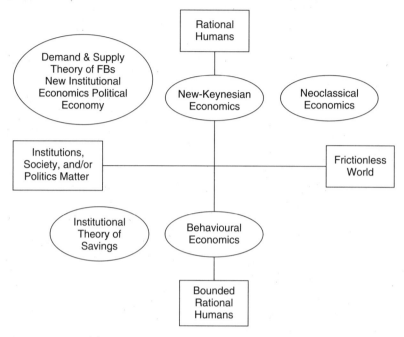

FBs = fringe banks

in explaining financial exclusion. These theories include the demand-and-supply theory, new institutional economics, and political economy. Moving clockwise to the north-east, we find new-Keynesian economics, which holds onto the human rationality assumption but is more concerned with institutions than is neoclassical economics. Further clockwise, we find theories that hold onto human rationality and assume that social reality is best understood as a series of frictionless markets. The influential neoclassical economic school fits into this category. Moving further clockwise, we arrive in the bounded rationality portion of the map, beginning with behavioural economics which, due to dropping the assumption of individual rationality, opens up the economy to considerable social friction. Finally, moving to the last quadrant that is characterized by bounded rationality and a role for institutions, we find the institutional theory of savings.

Economic Theories

From the 1980s, economic theory and policy became more deeply influenced by neoclassical economic theory. Neoliberalism, the policy regime shaped by neoclassical economic and political thought, finds the market (the firm and the consumer) the central means to the common good, with the state playing a secondary role. The firm and the consumer are understood to act as rational agents looking after their self-interest. While subjected to continuous challenge by other theories, the U.S. sub-prime mortgage crisis has presented, at least in the short term, a major challenge to this orthodoxy, particularly from behavioural economics.

From the 1940s to the 1970s the neoclassical school was less influential in economics and policymaking as it vied with other economic and interdisciplinary schools, most notably Keynesian and Marxist. However, the popularity of these latter two schools declined dramatically through the period of stagflation (high inflation and unemployment) during the 1970s, the collapse of the Berlin Wall, and growing debt in the global South. 'There is no alternative' was an expression, often in a tone of frustration, signifying that the only viable strategy for achieving social and economic good was through market-centred capitalism. Evidence of shifting economic policy can be found around the world, perhaps most profoundly in comparisons of before and after Prime Minister Thatcher in the United Kingdom, President Reagan in the United States, and Structural Adjustment Programs in many Southern nations. Canada too during this period was subject to neoliberal policies. Precisely why neoclassical economics came to such prominence is beyond the scope of this section. One interpretation is that the 1980s and 1990s witnessed a period in which markets became disembedded from society. 'In [Polanyi's] conception, markets and societies always existed locked in a lurching relationship and struggle, which progressed unevenly (or could even be destroyed) as, in a two stage or "double" movement, markets disembedded themselves from social constraint, and were then re-embedded and thereby secured and sustained, as well as constrained in the reactionary phase' (Craig and Porter 2006, 3).

NEOCLASSICAL ECONOMIC THEORY
It is hard to distinguish mainstream economics from neoclassical economics today. Even the sub-discipline of development economics, a

relatively interdisciplinary area of study within economics, has become deeply influenced by neoclassical economics.[1] What is neoclassical economics? The school has its roots in a broader study that was known as political economy in eighteenth- and nineteenth-century Europe. Political economy was associated with figures such as Adam Smith, David Ricardo, and John Stuart Mill. These theorists applied enlightenment ideals, in response to mercantilist pressure, to demonstrate the economic benefits of competitive markets, specialization of labour, and international trade. The neoclassical economics school, often defined as 'the study of the allocation of scarce resources,' dates from the end of the nineteenth century and the early part of the twentieth century. Proponents of neoclassical theory were William Jevons, Leon Walras, and later Alfred Marshall. These architects identified key concepts from the classical school – such as human self-interested rationality, competitive markets, and a limited role of the state – that became foundational assumptions for subsequent theorizing. Within the neoclassical school, instead of re-examining these assumptions as some disciplines have done (for example, anthropology), neoclassical economics has concentrated its energy on the development of quantitative methods that would allow for more sophisticated testing of data as if these assumptions held. The economics discipline has been quick to embrace advances in statistical analyses and mathematical modelling as means to improve its analytical abilities.

Neoclassical economics concentrates focus on economic agents and places the state in a secondary role. The state's role is to provide for, and enforce the property rights of, economic agents. The chief economic agents are firms and consumers whose behaviour is assumed to be rationally self-interested, well informed, and competitive. What does this mean? First, agents are rationally self-interested when they behave in ways that maintain or raise their well-being (for a producer this refers to profit, and for a consumer it refers to satisfaction or utility). An agent would not act in such a way as to undermine his or her well-being. For instance, a consumer would not take out a payday loan unless it was to her advantage. In fact, taking out the loan is an indication of the rationality of the use of payday loans. Next, a well-informed agent is one who has all the information necessary to make rational decisions to maintain or improve his well-being. The payday loan consumer obtains all the necessary information to make a rationally self-interested decision. It is assumed that she or he will collect information about the fees and benefits of loans from various payday and other types of lenders. This allows the consumer to shop around to find the best deal and to understand the full implications of the loan before completing the transaction. This assumption was seriously checked by the actions of the holders of sub-prime mortgages in the United States. Finally, it is assumed that the markets in which producers and consumers are operating are 'perfectly' competitive. This means that no one agent is able to influence the outcome in the market. The opposite of the perfectly competitive market is a monopoly (one producer) or a monopsony (one buyer), which, along with its imperfectly competitive cousins such as oligopoly and monopolistic competition, is generally ruled out in the neoclassical model. Thus, the payday loan consumer can trust that no one payday lender or group of lenders influences the market. In a perfectly competitive market, consumers can be assured that inefficient and corrupt lenders will be outcompeted and pushed out of business.

A weakness of the neoclassical economic school is a lack of self-reflexivity. Unlike some other disciplines, most notably anthropology and geography, economics has not rigorously examined its foundational assumptions. As a result, economics models are not sufficiently broad for accurately understanding the social world that it seeks to examine. Moreover, if economic analysis results in structures that do not allow agents to behave in ways that it predicts, then it might conclude that structures need to be more like the assumptions, thus becoming a theory that changes rather than explains the social world. However, the neoclassical model provides insights into human behaviour and allows for quantification of certain variables. Useful neoclassical economics tools that are applied in order to understand financial exclusion include the simple calculation of the net benefits of a loan.

What does neoclassical economics say about financial exclusion? With foundational assumptions about rational consumers and functioning markets, it concludes that financial exclusion is the result of consumer choice and/or mistaken government policy. One possibility is that consumers choose not to participate in mainstream markets because the economic benefits are outweighed by the economic costs, and instead they use fringe or informal financial services. A second, and not mutually exclusive, possibility is that government policy such as a usury ceiling creates distortions in credit markets that lead to exclusion of certain population segments. In this case the usury ceiling prohibits the bank from charging an interest rate that is sufficient to cover the transactions and risk costs associated with consumers' requiring smaller loans and having more limited security. In this case the mainstream bank does not offer the credit. The solution, according to neoclassical economic theory, is the abolition of the usury cap.

The Life Cycle–Permanent Income Theory. The life-cycle theory developed by Franco Modigliani and the permanent income theory developed by Milton Friedman have common elements that inform the neoclassical economic analysis of consumer behaviour over a lifetime. The model makes the standard assumptions about human rationality and access to information and assumes that the consumer has access to 'mainstream' credit markets. The model argues that in order to optimize long-run satisfaction, consumers make consumption decisions not on present income but on their expectation of their lifetime income.

One application of the life-cycle theory is to explain the higher debt load of young people compared to that of the middle-aged. At ages when the present income falls below the lifetime average income, for instance in early adulthood, the model predicts that the consumer will borrow in order to fill the gap. Conversely, where the present income exceeds the long-run income, as is typically the case in middle age, the consumer will save a portion of income. Life-cycle theory may be used to explain why it is that young people are more likely to use payday loans than are middle-aged people. Since their income is more likely to be below their lifetime average, they will seek out ways to borrow money to fill the gap.[2]

Credit Expansion and Sub-prime Loans. Levels of consumer credit have grown dramatically in Canada (and elsewhere) in the last twenty to fifty years (as discussed in chapter 1), and this growth may be linked to financial exclusion if high debt levels have pushed some people into sub-prime credit and payday loans. What is the neoclassical economic view of consumer debt? Debt on its own is not seen as a problem from a neoclassical economic perspective. If debt is used to finance an investment that raises the agent's economic position and thereby his ability to service debt obligations, then debt is justified. For instance, at the macroeconomic level, the concept of sustainable debt load was used by the World Bank to analyse the financial position of Southern debtor nations (see Perkins et al. 2001, 538). Other important variables that affect sustainability are the interest rate on debt and the factors influencing a country's access to hard currency (for example, exchange rates and import and export prices).

Neoclassical economic views about *consumer* credit levels are similarly fashioned: consumer debt is not a problem unless it results in a crisis. Montgomerie (2007, 115) argues, 'Neoclassical economics claims that individuals act as self-regarding utility maximizers, by virtue of their *a priori* rationality, in exchange relations. Reliance on this assumption about the motivations of individual behaviour has prevented any systematic action from being taken because rising debt levels are considered beneficial to household prosperity. The Anglo-American governments internalised these neoclassical principles and accepted that any product of the free functioning of markets is unproblematic unless it results in systemic crisis.'

Montgomerie points to the works of Maki (2002) and Calder (2002) as examples of the neoclassical economic approach to consumer debt. Maki shows how consumer expectations can downplay the significance of growing consumer debt, and Calder explains how changing cultural factors and instalment credit show that higher consumer debt is not a problem. Bostic argues that consumer debt has increased owing to expectations of rising future income (2002). Calder argues that instalment credit is the innovation that has allowed for accumulating consumer debt to be consistent with 'budgetism,' which involves the 'treadmill of regular monthly payments' (2002, 30). The discipline of monthly payments, he argues, is as rigorous a discipline as postponing consumption until saving the fee.

As was seen with the U.S. sub-prime mortgage crisis, the assumption of human rationality can sometimes and in some ways be a troublesome element of this analysis. People expected housing prices to continue to rise, but the housing-price bubble burst, leading to declining prices and reduced consumer ability to service debt. Thus, even amortized payments, what Calder calls *budgetism*, is not sufficient to ensure that high debt rates are sustainable.

Thus neoclassical economic theory is agnostic about consumer debt levels unless they become unsustainable, which would be indicated by a crisis (like the sub-prime mortgage crisis in the United States). But what if rising debt pushes some consumers to rely more heavily on sub-prime and payday loans? Is this a rational behaviour? The neoclassical economic tool of discounted benefit-cost analysis has been applied to examine this particular question. Net present value (NPV) analysis, for example, provides a tool in which is embedded the theory of time preference or of opportunity cost. Time preference and opportunity cost are two theories used to explain the existence of a positive interest rate. Time preference theory simply posits that, when given the option, people prefer one dollar today to one dollar tomorrow. Opportunity cost theory has to do with the productive use of capital; here, a person prefers one dollar today because it can be invested today to yield more than one dollar tomorrow. Time preference and opportunity cost together provide a theory behind the existence of a positive interest rate charged on credit.

To examine the net benefits of a credit transaction, NPV analysis uses an interest rate in 'reverse' in order to discount future costs and benefits. It does so by applying a discount rate to all future benefits and costs. One formulation of this analysis involves borrowing money in one period to make an investment that leads to savings in subsequent periods.

$$NPV = I + \Sigma \ (S_t/(1 + d)^t),$$

where I is the investment in period 1 (this would be a negative number); S_t is the savings in period 't'; and d is the period discount rate.

The costs and benefits in each period that are further away from the present are discounted more greatly. If the NPV is positive, then borrowing money to make the investment is economically advantageous. If the NPV is negative, then this credit transaction is not justified economically.

Elliehausen and Lawrence (2001) have used NPV analysis to demonstrate the rationality of payday loan use. In their analysis a consumer takes out a payday loan for an immediate car repair that otherwise would have forced him to take a long bus ride to and from work each day. On payday two weeks later he returns the principal and pays the fees, which amount to 391% APR. The NPV works out to be mildly positive, concluding that taking the payday loan is economically advantageous. While this analysis suggests that payday loans can be economically advantageous, it is based on a scenario that may not apply in many cases. In particular, it may not be safe to assume that borrowers apply their wage rate to time spent on the bus and that payday loans are always invested; they may be used to finance consumption or, worse for the NPV calculation, pay off another payday loan. Minor tinkering with the data in this analysis can lead to significant changes in the results, often leading to a negative NPV.

Financial Literacy Neoclassical economics requires that consumers behave rationally in pursuit of their short- and long-term interests. In order to pursue their interests, consumers – particularly those living in wealthy households, in households with major financial goals, and in complicated economies – must be financially literate. As discussed in chapter 1, in the last ten years the issue of financial literacy has become more prominent among policymakers, academics, and the media. High consumer-debt levels, the sub-prime mortgage crisis in the United States, and the rapid rise of payday lenders all raise questions about the literacy of individuals with respect to their finances. Moreover, state and employer withdrawal from benefit plans such as pensions, and the growing sophistication of the financial system, require that people have greater financial literacy.

NEW-KEYNESIAN THEORY

While the Keynesian school of macroeconomics has largely fallen from favour in economics since the stagflation of the 1970s, new-Keynesian analysis has shifted to study the foundations of the macroeconomy. Thus, new-Keynesian analysis is consistent with neoclassical economic theory on this count: both see macroeconomic analysis as best undertaken by starting with a focus on microeconomic actors, firms, and consumers. However, new-Keynesian analysis concerns itself with the market distortions embedded in the microeconomy, such as information asymmetries. The analysis finds that, when scaled up to affect large numbers of consumers, these asymmetries can damage the entire macroeconomy.

The core new-Keynesian theory in relation to financial exclusion relates to the notion of credit constraint. The classic credit-constraint analysis was presented by Stiglitz and Weiss whose study (1981) demonstrated that creditors, with imperfect information about borrowers, may depress interest rates and may ration credit in order to avoid risky borrowers, which leads to market distortions and 'credit' exclusion. Their analysis uses the principal-agent concept: the agent or borrower has information about his or her ability to repay that the principal or lender lacks. In order to avoid lending to risky borrowers, the creditor drops the interest charge and rations the credit to his or her best clients. 'The core idea of this alternative ... is that while borrowers need lenders' money, they often have informational advantages of two kinds over lenders: information concerning their competency, which affects their probability of success (their "type"); and their plans for using and repaying the loans they receive, which affect the likelihood of repayment (their "effort")' (Dymski 2005, 445).

In a novel and useful paper (2005), Dymski built a new-Keynesian model, drawing on the asymmetric information assumption, to understand the two-tier credit market found in U.S. urban markets. Dymski applied the Stiglitz-Weiss model to analyse, among other things, the coexistence of fringe and mainstream banking markets in the United States. He argues that the Stiglitz-Weiss model provides a theoretical underpinning for the bifurcation of banking in the global North and South and that it results in financial or credit exclusion. He begins by pointing out that the Stiglitz-Weiss model understates the importance of the secondary or fringe credit market. He addresses this gap with a model that explicitly theorizes a coexisting fringe and mainstream credit market.

The model flows from the initial assumption of asymmetric information between creditor and borrower. Changes in the way in which banks deliver credit (for example, credit cards and lines of credit) and screen clients (automated credit checks) lead to a selection of particular consumers who are deemed to have very low risk. Pooling these loans and selling them off through securitization further reduces bank risk exposure to these loans. 'Credit-included' consumers face a relatively low interest rate, but those consumers who are screened out of the primary market face credit rationing due to rate cap regulations. Consequently, credit-excluded customers face higher interest rates, and their economic situation deteriorates over time to a point where they are unable to even service their debts: 'the borrower begins as a fragile unit and moves inexorably toward being a Ponzi [or more fragile] unit' (Dymski, 2005, 452–3). The bifurcating credit market reinforces income and asset inequality: 'credit markets are no longer unified (if they ever were), but instead are fragmented and diverse; and financial exclusion grows as do the wealth/income and security/insecurity divides' (Dymski 2005, 454).

Interdisciplinary Theories

There are a number of approaches for understanding financial exclusion that are interdisciplinary in nature. An interdisciplinary theory is one that is informed by insights from more than one discipline. This group of theories includes a variety of approaches such as institutional theory, political economy, and poverty-and-community analyses. Each of these theories in turn has been influenced by more than one discipline, including economics, psychology, sociology, and geography.

BEHAVIOURAL ECONOMICS

Behavioural economics seeks to unpack the important assumption within neoclassical economics about human rationality. This is not to say that behavioural economics assumes people are irrational but that it seeks to gain a more complete image of human behaviour, sometimes described as *bounded* rationality. Whereas neoclassical economics assumes that people will always act in their short- and long-term interests, behavioural economics tests this assumption and seeks to gain a more thorough and nuanced understanding of human behaviour. It tests human behaviour using experiments and field tests. Since it drops the human rationality assumption, however, it also raises the importance of economic structure.

Behavioural economics finds that human behaviour faces important limitations to the neoclassical economics notion of perfect rationality. Mullainathan and Thaler (2001) summarize the behavioural insights for economics as demonstrating that people have bounded rationality, bounded willpower, and bounded selfishness. Bounded rationality is evidenced in such things as using rules of thumb (heuristics), overconfidence, framing, status quo bias, and discounting (Thaler and Sunstein 2008; Mullainathan and Thaler 2001). Bounded willpower is evidenced in behaviour such as using one's credit card to its limit, not regularly saving, and not learning about different investment options. Bounded willpower is engaging in behaviour that is against one's own best interests. Finally, Mullainathan and Thaler argue that humans cooperate more than unbounded selfishness would predict:

> Finally, people are boundedly selfish. Although economic theory does not rule out altruism, as a practical matter economists stress self interest as the primary motive. For example, the free rider problems widely discussed in economics are predicted to occur because individuals cannot be expected to contribute to the public good unless their private welfare is thus improved. In contrast, people often take selfless actions. In 1993, 73.4% of all households gave some money to charity, the average dollar amount being 2.1% of household income. Also, 47.7% of the population does volunteer work with 4.2 hours per week being the average hours volunteered. Similar selfless behavior is observed in controlled laboratory experiments.

Subjects systematically often cooperate in public goods and prisoners dilemma games, and turn down unfair offers in 'ultimatum' games. (2000, 7)

Behavioural economics offers important insights about financial exclusion. By relaxing the assumption about human rationality and using experimental methods it can help to unpack the consumer side of the financial exclusion question. Behavioural economics has demonstrated important limitations to human rationality, including financial behaviour. To the extent that people freely choose to be financially excluded, this approach offers insights; however, by the relaxation of only one assumption of the neoclassical economic school, its scope is not as broad as that of some other interdisciplinary approaches such as institutional analyses.

Behavioural economists must take care in their analysis of the behaviour of low-income people. Without understanding the structural obstacles that poor people face, behavioural economics might lead to conclusions consistent with the 'Culture of Poverty' thesis, which found that poor people were poor because of behaviours and ways of knowing that are self-destructive. This is not the case in the work of Mullainathan and Shafir (2009): 'We propose an alternative perspective, one largely informed by recent behavioural research. According to this perspective, the behavioural patterns of the poor may be neither perfectly calculating nor especially deviant. Rather, the poor may exhibit fundamental attitudes and natural proclivities, including weaknesses and biases, that are similar to those of people from other walks of life. One important difference, however, is that in poverty the margins of error are narrow.'

Analysis of Consumer Credit Choice. Behavioural economics has been applied to understand consumer credit choice. In one interesting study in South Africa, researchers worked with a bank in the design of mail-out advertising for a loan product (Bertrand et al 2005). The experimental design involved advertising a loan with different interest rates and providing different additional information. In some cases the information included the competitor's interest rates; in other cases it included ways in which the loan might be used; and, finally, in some cases it included graphics such as photographs. The results found that some psychological factors affected credit choice: 'As economic models predict, the interest rate strongly affects take-up. There appears to be a robust, negatively sloping, demand curve in this market. Yet, some of the

psychological factors also strongly affect demand in ways that are difficult to reconcile with the rational choice model. For example, consumers are more likely to take-up a loan if only one maturity and size are
described in the offer letter than if many examples are provided. For another example, male customers' take-up increases with the inclusion of
a woman's photo in a corner of the offer letter' (Bertrand et al. 2005, 4).

Investigating the ways in which people treat future income and costs
is another avenue of study in behavioural economics. In neoclassical
economic theory it is assumed that people discount future income in
a consistent manner. Recent studies on hyperbolic time discounting
found evidence that this was not necessarily the case. One study found
that payday loan borrowers display behaviour consistent with hyperbolic discounting (Skiba and Tobacman 2008).

The application of these behavioural economic insights to financial
exclusion is significant. A common question asked about financial exclusion is, why do some people choose to be excluded? Why don't they
open an account at a nearby bank? Conversely, why do people, in the
face of higher cash costs, cash their cheque at a cheque casher or take
out a loan at a payday lender or pawnshop? Behavioural economics
can offer important insights into these questions. The cheque casher
and the payday lender are more expensive than are the mainstream
bank equivalents (direct deposit in bank account, credit card, or line
of credit), but they offer the immediate, convenient, and specific services that people want. Thus, cheque cashers and payday lenders have
learned about human behaviour in designing their products and locating their outlets.

Behavioural Life Cycle. The life-cycle theory was discussed under neoclassical economic theory. An important revision to this model has
come from behavioural economic school. The behavioural life-cycle
theory was first developed by Shefrin and Thaler (1993). The behavioural life-cycle theory relaxes the assumptions about human rationality, in this case with regard to the savings and borrowing decisions over
one's lifetime. Households may not save as predicted by the life-cycle
model, because of human characteristics such as self-control, mental accounting, and framing that lead consumers to behave impatiently and
with less than optimal willpower. This leads to a savings rate that is
lower than the one predicted by the life-cycle hypothesis.

One of the most contentious issues in which the behavioural and regular life-cycle theorists engage has to do with retirement savings in the

United States: is it optimal or less than optimal? Life-cycle adherents argue that low savings rates demonstrate a rational choice on the part of Americans of working age (Thaler and Sunstein 2008). Behaviourists argue that the low rate is troublesome because it means that when retirement hits, people will face a significantly lower standard of living or they will place growing political pressure on social security. Where the truth lies is beyond the scope of this section, but what is clear is that it is easier to deal with excessive saving than with insufficient savings in retirement (Thaler and Sunstein 2008, 106).

Once again a limitation of this application to understanding financial exclusion is that it does not take into account the institutional barriers faced by low-income people in terms of savings (discussed below).

INSTITUTIONAL THEORIES

Institutional analysis comes in many forms, rooted in politics, sociology, and economics. In general, institutional analysis refers to analyses that seek to understand the broad context and the key institutions involved in the social reality being studied. For the purposes of this discussion we focus on the institutional analysis that highlights the economic component. Examples of this approach include new institutional economics, the demand- and supply-side of financial services, the institutional theory of savings, and the theory of asset building.

New Institutional Economics. The new institutional economics begins by challenging the neoclassical economics assumption that information collection and analysis is costless. This field of study rejects that notion and finds that information is costly to obtain and is asymmetrically held (some have more of it, and some have less of it). However, unlike the new-Keynesian school, it assumes that information constraints can act as a means to innovate new institutions that overcomes asymmetry and leads to mutually beneficial outcomes.

This field of study requires both historical (path dependence is an important concept here) and contemporary economic interdisciplinary study (North 1990). For instance, to understand governmental form across countries today requires an examination of past governmental forms. Contrasting U.S. with Latin American governmental forms, North finds that the United States' more decentralized and democratic structure today had its roots in the English system as early as the thirteenth century (1990, 113). While England was moving to more decentralization (as evidenced in the Magna Carta), Spain became more centralized after defeating the Moors (113–14). These changes led to long-term dynamics spilling over into the New World: 'The divergent paths established by England and Spain in the New World have not converged despite the mediating factors of common ideological influences. In the former, an institutional framework has evolved that permits the complex impersonal exchange necessary to political stability and to capture the potential economic gains of modern technology. In the latter, personalistic relationships are still the key to much of the political and economic exchange' (117).

The new economic institutional literature has identified many institutional and technological changes that have developed to plug information and institutional 'holes.' For instance, while neoclassical economics bemoans the tragedy of the commons when natural resources are exploited, institutional studies point to the innovative ways that communities have managed their resources (Ostrom 1990; Berkes 2004). More directly related to the topic of finances, studies have examined the ways in which different forms of community-based credit fill financial service voids. The best known of these is microcredit, popularized by the Grameen Bank in Bangladesh. However, the ROSCAs (rotating savings and credit associations) and the ASCRAs (accumulating savings and credit associations) are much older, traditional forms of financial services that are rooted in small communities. They are examples of what is known as *club goods*. Private goods are excludable (the owner can exclude others from using them) and subtractable (consumption by one person reduces what is available for others). Public goods are neither excludable nor subtractable. Club goods are excludable but not subtractable (Todaro and Smith 2006). Club goods allow communities to exclude non-members, but their existence does not reduce the availability of that resource for others. For instance, through decentralized peer monitoring and support, a ROSCA allows a limited group of people (exclusive membership) to benefit from group savings without the existence of a bank, and this process does not reduce the availability of financial resources for others. Microcredit organizations have used peer monitoring and support and combined it with large-scale organizations to develop highly effective micro-loan delivery. Asset-building programs such as individual development accounts (IDAs) (see below) are another example of an approach that uses the club goods notion (peer support) within an organizational structure to build the financial assets of the poor.

New institutional economics is a useful theory for understanding financial exclusion. It points to the role of history, as well as the important role of institutions in effective markets, governments, communities, and societies. Perhaps, most important, this theory sheds light on community-based means for promoting financial inclusion. By drawing on the concept of club goods, financial inclusion can be promoted. A weakness of this approach is that it ignores political-economic considerations such as the role of class and the changing role of the state.

Caskey's Demand- and Supply-Side Institutional Economic Analysis. A general institutional economics approach is best demonstrated in the work of John Caskey. His book *Fringe Banking: Check-Cashing Outlets, Pawnshops, and the Poor* represents a groundbreaking study of fringe banks in the United States from an interesting institutional economic perspective. It is institutional in the sense that Caskey identifies and analyses several key (demand- and supply-side) institutional factors that have a bearing on the growth of fringe banks. This is different from the neo-classical economic approach, which limits analysis to one key variable, or to a few, allowing for mathematical modelling and econometric analysis. However, Caskey's analysis seems to assume rational human behaviour.

Caskey points to the growth of fringe banks, with a focus on pawnshops and cheque cashers in the United States during the 1980s and 1990s; his study preceded the rapid growth in payday lenders. In chapter 4, 'Who Uses Fringe Banks and Why?' and chapter 5, 'Explaining the Boom in Fringe Banking,' he examines the demand-side (why customers use fringe banks) and the supply-side (why fringe banks offer financial services) of the fringe-bank growth situation. On the demand-side lie a number of factors including a preference for convenience, the need for quick cash, the inappropriateness of bank accounts, and stagnating incomes at the bottom of the income hierarchy. The supply-side factors that he identifies include bank branch closures, the introduction of deposit-account transaction fees, and the declining availability of small loans.

Caskey's study was groundbreaking and continues to influence our understanding of financial exclusion. His holistic analysis points out the large numbers of factors bearing on financial service choice. It should be noted that his analysis does have limitations. First, at least in his 1994 work, he assumes that human rationality holds. Second, his analysis does not consider political-economic factors, such as the role of class and gender, nor the immense process of financial service deregulation that was then taking place (a point highlighted more in the political-economy approach, for example, Leyshen).

Institutional Theory of Savings. Another important institutional analysis applied to the study of financial exclusion is the work of Michael Sherraden and Michael Barr (2004, 2005). They developed a multifactor model to examine savings that was rooted in institutional economics. It rejects the assumption of neoclassical economic theory that all consumers, poor and rich, operate within frictionless and competitive markets. Their theory sees institutions, including markets, as important intermediaries of human behaviour. It also rejects the idea associated with the culture-of-poverty theories that the poor are inherently different than the non-poor. The institutional theory of savings assumes that poor people behave like non-poor people; however, they face a different set of institutions. The model assumes that individuals are 'complex and their cognition and emotions can affect action,' consistent with the understanding of human behaviour in behavioural economics (Sherraden and Barr 2004, 8). The model seeks to explain savings behaviour and identifies seven key factors affecting savings behaviour, including access, information, incentives, facilitation, expectations, restrictions, and security.

As with Caskey's model, the institutional theory of savings seeks to encompass a large number of relevant factors bearing on financial exclusion. Some notable differences between the two relate to their assumptions about human behaviour and to the level of focus; the focus of savings theory is at the micro-level, and the focus of the demand-and-supply model is at the macro-level. Neither model integrates salient political-economic factors.

Asset Building. Asset building is an example of praxis, the merging of theory and practice. It is both a theory and, associated with individual development accounts, an anti-poverty program. As a theory, asset building accents the role of assets, which are distinct from income, in achieving human well-being. Sherraden (2005) has contributed to social policy discussion by explaining how an individual's assets can be of assistance in achieving his or her economic goals. He argues that asset building is consistent with a long-standing approach in international development studies that highlights capacity building, and that asset-building programs are consistent with approaches that strengthen human and social capital. Finally, he argues that asset building supports a shift from the state as service provider towards the state as enabler: 'The welfare state, created in the twentieth century, may be undergoing a major change. Gilbert describes a shift away from social entitlements and toward private responsibility, with an "enabling state" treating individual actors who are capable of looking after themselves with some assistance from the government, not as totally passive recipients of public assistance' (Sherraden 2005, 6).

Asset-building theory has been used to demonstrate the importance of asset-building strategies. Middle-income households in Canada and the United States have access to tax incentives for retirement savings, but the same is not true for low-income people. In Canada the bulk of the registered retirement savings is made by middle- and upper-income Canadians.[3] Low-income Canadians do not benefit from these same tax breaks. Thus it is argued that, for equity's sake – not to mention as a means to promote well-being – similar types of asset building should be available for low-income people. This is a rationale for individual development accounts (IDAs), a donor-matched savings scheme that releases the match for an asset-building scheme once the participant has completed his or her saving goal. The asset building may be for education, job training, business development, a home purchase, or a household item purchase.

Individual development account programs have a number of interesting connections to financial exclusion. They involve matched savings and participation in financial management training, and they require the participant to have a bank account. These aspects of IDAs can encourage people to move to financial inclusion. How useful they are in overcoming financial exclusion is addressed in chapter 5.

POLITICAL-ECONOMY THEORIES

For the purpose of this study, political-economy theories refer to those that examine the social world, cognizant of social, state, and political structures. Flowing from the Marxist tradition, this approach is sometimes referred to now as a neo-Gramscian approach; 'within a historical structure, three elements reciprocally interact: ideas, material capabilities and institutions' (Montgomerie 2007, 113). This theoretical framework often begins by contextualizing the macroeconomic policies instituted since the Second World War, with particular attention to neoliberal policies since the 1980s. With respect to financial exclusion studies, the approach finds that the neoliberal policy environment has created the context in which some firms, and consumers, find themselves serving or being served outside of the mainstream banking system.

The stagflation and the accumulation of international debt in the 1970s made it a watershed period. It shifted economic policy from the Keynesian model and ushered in the neoliberal policies. The rise of new classical macroeconomics (for example, Robert Lucas and rational expectations) at the expense of Keynesian macro-policies shifted monetary policy from being expansionist to focusing on the reduction of inflation. Neoliberalism is also associated with labour and financial service deregulation (Leyshon and Pollard 2000; Montgomerie 2007). Labour market deregulation was justified in order to reduce pressure on prices from the labour-side of the inflation equation (Leyshon and Pollard 2000, 207). Neoliberalism also called for relaxing the international restrictions to trade and investment in order to stimulate growth, thereby stimulating economic globalization, which was symbolized in the 1995 creation of the World Trade Organization.

Anglo-American countries were particularly inclined towards neoliberal policies. Election victories by Ronald Reagan, Margaret Thatcher, and Brian Mulroney in the early 1980s were important events that ushered in these policies in the United States, the United Kingdom, and Canada, respectively. Liberalization was possibly most extensive in the United States, evidenced by liberalization of power-generation markets, which later failed in the Enron collapse. Continental Europe, by and large, did not embrace the neoliberal agenda to the same extent. Northern European countries, France, and Germany maintained more extensive state intervention in spheres such as health care and employment insurance (Sen 1999). This distinction continues today as evidenced by state support for the unemployed (OECD 2008, cited in Osberg 2009). OECD data find that the highest levels of employment support are found in northern Europe, France, and Belgium, and the lowest levels are found in Australia, Canada, the United States, and the United Kingdom.

It was during the 1980s that financial services were deregulated. The state was to pull back from controlling foreign exchange and credit markets. For example, neoliberal policy calls for credit ceilings to be removed or raised to allow suppliers to offer higher-priced credit to higher-risk consumers. As discussed in the previous chapter, consumer credit was also used during the neoliberal period as a way to stimulate economic growth. Under the WTO's General Agreement on Trade in Services (GATS), retail banking would increasingly be traded internationally. Finally, the post-war separation of retail banking, insurance, and trust services diminished, allowing financial service providers in one area to compete with providers in another area.

Facing more competition, banks responded by seeking ways to raise profits or reduce unnecessary costs. This led them to close marginally profitable (or unprofitable) branches in more marginal neighbourhoods and areas (Leyshon and Thrift, 1997). Moreover, labour market deregulation has reinforced this process by reducing the incomes of people at the bottom of the income hierarchy (Caskey 1994; Buckland and Martin 2005). The result is the 'tiering' of financial service markets: private banking for wealthy clients, regular mainstream banking for middle-income people, and fringe banks for those low-income people who find themselves financially excluded (Leyshon 1997; Caskey 1994).

The political-economy framework to financial exclusion is critical of bank bifurcation because it segments the most marginal customers in the least attractive services; it may lead the most marginal customers to the financial coercion associated with high and complicated fees, encouraging repeat borrowing and aggressive collection practices, for example (Aitken 2006, 484). In addition, it is argued that bank tiering can lead to impoverishing pressures in inner-city neighbourhoods (Leyshon and Thrift 1997, 230; Dymski and Veitch 1992, sited in Leyshon 1997) and deepening poverty and inequality.

The political-economy framework provides a useful method for theorizing financial exclusion. By highlighting the deregulation of financial services and the shifting role of the state and financial service providers, it brings to the fore a critical contextual process that is missed in some other approaches. However, it may also overstate the role of power in the social world and thereby understate the importance of human agency and community capacity.

Financialization. Financialization is a relevant concept here. It refers to 'the increasing role of financial motives, financial markets, financial actors and financial institutions in the operation of the domestic and international economies' (Epstein 2005, quoted in Dore 2008). It is related to the concept *homo economicus* in that it places increasing emphasis on the financial or economic aspects of human life, to the exclusion of the psychological and social aspects. Like economic globalization, it is a fluid concept with many, and at times diverse, meanings, but it points to the shift from the managerial capitalism of the 1960s to the investor capitalism of the 2000s (Khurana 2007, cited in Dore 2008). It can help to explain the growing diversity of types, and size, of investments, ranging from mutual funds to asset-backed securities to derivatives. Financialization can also explain the boom in retail banking, including consumer credit products and volumes.

Evidence of financialization in the overall economy is found in many indicators. One common example – often connected with indicators of economic globalization – is the US$3 trillion that is exchanged in money markets each day (Dore 2008, 1099). Another empirical example highlighting financialization is the size of the derivative market compared with total world national incomes. Derivatives are 'instruments whose price depends on something else, which could be the value of a physical commodity, a coupon like a share or bond, or a financial ratio like an interest or exchange rate' (Erturk et al 2008, 6). Dore notes that, by 2007, over-the-counter derivatives (a particular type of derivative) were valued at US$516 trillion (2008, 1099). This is almost eight times the size of the total world national income of US$66 trillion. The precise meaning of this relationship is more complex than this presentation allows. That this component of the derivative market is so much larger than 'real' national income is an indicator of the size of financial transactions.

The prime example of problematic financialization is the sub-prime mortgages behind the U.S. sub-prime financial crisis. In these we see both 'upstream' and 'downstream' aspects of financialization. Upstream financialization (affecting the supply of credit, the investment side) is evidenced in securitization whereby mortgages are packaged with other credit products in asset-backed securities and then sold to investment companies and banks. Instead of being held by the bank that provides it, the mortgage is bundled with other assets and sold to other investors. These investors did not know the full risks involved in their investments. Downstream financialization (affecting the consumer through retailing) is evidenced in how the mortgage is marketed. Recall from the discussion in chapter 1 that people who have previously been unable to access a mortgage are now able to obtain one due to a low, or 'teaser,' interest rate and low or no down payment. The teaser rate is low but fixed for a short term, say one year to three years. When the term expires, the rate floats to a level that is several percentage points above the prime rate (and thus 'sub' prime). The consequences of the sub-prime mortgage crisis are still unfolding, but in the meantime upstream investments, asset-backed securities, have collapsed, bringing down huge investment companies and banks. The downstream effect is that millions of American homeowners have lost their homes. Recession in the United States, the United Kingdom, and several other countries directly affected by the crisis spread internationally to create a major global recession.

POVERTY AND COMMUNITY-BASED ANALYSES

An important theoretical approach, with links to political-economy because of its focus on structural barriers, is what we refer to here as poverty and community-based analyses. Owing to its importance in understanding financial exclusion, this theoretical perspective will be examined in more detail in chapter 2. It differs from the political-economy approach as it highlights the realities and experiences of the voiceless, in this case financially excluded people. It is an approach that begins with the experiences of low-income people and includes an understanding of the structures that reinforce inequality and poverty. Poverty and community-based analyses pay particular attention to class, gender, ethnicity, and inner-city locale as the causes of poverty. Often this research is associated with qualitative field methods such as neighbourhood surveys and life histories (Squires and O'Connor, 1998; Buckland and Martin 2005). These approaches seek to understand the 'why' behind different behaviours, with the assumption of human rationality. Results reveal that low-income consumers often behave in highly rational ways based on the relative costs and benefits of the different types of financial services they face. In addition to examining class and gender, these analyses consider the inner-city locale as a location of impoverishment (Buckland, Hamilton, and Reimer 2006; Dymski 2000). Here it is understood that the inner city is separate from the suburbs and that its impoverishment is related to a lack of resources or capacity.

GEOGRAPHIC SPATIAL ANALYSES

Spatial analyses examine if, and to what extent, location is a factor in financial service provision. In relationship to financial exclusion, these studies often seek to determine if mainstream banks are under-located and fringe banks over-located in low-income neighbourhoods. If this type of spatial location pattern were the case, then it would likely lead to poor people paying more for financial services than do others. Thus spatial analysis relates to Caplovitz's *The Poor Pay More* (1967) in which he documents how inner-city New York residents face higher priced goods and services compared to those of their suburban neighbours.[4] As these studies have tended to be largely empirical and are of importance to this study, they will be examined more comprehensively in chapter 3.

HOUSEHOLD ECONOMY

The study of the household economy is associated with sociology, human ecology, and the study of international development. Studying the household economy allows the unpacking of a complex site of negotiation, the household. Unpacking the household sheds light on its decision making, resource allocation, and gender relations. Studies in the Northern context have recently examined the rapid change in household characteristics (for example, Burgoyne 2008; Pahl 2008; Phipps and Wooley 2008), while studies in the global South have often focused on gender relations within the household (Agarwal 1997). Both of these types of studies have been interested in examining the role of finances – and in some cases banking – within the household and thus cast light on the theory of people and financial services.

For instance, in a 2008 special issue of the *Journal of Socio-Economics* on the household economy, two articles in particular examine financial issues in the household. Pahl's (2008) study of UK data finds evidence of a growing individualization of finances within the household, leading in some cases to greater intra-household inequality. She likens this contemporary reality in the United Kingdom to the traditional division of labour and finances – between subsistence and cash cropping – in sub-Saharan African farm households. While Northern household individualization and traditional sub-Saharan division of labour and finances may work at a metaphorical level, deeper links are troublesome. The gaps between these two regions in terms of contemporary reality and recent history are just immense. Nevertheless, this relationship points to a common feature across societies: gender bias.

International development studies have been fascinated with microcredit (and now a slightly broader approach, microfinance) in literature and practice. Besides examining financial costs and consequences, the literature has dug into the question of gender impact. Most studies have found that the financial impact of microcredit on the household has been positive, but there is more debate about the impact on females in the households that are receiving credit. Some studies on the impact of microcredit in Bangladesh, for instance, have concluded that all household members have benefited from taking out a small loan (Hashemi, Schuler, and Riley 1996). Another group of studies has questioned the nature of the impact on and the degree of benefit to female household members (Kabeer 2001; Goetz and Sen Gupta 1996). These studies find that the gender division of labour, which disallows women easy access to the market, and gender bias in household decision making means that men control decision making; this works to the betterment of the men more than to that of the women even if the women receive the loan.

To the extent that financially excluded people are members of households, studying the household economy is important. Financial exclusion may in part be caused by the structure of the household; therefore, pathways towards inclusion are only solved by addressing these structures.

CANADA

In addition to including studies on financial exclusion in Canada in the relevant sections above, we discuss them here as a unit in order to understand the general focus of these studies.[5] Ramsay's analysis (2000, 2001) was framed around the idea of the financially excluded as vulnerable consumers, and it examined fringe-bank fees and practices. Robinson (2006) examined the cost structure of payday lending, while considering important ethical issues associated with the rise in payday lending. Aitkin (2006) examined financial exclusion from a political-economy perspective, along the tradition of Leyshon. Buckland and Martin's work (2005) focused on a socio-economic case study of financial exclusion in a particular inner city in Winnipeg, akin to work by Squires and O'Connor (1998) in Milwaukee, Wisconsin. The Public Utilities Board in Manitoba held public hearings to determine a cap to fees for cashing government cheques and for obtaining payday loans. These two processes led to significant research on both the demand- and the supply-side of payday lending. The Public Interest Advocacy Centre (PIAC) has done some interesting quantitative surveying, and ACORN Canada has sponsored Robinson's original analysis of payday lending costs and profitability. Both of these groups have been active in advocacy with government.

What are some common elements to these studies? One element is that most of them take an interdisciplinary approach to the topic. Additionally, most of these studies explicitly apply some type of ethical analysis to their research: Ramsay's vulnerable-consumer idea, Robinson's advocacy for fee-cap regulation because of asymmetric power,[6] Aitken's notion that fringe lending is coercive, and Buckland and Martin's notion of two-tier banking. One way to further characterize Canadian studies on financial exclusion is to compare them to studies from other countries. For instance, in a comparison with studies from the United States some interesting differences are evident. While there have been studies in the United States that have been interdisciplinary and ethically oriented, there have been a significant number of studies that are more firmly lodged in an economic perspective and some that are less willing to assign an ethical critique to fringe banking. For example, Elliehausen and Lawrence's analysis (2001) of payday lending offers very little insight into the complex social and political dynamics at work for payday loan borrowers.

Conclusion

This chapter has reviewed key theories that have been used to inform the analysis of financial exclusion and related matters. It began with an overview of the ways in which theories about financial exclusion are constructed, and considered the principal constraint, the breadth (disciplinary versus interdisciplinary), the topic, and the object of this particular study. There is a significant range in the assumptions made within different theories. One way to map these differences is to consider the different assumptions that are made about human behaviour and the role of institutions. Figure 2.1 provides a summary of this analysis.

The many theories examined here were grouped into two broad categories, economic and interdisciplinary theories. Economic theories are more abstract and allow for high-level quantitative analysis, but they lack the breadth that the interdisciplinary theories can provide. Economic analysis allows quantitative methods that can lead to prescriptive decisions, but intellectual rigour in analysis does not ensure that these will be relevant. For instance, as discussed above, econometric analysis of financial literacy may find, based on a common set of indicators, that low-income people are less financially literate than are other people; however, the use of a common set of indicators of financial literacy may not be appropriate. Why should a person with few financial assets – as well as one with many assets – understand the variable risk and rewards of different types of investments? This is a benefit of applying an interdisciplinary perspective to the analysis. Moreover, what do low-income people think about financial literacy? Is it, in their minds, an important barrier or a resource?

No one theoretical perspective can holistically frame our understanding of the social world. Its complexity does not allow this. Yet trying to use every theory to understand financial exclusion would be problematic. What theories will be particularly useful to the study for the purposes of this book? This book is particularly grounded in institutional theory (especially chapters 1, 4, and 5) and community and poverty theories (chapter 3). These theories reject an analysis of financial exclusion based solely on consumer choice (associated with neoclassical economic approaches) and, rather, see the structures and processes that are rooted in locales (for example, inner cities), markets, and policies as providing a more complete understanding of financial exclusion.

3 Choosing Banking Services When the Options Are Limited

This chapter examines the reasons that low-income people choose the financial services they do in the face of major financial service barriers. It flows from a community- and poverty-study approach and presents a picture of the citizen choice that is made when banking options are limited. As a result of limited choices, many low-income people rely on fringe-bank services for some or all of their banking needs. However, these more expensive, weakly regulated services can aggravate poverty further. The data for this chapter come from secondary sources and from a variety of field research methods.

The chapter first presents a review of the literature on poverty and community studies that relate to financial exclusion. This is followed by background information on the field work, including a description of the neighbourhoods, the research methods, and the participating households. The core section examines the reasons that people choose certain types of financial services and describes respondents' recommendations for improving mainstream banking services.

Poverty- and Community-Based Studies

There are a number of poverty- and community-based studies that examine financial exclusion. They are interested in understanding the barriers to inclusion that low-income people face. These studies examine the ways in which factors such as class, gender, ethnicity, and neighbourhood of residence affect people experiencing financial exclusion. David Caplovitz's study *The Poor Pay More* is a seminal analysis of how markets in low-income New York neighbourhoods provide goods and services at a higher price than do the markets in wealthier neighbourhoods. This research has been reproduced for other cities such as Baltimore in the United States (Job Opportunities Task Force 2007). Studies from this perspective on financial exclusion are found for the United States (Blank and Barr 2009; Squires and O'Connor 2001), the United Kingdom (Kempson and Whyley 1999b; Rogaly, Fisher, and Mayo 1999), and Canada (Buckland and Martin 2005). Some of these studies use quantitative methods (Barr 2009; Kempson and Whyley 1999), and others use qualitative or mixed research methods (Buckland and Martin 2005). These interdisciplinary studies are rooted in areas such as the sociology of poverty, political geography, and community development.

An early study that focuses on the social context of financial exclusion is that of Squires and O'Connor (1998, 2001), which concentrates on low-income neighbourhoods in Milwaukee. Their book, *Color and Money: Politics and Prospects for Community Reinvestment in Urban America*, examines how race, ethnicity, and income affect people's access to mortgage credit and financial services. It was one of many studies documenting the fact that U.S. minorities, including African Americans, Hispanic Americans, and residents of marginalized communities, receive a disproportionately small share of consumer and mortgage credit (Squires and O'Connor 2001, 35). This process is called *redlining*, metaphorically crossing the neighbourhood off with a red pen to disqualify certain low-income neighbourhoods, used by service providers such as banks, mortgage providers, and insurers. It led to a major community backlash in the United States that helped to usher in the Community Reinvestment Act, among other reforms (Squires and O'Connor 2001, 141). *Color and Money* concludes with an examination of the ways to promote financial and mortgage services in redlined neighbourhoods through community action and community reinvestment.

The pioneering work of John Caskey in his book *Fringe Banking*, discussed in chapter 2, is an important contribution to the analysis of financial exclusion. While it does not centrally focus on social and poverty issues, it addresses them within a comprehensive framework that includes analysis of underlying institutional changes and examination of the business side of the banking equation. His book presents an analysis of the number of different types of fringe banks, the reasons customers use fringe banks, and an institutional analysis of the factors that explain the growth of fringe banking. In the process. he does refer to the social and poverty factors that have led to this growth, including the decline in deposit-account holders (due to bank fee increases and the closure of branches), income declines among people at the bottom of the income hierarchy, and an increase in the number of households with low income.

An important pioneering work on financial exclusion in the United Kingdom was Leyshon and Thrift (1997). It provided a critical political-economy analysis of the changes to the international financial system that were rooted in neoliberal policy from the 1980s. In addition to valuable theoretical insights, the authors examined the consequences of neoliberal reforms for low-income communities in the United Kingdom and the United States.

Some of the literature on financial exclusion from the United Kingdom has tended to have a policy orientation, perhaps because of the influence of the UK Financial Services Authority. Elaine Kempson and colleagues at the University of Bristol's Personal Finance Centre have produced a large volume of studies accenting the issues that have been highlighted by British policymakers, such as financial literacy and financial inclusion. In one report the authors examine the people who are financially excluded in the United Kingdom, the processes that lead to financial exclusion, and the consequences of being excluded (Kempson and Whyley 1999a). They conclude as follows on the underlying causes of financial exclusion: 'On the whole, then, large numbers of households are not being denied access to all forms of financial service provision; nor have they made an unconstrained choice to opt out. Instead, most of them face a range of barriers. This includes *price exclusion* – where some financial services are too expensive; *condition exclusion* – where the conditions attached to products make them inappropriate for their needs; and *marketing exclusion* – with no one trying to sell them financial products' (41).

The book *Poverty, Social Exclusion, and Microfinance in Britain* (Rogaly, Fisher, and Mayo 1999) takes a broad poverty- and community-based approach to understanding financial exclusion. It draws on the concept of *social exclusion*, which it defines as 'the processes which bring about lack of citizenship, whether economic, political or social,' where economic citizenship includes access to financial services (8–9). The book argues that stagnating low income, growing income inequality, weak employment opportunities, and declining social assistance reinforce social and financial exclusion. It finds that many Britons without a bank account use informal financial services including doorstep lenders (27). The book also examines microcredit efforts in the global South and considers various ways to address financial inclusion in the United Kingdom, such as improving provision from banks, the post office, and credit unions.

Research on the social aspect of financial exclusion in Canada was first investigated by Iain Ramsay (2000). Although his study was primarily concerned with policy and legal aspects of the 'alternative consumer' or fringe credit market, his use of the 'vulnerable consumer' idea highlighted social and poverty issues. By *vulnerable consumer* Ramsey referred to one who is excluded from the financial system, who must pay high fees to access banking services, and who might rely on credit to prop up stagnant wages (3). He called for a variety of policy reforms and improvements in service provision to people relying on fringe banks.

A Canadian study that was focused more centrally on the socio-poverty context was a study of fringe banking in a low-income neighbourhood of Winnipeg, the North End (Buckland et al. 2003). The research included examination of the number of bank branches in the neighbourhood over a twenty-three year period (162–3). In 1980 there were twenty mainstream bank or credit unions branches and only one fringe bank (a pawnshop). By the late 1980s there had been a rapid increase in the number of pawnshops, and in the 1990s there was a rapid increase in the number of cheque-cashing outlets. The number of banks declined throughout the period and then dropped precipitously in the late 1990s and early 2000s. By 2002 there were eighteen fringe banks and only five mainstream bank branches.

In addition, this study included a qualitative method survey of forty-one neighbourhood residents. The results were presented in a demand-supply framework, drawing on Caskey (1994) to explain respondents' financial service choice. Eight factors on the supply-side were identified: a distant bank or ATM location, high fees, a long period to hold cheques for cashing, difficult personal identification requirements, lack of control or trust over money, lack of anonymity, lack of access to credit and other banking services, safety concerns about carrying cash, and discrimination by bank staff. In addition to these factors, others were identified, including low income and assets, a spiral affect, and discrimination by welfare staff. The study used respondents' responses to highlight key points such as this point about the issue of accessibility: 'The growth of fringe banks provides accessible services to people in [Winnipeg's] North End. Our respondents explained [that] because of difficulties with mainstream banks, limited informal financial networks and limited income they often used fringe banks . . . In using fringe banks clients are not likely to easily move into a relationship with a mainstream bank. If this is the case, the growth of fringe banks will simply aggravate the problems of stagnating income among low-income Canadians and income inequality in Canada' (Buckland and Martin 2005, 178–9). Another study calculated the financial costs for a typical North End Winnipeg resident to rely on fringe bank services. It estimated that to cash two $500 cheques each month would cost a person who relied on a cheque casher $403 annually, compared to the person who relied on a mainstream bank's low-fee account, who would pay only $44 annually. The mainstream bank account holder would save $359 per year, representing 2.5% of the neighbourhood median after-tax income (for persons aged fifteen years or over) of $14,548 (Buckland, Hamilton, and Reimer 2006, 114).

The Neighbourhoods and Households

Poverty- and community-based studies are often rooted in the study of a particular group of people, sometimes within a particular geographic locale. The focus of this book is financial exclusion among low-income, inner-city people in Canada. The data from this section, and the next, draws on a field research project involving a mixed-method survey and the financial life history of just under one hundred participants in inner cities in Toronto, Vancouver, and Winnipeg (for more detail on the methods please refer to Buckland [2010] and Buckland, Fikkert, and Eagan [2010]). The field research was undertaken in three inner-city neighbourhoods: Toronto's Parkdale, Vancouver's Downtown Eastside, and Winnipeg's inner city. This section presents some background information about the neighbourhoods and the participants in the field research.

Each of these neighbourhoods, or portions of them, is distinctly disadvantaged (see table 3.1). Many residents have a low income, unemployment is common, and education levels are lower than the city's average. The neighbourhoods have been and continue to be important destinations for international and domestic migrants. In each neighbourhood there are a few mainstream banks and many fringe banks. Each neighbourhood is located in the inner city, a region adjacent to the downtown, where a disproportionate number of low-income people live. These inner cities have some common features such as availability

Table 3.1
Socio-economic data by neighbourhood

Characteristics	0004.00 (CT)	Toronto (CMA)	0059.06 (CT)	Vancouver (CMA)	0043.00 (CT)	Winnipeg (CMA)
Population in 2006	6861	5,113,149	6205	2,116,581	4137	694,668
Population in 2001	7417	4,682,897	4993	1,986,965	3803	676,594
Median age of the population (years)	37.3	37.5	44.4	39.1	32.8	38.8
Number of lone-parent families	380	237,430	50	88,115	385	35,010
Median income in 2005 – all census families ($)	34,995	69,321	33,877	64,332	31,993	64,316
Average household size	2	2.8	1.3	2.6	2.4	2.4
Total Aboriginal and non-Aboriginal identity population	6615	5,072,075	5805	2,097,960	4140	686,040
Aboriginal identity population	65	26,575	960	40,310	2015	68,385
Aboriginal identity as % of total population	1.0%	0.5%	16.5%	1.9%	48.7%	10.0%
Total population 15 years and over	5690	4,122,820	5715	1,752,390	3070	562,640
No certificate; diploma or degree	1380	813,595	2080	303,345	1605	130,370
No certificate; diploma or degree as % of total population ≥15 years old	24.3%	19.7%	36.4%	17.3%	52.3%	23.2%
Employment rate	56.9	63.7	40	63	43	65.1

(*Continued*)

Table 3.1 (*Continued*)

Characteristics	0004.00 (CT)	Toronto (CMA)	0059.06 (CT)	Vancouver (CMA)	0043.00 (CT)	Winnipeg (CMA)
Unemployment rate	9.6	6.7	13.9	5.6	17.8	5
Total population	6615	5,072,075	5805	2,097,965	4140	686,040
Total visible minority population	3415	2,174,070	1205	875,300	710	102,940
Visible minority as % of total population	51.6%	42.9%	20.8%	41.7%	17.1%	15.0%
Government transfers as % of total income, 2005	18.1	8.1	32	8.8	38.7	11
% in low income after tax – all persons, 2005	40.4	14.4	63	16.5	52.2	14.6

Source: Statistics Canada, 2011 Census Tract (CT) Profiles; 2006 Census, Catalogue #92-597-XWE
CT = Census Tract
CMA = Census Metropolitan Area

of low-income housing and rental accommodations, poor infrastructure, and a paucity of retailers. An important difference between these sites is that the Toronto and Vancouver inner cities are facing more gentrification pressures than is the Winnipeg inner city. In fact, recent trends in neighbourhood dynamics in Toronto point to a worsening socio-economic situation in the inner suburbs (a region between the inner city, the outer suburbs, and the peri-urban regions) relative to the inner city (Hulchanski 2007). This section will provide some description of each of these neighbourhoods, drawing on census data.[1]

Parkdale is west of Toronto's downtown and was originally settled by the city's elite. In the mid to late twentieth century Parkdale increasingly became a home to working-class families and then to increasing numbers of new immigrants. Income and employment levels of the new immigrants were lower than those of other Canadians. From the 1970s, with the closure of two mental health facilities in the neighbourhood, a significant number of people living with or recovering from mental illness settled there. Given that Parkdale is located right next to down-town, it has been an appealing location for middle- and upper-income Torontonians to move to during the housing boom of the last few years. This has facilitated a movement of middle- and upper-middle-income people back into the neighbourhood, that is, gentrification. Neverthe-less, there are many low-income people in the neighbourhood today (box 3.1). There are few mainstream banks in the neighbourhood but several fringe banks, and there are more mainstream bank branches in nearby downtown. Parkdale is also home to one of two Cash and Save outlets, a cheque casher owned by the Royal Bank of Canada.

Box 3.1 South Parkdale, Toronto

South Parkdale is a lower-income neighbourhood in Toronto. From 2001 to 2006 its population dropped by 8.1% to 21,005 (City of To-ronto 2007). The incidence of low income in 2005 was 40.0% for economic families and 56.3% for individuals. South Parkdale is a multicultural neighbourhood with 55.5% of residents claiming that they are visible minorities, compared with the Toronto average of 42.9%. The vast majority of residents – 91% – rent their accommo-dation. Narrowing down to census tract number 0000:40, median income was $34,995, approximately one-half the average income in Toronto. Twenty-four per cent of the population fifteen years of age or older had no post-secondary education, compared with the Toronto average of 19.7%. The unemployment rate was 9.6%, com-pared with the Toronto average of 6.7%. Income from government transfers was 18.1%, compared with the Toronto average of 8.1%.

The Downtown Eastside (DTES) of Vancouver is a particularly mar-ginalized neighbourhood in Canada. Many residents have low incomes or are unemployed, and rely on social assistance (box 3.2). It is located on a narrow tract of land that runs for several blocks east of the down-town and lies between Chinatown and Gastown.[2] The DTES used to have a reputation as the home of retired natural resource workers such as loggers, but more recently it has become known for drug usage by its residents. It is one of the few places in Canada in which public drug use is tolerated by the police, and it has the country's only safe injection site (an office where drug users can go to obtain hygienic needles and inject their drugs). Like Parkdale, the DTES is facing gentrification pressures, which were aggravated by the city's preparations for the 2010 Winter Olympics. While there are no mainstream banks in the DTES itself, there are many located in nearby downtown and China-town. Since 2004, Pigeon Park Savings, a 'junior' credit union, has been providing basic banking services to area residents. There are several fringe banks in and around the DTES.

Box 3.2 Strathcona, Vancouver

The Strathcona neighbourhood includes the Downtown Eastside in its northern portion. Strathcona had a population of 11,920 in 2006, which was a 3.0% increase from 2001 (City of Vancouver, n.d.). In 2006 the median income for the neighbourhood was $15,558, one-third of the Vancouver median income of $47,299. A little less than 60.0% of families had incomes below the low-income level, which is substantially higher than the Vancouver average of 26.6%. Ap-proximately 86.0% of the residents rented their accommodations, compared with the Vancouver average of 51.9%. Census tract num-ber 0059.06 is located in the northern portion of the Strathcona neighbourhood, and its data are more representative of the DTES than that of the entire Strathcona neighbourhood. In 2006 this cen-sus tract had a population of 6205, a median income of $10,884, an unemployment rate of 13.9%, and a proportion of low income of 63.0% (table 3.1). Just under one-third of household income came from government transfers. Visible minorities made up 20.8% of the population, and 16.5% were of Aboriginal identity.

Unlike Parkdale and the DTES, the North End, a portion of Win-nipeg's inner city, is some distance from downtown; it is located just north of the major railroad tracks that run through the centre of the city. One of the poorest areas in Winnipeg (box 3.3), the North End is just north of the West Alexander and Centennial neighbourhoods, which are adjacent to the downtown. It has been the destination of various waves of immigrants, initially from Eastern Europe from the late nine-teenth to the mid twentieth century. The challenges of some of these newcomers are depicted in John Marlyn's novel *Under the Ribs of Death*. The North End continues to be the destination for newcomers such as Filipino Canadians, and since the 1970s it has become the destination for the domestic migration of Aboriginal people. The North End saw a precipitous decline in mainstream bank branches through the 1990s and 2000s, while the number of fringe banks rose in their stead.

Box 3.3 Point Douglas South, Winnipeg

Point Douglas South neighbourhood is one of the more disadvantaged portions of the North End. Its 2005 population was 12,255, an 8.0% increase over its 2001 population (City of Winnipeg, n.d.). Average household income was $30,523, which was 48.0% of the average Winnipeg household income of $63,023. Low-income incidence among economic families was 45.3%, and among individuals was 62.4%, much higher than the Winnipeg averages of 11.1% and 34.8%, respectively. Forty-five per cent of the population identified themselves as Aboriginal, compared with the Winnipeg average of 10.2%. The proportion of people in the neighbourhood with visible minority identification was 16.8%, compared with Winnipeg's average of 16.3%. Zooming into census tract 0043.00, which is located in the central portion of Point Douglas South neighbourhood, we find that its 2006 population was 4,137. The census tract's median income after tax was one-half the neighbourhood's level at $14,548, there was a 17.8% unemployment rate, and 38.7% of household income came from government transfers. Just under one-half of the population identified themselves as Aboriginal, and 17.1% as visible minority.

The respondents from the field methods are from a highly marginalized group with roughly equal numbers in each city and by gender; the majority were of European origin, one-quarter were Aboriginal or Métis, and one-tenth formed a visible minority. Participants came from small households, and many had not completed Grade 12 (table 3.2). Many participants had very low average incomes, high rates of unemployment, and reliance on social assistance. The vast majority of the respondents had a mainstream bank account. However, 58% of survey respondents had a bank account *and* relied on fringe and/or informal bank services.[3] Respondents were asked to estimate the share of their financial services that they received from different types of providers, mainstream, fringe, and informal. The shares were 55% mainstream banks, 30% fringe banks, and 11% informal financial services.

Table 3.2
Respondent socio-economic data

	Survey	Financial life histories
Average household size	1.6	2.0
% Completing more than Grade 12	37.3	53.3
Average household income	$17,969	$12,725
% Receiving social assistance	63.9	86.7
% Holding mainstream bank account	82.5	67.7

Drawing on the financial life histories, this section presents an analysis of respondents' understanding of their economic situation. The narrative presents the ways in which different economic and social factors can reinforce one another to create immense pressures, pushing or maintaining one in poverty.

Most respondents identified low income as a fundamental constraint affecting many areas of their lives. Affording basic goods and services such as food and childcare was often a problem. These financial struggles led some respondents, sometimes, to borrow from lenders such as pawnshops and payday lenders. Respondents often linked financial hardship to physical and mental illness and to relationship break-up.

Many respondents commented that social assistance rates were too low, seriously restricting their spending. Many who relied on social assistance tried to supplement their income with part-time and often informal sector jobs, but these were poor paying. In addition, some respondents worried that earning extra income and/or accumulating savings would lead to reductions in their assistance levels. This created an additional reason to rely on a cheque casher; they felt that by keeping the income out of the mainstream bank account, it was more hidden and their social assistance support would not be reduced. While respondents faced serious financial challenges, many of them demonstrated effective short-term financial management skills.[4]

Credit from mainstream banks was generally unavailable, so respondents relied on pawnshops and payday lenders. Sometimes the accessibility of payday loans created more harm than good: 'Once you're in it [payday loans], you get stuck. We get stuck in it, the cycle is so vicious. It has 100% depressed my family. You're worrying about it all the time. I don't even want to [answer] the phone ... I've been suicidal because of it.'

Female respondents faced particularly strong barriers. As presented above, women also reported having less comfort than did men with fringe bank services in terms of the accessibility of information, a feeling of being in control of their funds, and a feeling of being respected by and of being comfortable with fringe bank staff. Several respondents experienced discrimination on the basis of gender, race, drug use, poverty, social class, and neighbourhood of residence from institutions such as banks, schools, and jobs. Several female participants found the barriers to mainstream banking to be more constricting than did male participants. These barriers included personal identification, access to mainstream bank credit, and information about account fees. One Winnipeg male had a particularly terrible racist experience at his workplace: 'My brother Brad stayed on his crew, and those guys didn't like native people. And my brother Brad should have told me about that . . . [They'd say,] ". . . get out of my way, Indian, I'll [expletive] show you how to do that". . . I would find drywall or something in my sandwiches. I'll [expletive] take a bite. That was the last straw, actually, that sandwich bite. I threw my sandwich up against the wall and said, "[Expletive], I'm out of here" . . . You're a different colour, you smell different, so what? If I cut the skin, you still bleed the same colour of blood as I do.'

Participants also commented on the difficulty they faced in getting funds to finance an education. Some respondents spoke of the way in which poor housing conditions reinforced their low-income situation. Mental illness was a serious challenge for several respondents. One Toronto respondent experienced declining mental health, and this affected his working: 'My first music job, we're talking about that . . . because of the unhappiness . . . midlife crisis when I had a nervous breakdown, my music career is broken in half . . . I've got no job skills.'

One Winnipeg single mother had relied on social assistance for several years and had had a substance-abuse problem. She recovered from her addiction and completed a training course that opened the door for her to a good but physically demanding job, sandblasting. She was then injured in a car accident, and her mother died. This pushed her back into a reliance on social assistance. Substance abuse took a huge toll on the lives of several respondents. One Vancouver respondent facing financial struggles turned to crime to finance his addiction: 'I was just selling drugs to make money to get high with, you know . . . for myself. So I wasn't saving money or anything . . . Just surviving. Supporting my habit, I guess . . . I could spend sixty dollars a day to not feel sick.'

Commonly, respondents faced multiple challenges including illness, financial challenges, unemployment, and declining self-esteem. In some cases, serious illness – such as HIV/AIDS – became the top, and only, priority with which the respondent could deal.

Choosing Financial Services with Limited Options

This section examines the reasons that low-income people choose the financial services they do. The presentation is premised on the notion that bank options for low-income people, particularly in inner cities, are limited. These limitations are presented below under the headings 'Access,' 'Fees,' 'Product Design,' 'Services beyond Cheque Cashing,' and 'Staff Culture' categories that flow from the results of a community and poverty-based field research project that was completed in three inner cities in Canada. Data for each category come from two sources: secondary sources (academic studies, national surveys, and bank service fee schedules) and field research. The field research results that follow rely on a neighbourhood survey[5] and on the financial life history method,[6] involving just fewer than one hundred interviews that were undertaken in one to three inner cities between 2006 and 2008 (table 3.2). These methods are examples of a mixed-method (or quantitative-qualitative) research approach[7] that is useful particularly for problem identification and theory building.[8]

The results of various surveys provide insights into the reasons people sometimes choose financial services that appear, on the surface, to be not beneficial for them. The assumption going into these surveys was that low-income people, like all other people, behave in rational, if complex, ways. This rationality is evidenced by the way in which people examine the costs and benefits of different types of banking services and choose services with the highest net benefit (table 3.3). Relevant costs and benefits are classified as direct economic, related economic, and related social. Direct economic costs are the fees for a particular service, such as a cheque-cashing fee at a fringe bank or a fee for a low-fee account at a mainstream bank; direct benefits of a cheque-cashing service include the speed with which one receives the cash. Related costs and benefits include both economic and social. A related economic cost would include the transportation cost to get to the bank, while a social cost would include the friendliness of the service provision. We assume that people choose financial services in order to maximize the net benefit they receive from them. In inner-city locations

Table 3.3
The net benefit calculation for choosing financial services

	Benefits	Costs
Direct economic	Immediate access to cash (higher benefit) vs. hold period (lower benefit)	Fees
Related economic	Access to other appropriate services (e.g., other transactions or other developmental)	Travel to branch, i.e., time and cost
Related social	Friendly service provision	Unfriendly service provision
Net benefit equals	Total benefit, less	Total cost

where there are few mainstream banks and service provision is weak, fringe bank services may offer a higher net benefit, at least for some financial services.

There are limited national-level data on the question of bank accessibility for poor people. National surveys find that some people are simply denied bank services. A survey sponsored by FCAC (2005) found that 4% of respondents were refused a bank service. The most commonly denied service was a credit card (41%), and the next most denied service was a chequing account (24%) (Ipsos-Reid 2005, 7–8).

The field methods focused primarily on respondents' experiences with different types of banks and bank services. Respondents were asked to explain the reasons for their choice of banking services. The responses have been categorized into five areas, which are discussed next.

Access

An important argument found in the financial exclusion literature, and discussed in chapter 1, is that low-income areas such as inner cities prominently feature fringe banks and have few mainstream banks; this spatial distribution of banks leads low-income people to rely more on fringe banks than on mainstream banks. For the United Kingdom, Leyshon (2004) argues that the roots of the geographic analysis of finances lie in David Harvey's *Social Justice and the City* (1973). Leyshon (2004, 461) contends that this early emphasis on financial geographies was usurped by the analysis of the dynamics of housing markets.

However, by the 1990s, because of financial service liberalization,the analysis of financial geographies had become more popular. Through the 1990s and 2000s there were several studies of bank spatial dynamics in the United Kingdom (Leyshon, Signoretta, and French 2006; Leyshon and Thrift 1997) and in the United States (Caskey 1994; Graves 2003; Temkin and Sawyer, n.d.; the Brookings Institution 2006). There have been some studies on the topic in Canada (Buckland et al. 2007; Jones, Bermingham and Erguden 2005; Meyer 2007; Stratcom Strategic Communications 2005).

The majority of these studies test that the locations of various types of banks (mainstream and fringe) are (positively or negatively) related to the income or dominant ethnicity of the neighbourhood (census tract, census ward, neighbourhood, and neighbourhood cluster). Generally, the hypothesis is one of two types: (1) mainstream bank branch networks are denser (or becoming denser over time) in better-off, compared to poorer, neighbourhoods; (2) fringe bank networks are denser (or becoming denser over time) in poorer, compared to better-off, neighbourhoods.

In their review of changes to banks and building society branches in the United Kingdom from 1989 to 2003, Leyshon, Signoretta, and French (2006, 2) found that banks closed just over one-third (36%) of their branches, while building societies' branches declined by between 17% and 22%. When these closures were categorized by type of neighbourhood, the highest closure rates were found in 'multicultural metropolitan,' areas that include inner cities with low average income. Lower than average rates of closures occurred in better-off areas including 'suburbs and small towns' (3).

Caskey's study (1994) of fringe banking in the United States includes an effort to explain the growth of fringe banks, and to do so he provides a spatial analysis of banks in three time periods (1970, 1980, and 1989) in five U.S. cities (Atlanta, Denver, New York, San Jose, and Washington, DC). Caskey finds that bank branch closures during this period disproportionately hit low-income neighbourhoods in Atlanta and New York, and neighbourhoods with a majority African-American population in all cities but San Jose (96–7). Temkin and Sawyer (n.d.), examining eight cities in the United States, found results consistent with those of Caskey. Graves (2003) examines the density of bank and payday lender outlets by neighbourhood in Louisiana and in Cook County (Illinois) and found that 'the results of the difference in means tests suggest that payday lenders are locating in neighbourhoods that are poorer and have higher concentrations of minorities than their county of location as a whole. The test reveals an even stronger pattern of locational bias among banks, one in favour of neighbourhoods that are wealthier and whiter than countywide means' (311). The Brookings Institution (2006), examining twelve U.S. cities and considering financial services with other retail services (such as grocery stores), concludes that 'low-income families tend to pay higher than average prices for a wide array of basic household necessities – often for the exact same items – than higher income households' (4).

Spatial studies in Canada have been more limited in scope. One case study examined banking locations from 1980 to 2003 in an inner-city neighbourhood in Winnipeg (Buckland et al. 2003). The study found that mainstream bank numbers declined from twenty to five, and fringe bank numbers (including pawnshops, cheque cashers, payday lenders, and rent-to-owns) grew from one to eighteen (figure 3.1). In a study

Figure 3.1: Breakdown of mainstream and fringe bank branches in Winnipeg's North End, 1980–2003

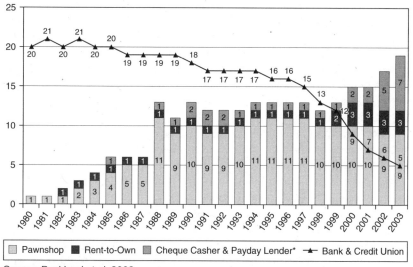

Source: Buckland et al. 2003.
*Payday loan and cheque cashers are the number of payday loan outlets plus the number of Money Mart outlets. In 2003 there was only one cheque-cashing outlet that did not offer payday loans.

of payday lender locations in Canada it was concluded that payday-lender outlets often locate near mainstream banks (Jones, Bermingham, and Erguden 2005). In a 2007 study of payday lender outlets it was found that 'the mapping of payday lenders in Winnipeg demonstrated a bias in locating in inner city and poorer suburban over suburban and higher-income suburban areas. In some cases these locations are on principal roads and possibly attract people from a variety of neigh-bourhoods. While no statistical methods were applied, it was apparent from the maps that payday lenders disproportionately locate in neigh-bourhoods with poorer income indicators (e.g., lower median income, higher incidence of low-income), lower social indicators (e.g., average education levels) and certain ethnic characteristics (higher rates of ab-original people and visible minorities)' (Buckland et al. 2007).

Spatial studies are important contributions to the study of financial exclusion. They demonstrate a bank-locational bias: a low density of mainstream banks and a high density of fringe banks in low-income neighbourhoods.

Secondary research on the topic of bank access has identified it as an important factor behind bank service choice. Branch access was identified by the MacKay Report as an important issue regarding bank access: 'Branch closures have a disproportionate impact on particular groups in society . . . primarily a concern of those who live in small rural communities and low-income neighbourhoods in urban centres' (Task Force on the Future of the Canadian Financial Services Sector 1998b, 32). In a national survey sponsored by the FCAC it was found that 62% of respondents felt that convenience of the location was im-portant and 51% of respondents felt that hours of operation was a criti-cal factor (EKOS 2001, 35).

Field research conducted in three Canadian inner cities found that branch location and hours of operation weighed heavily on partici-pants' choice of bank. Some respondents reported that because main-stream banks had closed branches and fringe banks had opened outlets in the inner city, the latter had become more convenient than had the former. 'It is nearly impossible to bundle up my four small children in order to walk five or six blocks to the bank to cash a cheque, let alone travelling out of the North End altogether' (Buckland and Martin 2005, 168). As we know, financial exclusion rates are highest among low-income people, those people least likely to have personal trans-portation, Internet hook-up (for Internet banking), and possibly even a telephone (for telephone banking).

A higher proportion of survey respondents (86.4%) found fringe banks to be more convenient than mainstream banks (61.4%). Conversely, more survey respondents found mainstream banks (22.9%) to be inconveniently located as compared with fringe banks (6.1%). Winnipeg respondents found mainstream banks to be least convenient, and Vancouver respondents found them to be most convenient. This is not surprising considering the small size of Vancouver's DTES and its location adjacent to the downtown and Chinatown, both of which contain many mainstream banks. Winnipeg's North End, on the other hand, is physically larger and is removed from a relatively affluent neighbourhood with more banks. Men were more impressed than were women by the convenience of fringe banks compared with that of mainstream banks.

Respondents felt that fringe banks had better operating hours compared with those of mainstream banks. Eighty-four per cent of respondents in the survey stated that fringe banks had convenient hours of operation, whereas only 40% stated that mainstream banks' operating hours were convenient. '[The] mainstream bank [is] not really a problem, but sometimes [I] wish that they were open Saturdays. Fringe banks are there when you need them, and they are open longer.'

Fees

A premise of this book is that inner cities have a variety of types of financial service providers. Informal, fringe, and mainstream banks are the principal categories used here. However, these different types of providers operate in quite different ways. The differences relate to a number of issues: the size of the organization, the level of regulation, deposit taking, and the type of services provided.

While mainstream and fringe banks offer different sets of financial services, which makes fee comparison challenging, there are obvious similarities. For instance, it is possible to cash a cheque at a mainstream bank and a fringe bank. Mainstream banks are required by law to charge no fee for cashing federal government cheques of less than $1,500. In some provinces (for example, Manitoba and Ontario) there is a cap on the fees allowable for cashing cheques from other levels of government. Mainstream bank fees for other types of cheques do not have a standard, but commonly the fee is $5. Cheque cashers charge higher fees. For instance, the average fee among ten cheque cashers for cashing a cheque in Winnipeg in November 2006 was $2.24 plus 2.94% of the face value of the cheque (for a $100 cheque, fees ranged from $3.67 to $5.98) (Buckland 2006b). For a $100 cheque the difference between fringe and mainstream bank fees is not significant. However, since the fringe bank fee is made up of two components, a fixed dollar value and a percentage of the cheque's face value, the fees rise for higher-value cheques. Consider a $500 cheque (not from the federal government): the typical mainsteam bank will charge $5, while the average fringe bank will charge $2.24 plus $14.70, for a total of $16.94, which is a difference of $11.94 or 3.4% of the cheque's face value.

Another option to cheque cashing is opening an account at a mainstream bank and having the funds electronically deposited. This option also appears to be more attractive than fringe bank cheque cashing. In this case, the client must open and maintain an account, which involves having appropriate personal identification and allowing the bank to assign fees to the account on a regular basis (as opposed to a one-time basis in the case of cheque cashing). Most banks and credit unions have developed a relatively low fee account, allowing a reasonable amount of free transactions per month. The fees range from $4 to $5 per month for ten to twelve (in one case, thirty) transactions per month. Thus a person cashing a $500 cheque (with a hold period applied) would pay, say, a $4.50 monthly account fee and be able to cash the cheque and make nine to eleven more transactions for free. Now, if that same person is able to have his or her income direct-deposited, then he or she faces the same low fee ($5 per month), gets cash immediately, and gets an additional nine to eleven transactions for no additional fees.

For evaluation purposes, fees for different fringe bank credit products are often lumped together and then transformed to generate an equivalency to an annual interest rate, most commonly using the annual percentage rate (APR). Most of these types of credit are for terms that are much shorter than a year, but the APR allows the consumer to compare across credit products. Almost universally, this transformation generates APRs that are well in excess of interest rates on mainstream bank credit products, such as a credit line and a credit card, and above the criminal rate of interest. Mainstream bank credit products are generated at some percentage points above the prime rate set by the Bank of Canada. However, the current economic recession and the financial crisis have placed a premium on interest rates such that many banks are currently charging 12% to 20% interest on their credit cards. Credit cards offered by retailers often charge higher interest rates. However, the APRs on fringe bank credit products are much higher. The following is a sampling of the rates for products that are comparable:

- In September 2007, average fees for a $250 payday loan from eight firms in Winnipeg were: total fees of $64 (ranging from $44 to $109); APR of 778% (ranging from 535% to 1321%) (Buckland et al. 2007).
- In 2003, pawn fees were higher for smaller loans ($10–$50) compared to those for larger loans ($100–$200), with an APR ranging from 240% to 540% (Buckland and Martin 2005).
- In 2003, rent-to-own fees amounted to APRs ranging from 120% to 489% (Buckland and Martin 2005).
- In 2003, tax-refund advance loans, on average, charged 286% APR (Buckland and Martin 2005).

Calculated as lump sums or APRs, fees charged for financial services provided by fringe banks are higher than fees for similar services at mainstream banks. However, it does not follow that people who use fringe banks are irrational. There are a variety of other economic and social factors that bear on the decision to choose a financial service. There is some evidence that, at least in the case of cheque-cashing fees, customers have a good idea of fringe bank fees. An FCAC-sponsored survey found that 44% of the respondents who used the cheque-cashing service said that the fee was between 3% and 5% the value of the cheque (Ipsos-Reid 2005, 17).

From the field research, many respondents who used fringe bank services understood that they paid a premium on the fees for fringe bank versus mainstream bank services, but they explained that they integrated other costs and benefits into their calculations that made fringe banks the rational choice. Even when respondents in the survey were asked directly about relative banking fees, they often referred to other factors, such as accessibility and convenience, that explained their choice to use fringe bank services.

Respondents' perceptions of the size of bank service fees varied. They generally reported that fringe bank fees were higher than mainstream bank fees. In the survey, 71% of respondents, uniformly high in all three cities, felt that fringe bank fees were more expensive than mainstream bank fees. However, some respondents, men in particular, felt that the fees for comparable banking services between fringe and mainstream banks were close, as this quotation highlights: 'Everyone's gotta make a buck. That's why [fringe] service charges are high and why they are open twenty-four seven . . . The mainstream banks seem to make up charges as they go along.'

Part of the reason that some respondents claimed fringe and mainstream bank fees to be comparable, as implied in the above quotation, has to do with what some participants referred to as 'hidden' fees in mainstream banking services. These are fees that they claimed appeared in their bank statement and for which they felt they were not responsible. This is juxtaposed to the cheque-cashing transaction where the fee is taken at the point of the physical transaction and the balance of the cheque is given to the client in cash: '[At the] fringe bank all you are doing is cashing the cheque, and they are taking the cost off the top. The banks are taking the fees out from the account, and you don't know what is being taken out from the account.'

Men were more likely than women to express concern about unexpected or hidden fees for mainstream bank services. Men were more likely to admit that fringe bank fees were high but that they were up front. Women were more likely to feel that mainstream bank fees were well laid out and that fringe bank fees were always increasing.

Product Design

Product design is critically important in determining the usefulness of a product. By *design* we refer to the particular requirements and criteria for using the financial services. The design features that present the greatest barriers for low-income people relate to the fees (as discussed above), the hold periods on cheques, and the personal-identification requirements. In all of these cases fringe banks have product design that makes their products more attractive for some people who have limited options.

In order for a person to cash a cheque at a bank – as opposed to depositing it and withdrawing a similar amount of funds, which is already present in the account – a seven-to-ten-day hold is placed on it. This allows the bank the time to clear the cheque with the bank that is the source of the cheque. Cheque cashers are in the business of cashing cheques immediately, and they do this by charging a hefty fee.

Yet cheque cashers are popular, as evidenced by the over 1,300 payday-lender outlets – most of which offer cheque-cashing services – in Canada. The hold period on cheque cashing at mainstream banks has been a well-documented barrier for low-income people. The MacKay Report identified this as an issue that needed to be addressed (Task Force on the Future of the Canadian Financial Services Sector 1998b, 30; Association coopérative d'économie familiale du Centre de Montréal 1996, 59). A 2005 FCAC-sponsored survey found that 7% of Canadians have used a cheque casher in their lives (Ipsos-Reid 2005, 11). The majority of cheque-casher users (53%) explained that they used the service because it was faster than the service of a mainstream bank (Ipsos-Reid 2005, 11).

Respondents of the field research found it easier to cash their cheques at a fringe bank versus a mainstream bank. Cheque cashing was seen by almost three-quarters of the survey respondents as an easy transaction to complete at a fringe bank. Forty-one per cent of respondents claimed that cashing a cheque at a bank was easy. Conversely, just over 9% of respondents found cheque cashing at fringe banks to be problematic, while just under 40% of respondents found it to be problematic at mainstream banks. Toronto respondents, as compared to Vancouver and Winnipeg respondents, found cashing cheques at mainstream banks to be the most difficult. Women, as compared with men, felt that cheque cashing was difficult, whether at mainstream or fringe banks. '[I] hate it when banks hold cheques. [You] work two weeks to cash your cheque and then you would have to wait another ten days to get cash. [I] would go hungry, [I] lost places to live. Holds had a huge impact on my life [between] 1979 and 1981.'

A second major rule that influenced financial service choice among respondents was the personal identification (ID) requirements. Banks require, and are required by law, to have clients verify their identity through the use of certain agreed-upon forms of ID. As discussed in the introduction, the banks have voluntary codes for the personal ID that they will allow for a bank transaction. The trouble is that many low-income people do not have adequate ID to meet these requirements. Thus many respondents, in various surveys, have pointed to the lack of personal ID as a major constraint to using mainstream banks. Fringe banks, however, typically require less ID, and some have their own ID systems.[9] Some community banking projects have also introduced their own ID systems.

Secondary data have identified personal identification as a barrier to financial inclusion. For instance, research that informed the MacKay Report identified personal ID as a major barrier to accessing a bank account (Association coopérative d'économie familiale du Centre de Montréal 1996, 44). The 2005 FCAC-sponsored survey found that 5% of respondents without a bank account claimed the reason to be the lack of ID (Ipsos-Reid 2005, 6).

Respondents in the field research survey claimed that ID was more challenging at mainstream banks than at fringe banks. Sixty per cent of survey respondents found identification at fringe banks to be easy, while 47% found it to be easy at mainstream banks. Only 20% of respondents found it difficult to meet ID requirements at fringe banks, while 45% of respondents found ID requirements to be problematic at mainstream banks. However, 85% of respondents made a high number of qualitative, additional responses to this question. It was the highest rate of response for all qualitative questions. This shows that personal identification is an important issue for the participants. Several respondents commented on the convenience of the photo ID system of one particular fringe bank: 'Money Mart just needed a photocopy and proof of residence. They took my picture, and that's it. I just give them my name and some info, and they compare [it] with my file picture and info.'

Services Beyond Cheque Cashing

Various studies have found that low-income people face a lack of options in terms of access to savings and credit services.

In a financial-diary method undertaken with low-income participants in South Africa, it was found that respondents relied heavily on informal sources of savings, many of which were convenient (Collins et al. 2009, 116.). Examining a large-sample randomized survey of low-income and modest-middle-income people in Detroit, Barr (2009) found that both informal and formal sources of savings were used. One-half of the sample used bank savings accounts, one-third used retirement vehicles, and more than one-half of the respondents behaved with their income tax returns in such a way as to postpone their full refund, as a means of saving (Barr 2009, 82). Commenting on the evidence about low-income Americans, Mullainathan and Shafir (2009, 127) note: 'Many low-income families are in fact savers, whether or not they resort to banks (Berry 2004). Without the help of a financial institution, however, their savings are at a greater risk (from theft, impulse spending, access by household members), will grow more slowly, and may not be readily available to support access to reasonable priced credit in times of need.'

In chapter 1 there was a reference to the growing prevalence of credit card use: the proportion of people without a card in Canada dropped from 21.1% in 1999 to 16.5% in 2005. Besides the large number of pay-day-lender outlets across the country, the sharp rise and the substantial level of payday loan use in Canada have been documented by several national level studies. The most recent Survey for Financial Security found that 2.7% of the respondents had a family member who had taken a payday loan in the last three years (Pyper 2007); an industry association survey found that 5% of the population has taken out a payday loan (Environics Research Group 2005). While the evidence is disputed, it is clear that, on average, payday loan clients have incomes that are lower than the Canadian mean (Buckland et al. 2007, 29). A study of low-income inner-city residents in Winnipeg found that small loans were available from family and friends, but, without access to mainstream bank credit, residents often looked to fringe banks as an important source of credit: 'Respondents often required finances for everyday living, unforeseen expenses or in emergencies . . . For these respondents, fringe banking was often seen as a viable option to obtain finances for these expenses' (Buckland and Martin 2005, 170).

In the field research survey, just over 50% of the respondents felt that they were ineligible for mainstream bank services, but just under 20% of the respondents felt that they were ineligible for fringe bank services. The proportions were reversed regarding eligibility for these services: 20% felt that they were eligible for mainstream bank services, while 50% felt that they were eligible for fringe bank services. With specific reference to credit, 24% of the survey respondents felt that it was accessible at mainstream banks, while 56% of the respondents felt that it was accessible at fringe banks. Men were more likely than women to claim that fringe bank credit was accessible. Indeed several men indicated that more fringe bank credit restrictions would be desirable because they had experienced debt problems in the past as a result of getting a loan from that source. Twice as many respondents (37.2%) indicated that credit was available from fringe banks compared with those (16.7%) who felt that it was available from mainstream banks. Winnipeg respondents felt the least constrained regarding access to credit. 'All you need is a job and references for fringe financial services. I am very ineligible for mainstream financial services because of my debt.'

Respondents were asked about the suitability of mainstream and fringe bank services to meet daily, long-term, and retirement financial needs. For daily needs, mainstream banks were considered suitable by 65.4% of respondents, and fringe banks were considered suitable by 33.4%. For long-term needs, the suitability shares moved to 59.0% for mainstream banks and 12.8% for fringe banks. For retirement goals, the suitability share was 50.0% for mainstream banks and 12.8% for fringe banks.

Staff Culture

There is evidence that certain groups of people have a less satisfactory experience at retailers, including banks, than do others. Mullainathan and Shafir (2009) note that it is not only one's experience with a retailer but also one's *perception* of the likely experience with that retailer that can be unsatisfactory. In other words, if a low-income person perceives mainstream banks as servicing better-off people, then that may stall them from using it. Conversely, if fringe banks are perceived as the 'bank for the poor,' then a low-income person may choose to use them. They note that 'a single mother who, without access to child care, needs to present herself at a bank in the company of her small children may be aware of the fact that, ideally, children are not brought into a bank. Along with a severely limited understanding of financial instruments, a poor client may feel reluctance, even shame, and a general sense that she can never be a valued bank customer' (Mullainathan and Shafir 2009, 134).

One way to understand consumer experience with a retailer is through customer surveys or mystery shopping. Mystery shopping, which is also called *mystery customer research* (Jesson 2005), is a way to measure the quality of a retail service. Mystery shopping is a form of participant-observer research that involves a covert element. Typically, a researcher, without identifying her or his research role, engages in a retail activity and observes some aspect of the shopping experience. These characteristics have made the mystery shopping method complex. Critiques of mystery shopping argue that due to its limitations its purpose should be constrained to diagnosis and triangulation, not quantification of social phenomenon (Jesson 2004; Alan Wilson 1998, 161).

Mystery shopping has its origin in the commercial sector (Jesson 2005), but it is increasingly used in the academic and policy fields. The academic literature using mystery shopping is rooted particularly in the United States (Ayres 1991; Yinger 1998). With mystery shopping, Ayres (1991) tested whether race and gender affected shopper treatment by car salespeople in Chicago and concluded that car dealers provided lower prices to white customers than to black customers.

Mystery shopping has also been used to inform policy. For instance, regarding the Canadian banking sector, mystery shopping has been used by the Financial Consumer Agency of Canada (2003, 2005) and, in the past, by a mainstream bank review completed by J.D. Power and Associates.[10] The FCAC mystery shopping, referred to in chapter 1, includes testing mainstream bank observance of the Access to Basic Banking Services Regulations, which require that mainstream banks, for free, open bank accounts and cash without a hold period a federal government cheque up to $1500 for anyone with adequate personal identification.

Through its mystery shopping, the FCAC found some weaknesses in mainstream bank service provision.[11] For instance, Conacher (2007) noted that the 2003 FCAC mystery shopping found that banks broke several regulations by not having a clear, publicly available policy on holds on cheques, by engaging in tied selling, and by failing to post notice of branch closure. Moreover, according to Conacher, the FCAC commissioner did not prosecute any of these banks, and as a result the names of the offending banks were not publicly reported. More challenges were identified in the most recent mystery shopping, in 2005, which tested bank policy on opening an account and cashing federal government cheques. The results found that, 'of the 292 attempts to open accounts, 48 accounts (16%) were declined. Of the 212 attempts to cash a federal government cheque, 20 (9%) were unsuccessful. Contrary to regulations, written letters of refusal by the banks were not provided in 90% of the cases involving refusing to open an account and 95% of the cases involving refusing to cash a cheque' (Conacher 2007). These FCAC mystery shopping methods demonstrate weaknesses in the provision of basic banking and in the enforcement of the basic banking service regulations by FCAC.

A mystery shopping method was used by a coalition of the consumer groups that were participating in the Manitoba Public Utilities Board hearing to determine a payday loan fee cap (Buckland et al. 2007). The process involved two steps: an enquiry phase and a borrowing phase. During the former, three mystery shoppers approached twelve payday lenders in Winnipeg. The shoppers asked an open-ended question, and then detailed questions, about payday loans, including about the fees. Some of the results from this research showed that in just under 60% of the cases the tellers said little or nothing about the payday loan fees in response to the open-ended question. Moreover, there was very little information posted or pamphlets available about fees. Even after the detailed question about payday loan fees had been posed, 75% of tellers provided answers that were 'unclear or not complete enough for the mystery shoppers to feel they fully understood' (Buckland et al. 2007, 53). In only one case was a shopper given the interest rate charged on the loan. 'When asked specific probing questions, usually the tellers were forthcoming with an answer, but rarely would they volunteer any additional details that would aid in clarification or understanding. They politely provided bare-bones answers, but not anything beyond that. Less frequently it happened that, no matter how many different times and ways a question was asked, no clear answer was given to the mystery shopper at all' (Buckland et al. 2007, 53).

Another mixed-method mystery shopping method examined the manner in which banks treated low-income shoppers. This method involved a pair of shoppers, one person portraying a low-income shopper and the other a middle-income shopper. They engaged a teller to find out about two financial services at sixty-three purposively selected mainstream and fringe banks in Toronto, Vancouver, and Winnipeg (Buckland, Brennan, and Fikkert 2010). For mainstream banks, the services were account opening and overdraft protection; for fringe banks, the services were cheque cashing and payday loan. Shoppers collected quantitative and qualitative observations relating to teller courtesy, information accessibility, information understandability, teller interest, and teller eagerness. Key results from this research were that low-income shoppers felt less well treated than did middle-income shoppers at mainstream banks; certain mainstream banks did better in this regard than did others; and information accessibility was an important challenge at fringe banks, particularly for payday loans.

Low-income shoppers were less satisfied with their experience of mainstream banks than were middle-income shoppers. The reasons identified for this difference included the following: the duration of shop was longer for the middle-income shopper than for the low-income shopper; the middle-income shopper was provided with more verbal and written information; the middle-income shopper was asked more questions by the teller; and more of an effort was made to ensure that the middle-income shopper had a follow-up appointment. Conversely, the low-income shopper received less written material, did not feel that the teller was eager for his or her business, and was often not encouraged to arrange a follow-up meeting.

While the sample size was small and no statistical tests were appropriate (as the sample was not randomly selected), the results found differences in shopper treatment by particular banks. Both the low-income shopper and the middle-income shopper had a relatively positive experience at two mainstream banks; both shoppers had a particularly negative experience at another mainstream bank; and at one mainstream bank the low-income shopper was dissatisfied and the middle-income shopper was satisfied. Shopper experiences with fringe banks ranged in the middle to the bottom in satisfaction.

Secondary data have identified issues related to the shop as having a bearing on financial service choice. In fact, the MacKay Report stated that 'people who want to hold accounts and perform transactions should be treated with courtesy and respect' (Task Force on the Future of the Canadian Financial Services Sector 1998b, 31). In a survey sponsored by FCAC in 2001, the factors considered most important, after access, in financial service choice related to the shop. Seventy per cent of respondents indicated that ease of understanding the product was an important factor, 69% of respondents stated that friendliness of employees was important, and 65% of respondents stated that the service fee was important (EKOS Research Associates 2001, 32). In another survey sponsored by FCAC, 6% of respondents who did not have a bank account said that this was because of a lack of trust and/or because an account was unsafe (Ipsos-Reid 2005, 6).

In the field research, respondents identified a number of aspects of the shopping experience that affected their choice of financial service. These factors include treatment by staff, trust in the institution, availability of information about the financial service, and time to complete the transaction.

The way in which respondents felt they were treated by bank staff was an important factor affecting their bank choice. The bank shop involves interacting with the teller and other staff (for example, security guards). Respectful treatment refers particularly to politeness and friendliness of the staff. Our research has found that the staff treatment of clients is an important and complicated factor in determining financial service choice. As with other questions, we asked the respondents about their experiences in terms of respectful treatment at mainstream and fringe banks. The results were interesting. They show that an equal number of respondents (66.7%) felt respected by mainstream staff as by fringe bank staff. However, a slightly higher proportion felt disrespected at mainstream banks (22.4%) than at fringe banks (15.6%). Winnipeg

and female respondents were more likely to feel respected by mainstream bank staff, and Torontonians and male respondents were more
likely to feel respected by fringe bank staff. 'People judge you on ap-
pearance and on where your cheque is from. When you are in a lower
income bracket, people tend to direct their hate and frustration at you.
[I] feel more judged at the bank than at Money Mart, where they may
be used to dealing more with low income folks.'

As discussed above, trust in the bank regarding fees is an important factor in determining financial service choice. If people see unac-
counted-for fees charged to their mainstream bank account, they may
perceive this to be unfair and become distrustful of the bank. Respondents were asked about their general level of trust towards the bank.
This includes transparency about service design and consistent application of service rules.

The quantitative survey results demonstrated a stronger level of
trust among respondents in mainstream banks versus fringe banks.
A higher proportion of respondents trusted mainstream banks (61%)
versus fringe banks (42%), and a higher proportion of respondents dis-
trusted fringe banks (32%) versus mainstream banks (21%). Slightly
more equal results were found for trust towards fairness of fees: 54%
of respondents felt that mainstream bank fees were fair, and 37% felt
that fringe bank fees were fair. However, somewhat in tension with the
quantitative results, there was a high number of qualitative responses
to this question that demonstrated that respondents were particularly
untrusting about fees at mainstream banks. Qualitative responses from
respondents indicated that many respondents preferred the simple off-
the-top fees of fringe banks to the fees of mainstream banks. Women
(66.7%) felt they had more control than men (51.4%) felt they had, regarding their funds in mainstream banks, while the reverse was the
case with fringe banks: men (64.5%) felt they had more control than
women felt they had (39.3%). 'The bank has all these hidden fees. At
Money Mart they tell you straight up.' 'The impersonality of being a
number in the system of a mainstream bank makes me feel like I can't
depend on them. They change their fees all the time, and people don't
pay attention, so the bank just keeps adding charges, and I don't trust
them . . . How is it that the banks have record profits? All the little
"dings" – twenty-five cents, fifty cents, two dollars – all these little
charges. They are a huge conglomerate of chomping and money, and
they didn't get that way by charging less.' 'At fringe it's upfront; you're
paying it and it's [the] end.'

In the area of fringe bank fees, pawnshop fees were seen as fair by the largest share of respondents (68.0%), followed by cheque cashing at Money Mart (33.3%), cheque cashing at other fringe bank (14.3%), and finally fees at payday lenders (12.5%).

A third factor that was identified by respondents as affecting their shopping experience was information about the service, particularly regarding the ease with which information was obtained. Of the respondents, 75% felt that it was easy to obtain information about mainstream bank services, and 65% felt that it was easy to obtain information about fringe bank services. In both cases approximately 12% of the respondents felt that obtaining this information was difficult. Male and female respondents felt similarly, and some members of both groups expressed doubt about the transparency of mainstream bank fees – men with respect to fees to open an account and women with respect to general fees. '[At the] bank, service charges seem to be added without authorization, but overall I trust them.' '[At mainstream banks] it's kind of hard to get through to anybody there. You really have to go down there, and it takes so much time and bus fare. Money Mart actually has somebody on the line that wants to talk to you.'

A final factor relating to the experience had to do with the time required to complete the financial transaction. The survey did not include a question about this time, but the issue surfaced in qualitative comments. Indeed, time to complete the transaction was one of the most commonly reported benefits of using fringe banks, and costs of using mainstream banks. Particularly because respondents were not directly asked about transaction time, the frequency and emphasis of the comments point out that transaction time is an important factor in choosing a financial service provider. Vancouver and male respondents voiced this point most commonly. 'I know I will have to pay more at Money Mart to cash my cheque but I know I will get my money faster.' '[The] bank takes more time, but fringe costs more.'

Evaluation and Suggestions for Improvements to Financial Services

Respondents were asked to evaluate the overall quality of different financial services. Credit unions and community banking projects ranked the highest for their overall quality, informal and mainstream banks fell in the middle, and fringe banks ranked the lowest. All respondents who referred to Pigeon Park Savings, Cash and Save, and credit unions said that they had good or very good quality services

Table 3.4
Comparing the quality of financial services

	% reporting good or very good quality	# of responses
Pigeon Park Savings	100.0	10
Cash and Save	100.0	6
Credit unions	100.0	7
Loans from family or friends	75.0	20
Mainstream banks	71.7	46
Pawnshops	56.7	30
Money Mart cheque cashing	56.0	25
Other fringe-bank cheque cashing	50.0	8
Payday loans	25.0	8

Table 3.5
Suggestions for improving mainstream banking services

Suggested change	Mentioned (#)	Category of suggested change Mentioned	%
More accessible locations	8	Access	22.1
Better hours	7		
Lower fees	11	Fees	16.2
Reduced cheque-cashing restrictions (hold period)	3	Design	22.1
Improved ID requirements	7		
Debt absolution or protection from garnishment	5		
More accessible credit	3	Services	4.4
Less wait time for transaction	9	Shop	22.1
Better communication	3		
Friendlier or more respectful staff	3		
General support for low-income clients	9	General	13.2

(table 3.4). Following a rank ordering, loans from friends or family ranked next highest (75%), then mainstream banks (71.7%), pawnshops (56.7%), Money Mart cheque cashing (56.0%), other cheque cashing (50.0%), and payday lenders (25.0%).

Respondents were asked what improvements could be made to improve existing mainstream banking services (table 3.5). The most common responses included lower fees, more support for low-income people's financial needs, and reduced time for transactions. Men more often suggested reducing the time for transactions, providing general support for low-income people, and enhancing transparency (for example, with regard to fees). Women commonly suggested giving more respectful treatment, targeting incentives to benefit low-income patrons, having fewer ID restrictions, and offering more accessible credit. After the suggestions had been grouped into categories, improving access, improving design for services, and improving the shopping experience all tied for first place, with each category representing 22.1% of the suggestions.

Conclusion

The rationality of respondents regarding financial service choice is evidenced in the sense that they examine the costs and benefits of the different types of banking services in order to choose the service. In the face of poor banking options, low-income people make rational decisions to use services that are not ideal, in part because of the limited options that they face.

Respondents were able to explain how they factored in direct economic, related economic, and related social benefits and costs to choose a financial service. However, decisions are not static, and often people use mainstream and fringe bank services simultaneously. Some respondents stick to certain types of services – for example, a cheque casher – for long periods, while others switch back and forth depending on the current relative costs and benefits. Banking characteristics such as access, fees, design, services, and the staff culture are important factors affecting the benefits and costs of particular services.

4 The Business of Inner-City Banking

While chapter 3 sought to understand the consumer side of the financial exclusion relationship, this chapter explores the business side of banks that operate in the inner city. It does this by examining important economic issues related to mainstream and fringe banks. These issues relate to the banks' entire operations, which are not limited to their inner-city operations, and include the size of banks, market structure, efficiency, scale, and costs. The chapter begins with a discussion of the ways in which financial services are understood to relate to economic development.

Data on the economics of banking will be presented, demonstrating that while non-poor Canadians benefit from mainstream banks that are oligopolies and reasonably efficient, many low-income Canadians rely for some or all of their financial services on fringe banks. These fringe banks are growing in number and variety (for example, payday lenders and second-hand shops that act like pawnbrokers).

Banks for Economic Growth and Decline

Structural change theory provides important insights into the role of different sectors in fostering economic development. The orthodox version of this theory finds that the expansion of certain sectors is the key means to fostering economic growth.[1] This structural transformation notion was highlighted by W. Arthur Lewis, who argued that the principal means by which a largely agrarian economy would economically develop was industrial expansion (Todaro and Smith 2006). Rates of return on investments in industry are higher than on investments in agriculture, and they help to stimulate economic growth. As industry expands, then agriculture will contract, if not absolutely then certainly relative to the whole economy. Depending on its trade regime, a nation might opt to expand the export of its manufactured goods and use the export earnings to import more food and fibre.

Contemporary proponents of structural change such as Hollis Chenery provided a more nuanced version of structural change theory, involving a continuing process where new and increasingly more capital-intensive industrial sectors become the leading sector. Once again, the difference between rates of return on capital-intensive versus labour-intensive industry is the catalyst for growth. Northern countries,[2] which were the model upon which this theory was based, since the 1980s have experienced further structural change and economic growth through the information and communications revolution. Here the leading sectors include information and communications companies, and companies from other sectors (agriculture and industry) adopt these new technologies. As the capital-intensive industrial sector expands, again depending on the trade regime, the country might expand its exports of these wares and increase the importation of labour-intensive manufactures and food that it needs.

Banking has a limited role in structural change theory, which relates the historical treatment of banking in economics. Historically, economics has described banking as separate from the 'real economy.' The real economy is where production takes place and includes industry, agriculture, and construction, for example.[3] Banking is considered as infrastructure to support the real economy. This 'unreal' or 'semi-real' label for banking may be useful in one sense – that it cannot itself produce goods. However, for a capitalist economy to function, the bank must provide important services, including services to producers (farmers, industrialists, and construction companies) and to consumers.

. Moreover, liberal trade regimes in Northern countries have led to the shifting of agriculture and labour-intensive manufacturing to low-wage Southern countries. However, banking has not shifted from North to South. It is a relatively simple task to build factories and farms in the South and then transport the product to Northern markets. Importing flowers to Canada from West Bengal (India) and toys from Guangdong Province (China), for example, means setting up farms and factories that meet the quality standards of a foreign market. Transportation is achieved through air in the case of perishable flowers, and sea in the case of toys. It is not quite as easy to get one's investment funds or retail financial services from an offshore bank.

There are other barriers to the provision of banking services from overseas or to the setting up of a branch in the country (discussed below). Theoretically, this suggests that national banking continues to play an important role in economic activity as the leading sector moves from agriculture to labour-intensive manufacturing to capital-intensive manufacturing and finally to the information and communication sectors. Regardless of the leading sector, companies need finance, and consumers need financial services. Some, but not all, of these services are more efficiently provided by banks based in the country.

This suggests that as a nation experiences economic growth, banking will continue to contribute to the national income. This is reflected in a growing contribution to national income and in banks continuing to experience what are called in economics *normal* or *adequate profits*. Banks stimulate, or at least facilitate, economic growth, but does this growth trickle down to every locale and person?

As finances are needed at the national level to facilitate economic development, so are they needed at the local level. Local economies need access to savings in order to stimulate investment that will support and strengthen their infrastructure, industry, and other activities. Individuals in these locales require financial services in order to pursue transactions and to save and borrow. Of course, investors and consumers are not limited to their locale in order to access financial services. However, a lack of accessible local financial services acts as a barrier to local economic development. Only mainstream banks mobilize savings for investors to invest in local development, but both mainstream and fringe banks provide consumer financial services.

An implicit assumption in this analysis is that, to a certain extent, mainstream and fringe banks compete with one another in providing financial services primarily to low-income and modest-middle-income people. The coexistence of fringe and mainstream banks in inner cities is apparent in a drive through of many Canadian inner cities. Therefore, the financial services of low-income and modest-middle-income people are provided by both mainstream and fringe banks. Arguably, this enhances the competition on the supply side of the market. However, adding two fringe banks to a market that is dominated by five or six mainstream banks does not make the market perfectly competitive.

Some locales may have more, and some locales may have fewer, mainstream and fringe bank branches. Where there are more bank branches there is the potential for greater local competition, but it is important to not assume that more firms automatically leads to more competition. One has to carefully examine the structure of the local market. If the local market features a few large firms that take advantage of efficiencies and coexist with many small firms that do not experience economies of scale, then the large firms can still influence the market. Since the costs of the large firms are lower than those of the small firms, the large firms can undercut the small firms or they may keep their prices at par with the small firms and enjoy super profits in that locale.[4]

Mainstream banks may compete with fringe banks for low-income clients and in inner-city neighbourhoods. Another possibility is that mainstream banks may pursue strategies that discourage low-income people from using their services, which creates an unmet demand. That demand is met by fringe banks. This understanding of inner-city banking is consistent with the two-tier banking model developed by Gary Dymski (see the discussion in chapter 2). The model draws on work by Stiglitz and Weiss (1981) on the subject of credit constraint and posits that mainstream bank creditors do not operate in a perfectly competitive market. Rather, they face limited information about borrowers and the likelihood of their repaying loans. In order to avoid this problem – called *asymmetric information* in economics – the bank seeks a strategy to work only with low-risk borrowers. To do so, it uses automated credit checks to exclude higher-risk borrowers. The result is a market that provides rationed credit at a low interest rate to low-risk borrowers. As a result, high-risk borrowers are excluded from access to mainstream credit and are forced into the fringe or informal sectors for credit, where credit is more expensive.

The two-tier credit model is a useful starting point for understanding inner-city banking markets, but the analysis turns on credit, and there is no reference to either savings or transaction services. For many low-income people, transactions are possibly more important than access to credit. It is possible to extend Dymski's analysis from mainstream bank credit to include mainstream bank transaction services. The fee for a basic bank account is quite low (much lower than the fee at a cheque casher), but as chapter 3 documented, various factors – access, design, developmental services, and the staff culture – can act as barriers to using mainstream bank transaction services. Through location strategy, rules on cheque holds, and staff training, mainstream banks create obstacles to low-income people using their services. The consequences are that many low-income people rely on fringe bank transaction services.

As we shall see below, it is clear that at the national level both mainstream banks and multi-line fringe banks are oligopolistic. It is not clear how these two types of financial service firms interact in the inner city. There are two competing views of the inner-city financial service market: one in which mainstream and fringe banks (imperfectly) compete with one another to offer services, and one in which they bifurcate the market, based on the risk and the income level of the client. It is possible to synthesize these two views into one in which the two types of banks compete with each other for certain types of customers (modest middle income, middle-level credit risk) but then segregate the rest of the consumers. This would mean that middle-income, upper-income, and low-credit-risk clients are streamed to mainstream banks, and low-income and high-credit-risk clients are streamed to fringe banks.

Bank Size and Profitability

In economics, 'normal' profit, or a normal return on capital, is the rate of return that is required in order to adequately remunerate the holder of the capital. Adequate remuneration can be understood from a couple of vantages. First, given the level of risk, adequate remuneration is equal to, or greater than, alternative ways of investing the funds. This is the idea of opportunity cost. No profit-seeking investor will invest in a bank if the returns are lower than they are in comparably risky investments. Therefore, an adequate profit is one that is sufficient to attract investors from other sectors or to keep existing investors from moving their investments to other sectors.

A second way of understanding adequate profit is that it is the rate of return on capital in a perfectly competitive market. A perfectly competitive market is an archetypal neoclassical economic market with many small buyers and sellers. In fact, these buyers and seller are so numerous and small that no one of them can affect the outcome of the market. In this market, buyers and sellers are 'price takers': they cannot set the price of the good or service; they simply respond to the price with a level of production or consumption. The result is that capital earns an adequate return. We know this because, if there are higher than adequate returns in the market, new sellers from elsewhere will see a good opportunity and enter the market. As a consequence of more sellers entering the market, the quantity of goods on the market will increase, prices will drop, and profits will reach an adequate level. The perfectly competitive market is a useful hypothetical model for gaining insight into the workings of markets. However, most markets, including the banking markets, are not perfectly competitive.

Besides ensuring adequate profits, a perfectly competitive market leads firms to allocate resources in an economically efficient manner. This means that a firm will maximize its outputs for a given amount of inputs (for example, capital for plant and equipment, and operating funds for salaries and lighting costs). An inefficient firm that does not do so will face costs that exceed those of its competitors, and it will not be able to compete. It will fail. This point will be picked up below. The efficient firm will continue because its revenue will allow it to pay its input costs, including earning an adequate return on capital.

Mainstream Banks

For the purposes of this study, mainstream banks refer to federally or provincially regulated banks, trust companies, loan companies, or credit unions. By far the largest actors in this group are the banks, which are federally regulated. The credit unions and caisse populaires fall under provincial jurisdiction. From a regulatory perspective, there are three types of banks in Canada: domestic banks, foreign bank subsidiaries, and foreign bank branches. Each group faces different regulatory requirements. As of November 2009 there were twenty-two domestic banks, twenty-six foreign bank subsidiaries, and twenty-nine foreign banks with branches in Canada (OFSI 2010a).

The largest financial institutions in Canada are domestic banks, in particular the top six: RBC, TD, Scotiabank, BMO, CIBC, and National Bank. All told, domestic banks make up 86.0% of the assets of federally regulated banks, which amount to just under $3.1 trillion (OSFI 2010b). Foreign-bank subsidiaries hold 4.9% of these assets. The Desjardins Group and credit unions outside of Quebec hold assets representing 9.0% of the total (table 4.1).

Through liberalization processes in the last two decades, mainstream banks have also become active in other sectors including securities, insurance, and trust. Their retail branch banking generally covers the entire country, which is quite different from the United States where, until recently, regulation limited banks from providing retail services beyond one state. It is estimated that Canadian banks make up around 70% of the Canadian financial services sector (Allen,

Table 4.1
Allocation of total bank assets

Domestic banks	$2,660,583,204,000	86.0%
Foreign bank subsidiaries	152,373,038,000	4.9%
Desjardins Group	152,000,000,000	4.9%
Credit unions outside Quebec	127,700,000,000	4.1%
Total	3,092,656,242,000	100.0%

Source: Office of the Superintendent of Financial Institutions, Desjardins Federation, Credit Union Central Canada

Engert, and Liu 2006). The revenues of these banks represent just over 6% of Canada's gross domestic product (Allen, Engert, and Liu 2006). In 2000, chartered banks held 74.2% of personal deposits, 77.0% of residential mortgages, and 66.1% of consumer lending (Siklos 2004, 366).

By way of comparison, the two top payday lenders in Canada are Rent Cash Financial Inc. and Money Mart. Rent Cash Financial holds approximately $84 million in assets. Dollar Financial Corporation, Money Mart's parent company, holds US$923 million in assets. If we estimate that Money Mart represents one-third of these assets, its portion amounts to US$308 million in assets. Therefore, Money Mart's and Rent Cash Financial's assets amount to approximately $408 million, about 0.014% of the federally regulated bank assets.

The top five Canadian banks are some of the largest corporations in Canada, with RBC ranking number one (by revenue). They were ranked in the country's top twenty-five largest corporations in 2008 (table 4.2). But banking is not just a big revenue earner. Canadian banks are also profitable. With an average return on equity of 19.0%, as a sector it ranked number three (just behind food and staples retailing and telecommunications services) for return on equity over a seven-year period, 1997–2003 (Ernst and Young LLP 2004). This profit rate is considerably higher than that of capital goods (6.1%), steel (3.6%), oil and gas (3.3%), and automobiles and components (1.1%) (Ernst and Young LLP 2004). The profit levels did decline with the recession in 2008 but have rebounded faster than the rest of the economy, with a simple average return for the first quarter of 2009 of 11.9%. The highest return, 16.9%, accrued to Scotiabank (table 4.2). In the most recent Bank of Canada *Financial System Review* it is noted, 'Canada's major banks have remained broadly profitable throughout the crisis' (Bank of Canada 2009, 26).

Table 4.2
Revenue and return on equity of the largest mainstream banks

	2008 Revenue ($ billion)	2008 Ranking by revenue (Financial Post FP500)	2009 Return on equity (first quarter)
RBC	$37.6	1	12.0%
Scotiabank	26.6	10	16.9
TD	25.7	11	9.1
BMO	19.9	15	12.6
CIBC	12.7	25	8.8
Simple average			11.9

Source: Financial Post FP500 and Financial Post Sector Analyzer

Fringe Banks

Fringe banks, as noted above, are much smaller in size than mainstream banks. Nevertheless, their role in providing financial services to low-income Canadians makes them important actors in inner-city banking.

The largest publicly traded payday lenders in Canada are National Money Mart and Cash Store Financial, which operates The Cash Store and Instaloans. There are several middle-sized payday lenders, such as Cash Money (one hundred locations) (Cash Money, n.d.), and smaller organizations, such as Sorenson's Loans Til Payday (seventeen outlets) (Sorenson's Loans Til Payday, n.d.). National Cash Advance is owned by the largest payday lender in the United States, Advance America, but it had only opened thirteen outlets in Canada as of 2009. Some payday lenders are members of the Canadian Payday Loan Association (CPLA).[5]

Money Mart, based in Victoria, BC, is owned by Dollar Financial Corporation, based in Berwyn, Pennsylvania, which is a publicly traded U.S. transnational corporation with operations in Canada, the United Kingdom, and Poland. Money Mart began in 1982 (Money Mart 2006), with its principal service for many years being cheque cashing. Since the rapid rise in payday lending, this latter service has become a major source of its revenues. Cash Store Financial, based in Alberta and previously named Rent Cash, is primarily a payday lender but offers other financial services such as cheque cashing. It started operations in 2002, initially offering payday loans through The Cash Store and Instaloans, and rent-to-own through Insta-Rent Inc. It has a payday loan operation in Australia. Advance America, the largest payday lender in the United States, entered the Canadian market in 2008 with seven outlets, and as of December 2009 it had thirteen outlets (National Cash Advance 2009). It also has operations in the United Kingdom, and it reported in 2009 that it was operating at a loss (Advance America 2009).

Money Mart's revenue for the fiscal year ending 30 June 2009 was US$236.3 million, which represented 44.7% of Dollar Financial Corporation's total revenue (DFC 2009). For that year DFC reported a small net income of US$1.8 million, down considerably from its 2008 net income of US$51.2 million (table 4.3). The return on equity in 2009 was 1.0%, which, once again, was way down from the rate in 2008 of 26.5%. Information about the precise amount of the profit that accrues from its Canadian Money Mart operations is not available, but Money Mart is an important part of DFC's operations. In 2009, 44% of DFC's consumer-lending revenues came from its Canadian Money Mart operations, and 42% of DFC's total face value of cheques cashed came from Money Mart. Of DFC's revenue, 51% came from payday lending, 29% from cheque cashing, and the remainder from money transfer and other services (DFC 2009). DFC reported a loan volume of US$776.4 million and loan revenues of US$121.5 million.

Cash Store Financial reported a net income for the year ending 30 June 2009 of $14.7 million (up from $10.8 million in 2008) on total revenues of $150.5 million. These 2009 earnings were based on shareholders' equity of just under $66 million, so the return on equity increased to 22.2% (up from 15.2% in 2008). Over four-fifths (82.9%) of its revenue came from 'brokerage' fees (that is, payday lending), and 16.9% came from other services such as cheque cashing and debit card fees. It reported a 2009 loan volume of $594.2 million and an average loan size of $365.

Combined, payday loan volumes in 2009 from Money Mart and Cash Store Financial amounted to $1.42 billion. Robinson (2007) estimated that a typical Manitoba payday loan outlet provided approximately ten to thirty payday loans per day. On average an outlet could lend $1.5 million in loans per year. If one multiplies this average annual loan volume per outlet by the number of outlets (1,451), the result is an industry total loan volume of approximately $2.2 billion annually.

Pawnbroking has a much longer history than does payday lending. In the United States there is a variety of types of pawnshops, including

Table 4.3
Income and return on equity of publicly traded fringe banks

	Year	Net income and comprehensive income	Shareholders' equity	Return on equity
Cash Store Financial	2009	$14,647,0000	$65,852,000	22.2%
	2008	10,806,000	71,202,000	15.2
Cash Canada Group Ltd.	2008	682,535	5,952,531	11.5
	2007	476,874	5,254,996	9.1
Dollar Financial Corporation	2009	US$1,775,000	US$171,252,000	1.0
	2008	US$51,173,000	US$193,325,000	26.5

Source: Annual and 10-K reports

commercial and philanthropic (similar to those in Western Europe). There are small single-outlet shops and some large pawnshops with multiple outlets such as Cash America International (Caskey 1994). In Canada there are two identifiable companies with multiple outlets that are engaged in pawning, payday lending, or second-hand-good sales: Cash Canada and Cash Converters. These firms are seeking to expand their operations in middle-income neighbourhoods.

Cash Canada has an unusual business model, combining payday lending with pawning (Cash Canada, n.d.). According to its website, Cash Canada began in 1993 and has thirty-six outlets in western Canada. It sells used merchandise (from 'defaulted collateral loans') and provides 'collateral' loans and payday loans (Cash Canada, n.d.). It earned a significant profit in 2008 representing an 11.5% return on equity (Cash Canada Group Ltd. 2008).

Cash Converters, a second-hand retailer, has fourteen stores in four provinces (Cash Converters, n.d.). This Australian-based company claims to have 140 stores in Australia, 130 stores in the United Kingdom, and over 450 stores in twenty-one countries (Cash Converters, n.d.). Cash Converters International reported a record profit for the first half of 2008 at $7.94 million, up 9.3% from the previous year's result (Cash Converters International Ltd. 2008). At least in one location in Canada, Cash Converters offers something similar to a pawn loan, referred to as 'Option Buy Back' (Cash Converters, n.d.). Here the item is purchased from the customer and held for fifteen to thirty days. If the customer returns before the end of the term, he or she can repurchase the item for the purchase price plus fees. If the customer does not return, then the item is sold by the retailer.

The data presented above demonstrate the strong, if somewhat bumpy, financial performance of the larger fringe banks. However, these data are somewhat misleading references to the entire fringe bank industry in that they reflect the performance of large fringe banks. Many fringe banks are small operations, and data on these firms are difficult to access. Through the recent regulatory reform process regarding payday lending, some studies have provided insights into a broader cross-section of the industry. In their review of payday lenders, Ernst and Young LLP (2004) concluded that, on average, returns in the industry were 'comparable in other segments of the financial sector' (44). They reported returns to mainstream financial services for a seven-year period as just under 19%. The study also noted that seven of the nineteen payday lenders interviewed claimed negative net income for the study period. This means that the remaining twelve profitable firms are earning, on average, returns in excess of 19%.

Scale and Efficiency

There has been a great deal of research into the question of bank efficiency and scale. This section does not intend to review or summarize the literature. It presents some basic concepts that can assist the reader in thinking about the inner-city banking market.

Within orthodox microeconomic theory an important tension exists between competition and efficiency. On the one hand, perfect competition will ensure that no one actor controls the market outcome to its advantage. Moreover, if there is no advantage to large scale, then a perfectly competitive market is ideal. On the other hand, if bigger is better and, like the natural monopolies described above, there is some advantage to big producers, then markets that are dominated by a large number of small producers are second best. Economies of scale (also termed *increasing returns to scale*), as they are known in economics, mean that larger firms are more efficient than smaller firms. However, larger firms mean that the market is no longer perfectly competitive, and we cannot assume that firms have no market power.

Consider an extreme example. Electrical generation and supply are common examples of a natural monopoly. The plant and equipment are characterized by 'indivisibilities' that make large-scale production more efficient. Indivisibilities are identifiable both in electrical generation through dams and coal-fired plants (small dams and small plants are less efficient than are large ones) and in supply through electrical lines (one set of cables is less expensive than many sets). But, theoretically, electrical generation and supply could be done through a perfectly competitive market structure. It would require many small companies producing electricity (possibly through various means such as coal, hydro, and solar) at a predetermined price. A perfectly competitive market for electricity could be designed, but it would require many small producers and many sets of cables to deliver the electricity to the buyer. It would be inefficient and expensive.

Now most goods' and services' markets are not natural monopolies. However, for many goods and services, there are efficiencies to be gained from a larger scale. Thus, the archetypal perfectly competitive market turns out to be inefficient in some cases. Economies of scale result from the declining average costs as the production level rises, as well as from various internal and external factors such as indivisibilities (where certain plant and equipment have engineering limitations to efficiently produce a certain minimum size, for example, steel); specialization (where expansion allows workers to specialize and become better at one particular activity); and technological change (Bannock, Baxter, and Rees 1982).

Another source of efficiencies lies in economies of scope. These are improved efficiencies to the firm that stem from the addition to their offerings of similar goods and services using the same inputs. A cheque casher is a good example. This firm has outlets and staff that allow it to provide cheque cashing. Assuming the outlet is not completely busy all the time, there is the possibility of taking advantage of economies of scope. These same outlets can be the base of other types of financial services. The outlets form the infrastructure that gives the firm the capacity to offer more services from those same locations. Before payday loans became popular, cheque cashers commonly processed bill payments, generated money orders, wired funds internationally, undertook currency exchange, and completed income tax returns. With the popularity of payday loans, many cheque cashers have added that service as well, and it has become the biggest revenue winner for some of them, such as Money Mart. The cheque-cashing staff are trained to cash cheques, and these skills can be used to process other services. Thus, firms have an incentive to add services to their retail offerings that use the unutilized capacity of their locations and staff.

Economies of scale and scope are in tension with the perfectly competitive model. The rub is that perfect competition offers a market structure that avoids control issues but may be inefficient. Economies of scale suggest that imperfect competition may be a more efficient structure for some sectors. However, if firms are large, they will be able to influence the market.

Another type of economic efficiency is *allocative efficiency*, in which resources are allocated in such a way as to maximize the output from a given level of inputs.[6] However, with reference to imperfectly competitive markets, there is yet another type of efficiency to consider: *x-efficiency*. When a market structure is not perfectly competitive, we cannot assume that firms are efficient. With bad management, a large firm may earn only adequate profits. With good management, the oligopoly might be able to earn super profits. The efficiency associated is called x-efficiency. The gap between the costs that the firm would face if it were well run and its actual efficiencies is understood to be due to poor management, or x-inefficiency.

An obstacle to perfect competition is called an entry barrier.[7] Entry barriers prevent new firms from setting up shop even when existing firms are earning more than adequate profits. These super profits are meant to signal new firms to enter the market, but they are prevented by the entry barriers. These barriers give the firms in the market even greater control over it, as compared to the perfectly competitive archetype. Barriers to entry can result from 'natural' or 'generated' factors. The former are associated with natural monopolies, markets that are characterized by high efficiencies to large-scale production (see below). The latter are generated monopolies, markets that have been protected through such things as brand awareness, patents, and regulation.

It has been argued that mainstream banks in Canada have both natural and generated barriers. Conacher (1998) argued that mainstream banks in Canada benefit from barriers such as extensive branch networks and 'widespread consumer name recognition.' Natural barriers are associated with the extensive infrastructure necessary for banks to operate in Canada. People want to be able to access their bank anywhere in the country, thereby requiring banks to have an infrastructure throughout the nation. This acts as a barrier to all but the largest firms because the capital requirements for such a network are immense. Brand awareness is another barrier to entry into Canadian banking. Through advertising, the large Canadians banks have created a brand awareness that makes it difficult for others to break into the market. Finally, regulation can act as a barrier to entry. Although foreign bank regulations have been liberalized over the past twenty years, foreign banks that want to establish banking operations in Canada without establishing a subsidiary face regulations that are different from those faced by Canadian banks. These regulations do not prevent them from entering the Canadian market, but they present one more barrier – on top of natural barriers and brand recognition barriers – that may be a hindrance.

The majority of markets in Canada are imperfectly competitive. Some markets might approach perfect competition, such as the supply-side of farm output markets.[8] Imperfect competition includes a range of market structures such as monopolistic competition, oligopoly, and monopoly. A monopoly is a market where one firm alone supplies the market. This is the case with some goods associated with electrical generation, policing, and the military, for example, where there are natural monopolies. De Beers Diamonds comes closest to a monopolist outside of these natural goods monopolies. Unlike the perfectly competitive firm, the unregulated monopoly is able to manipulate the market in order raise its profits above what is adequate.

Oligopoly is a market in which a small group of sellers dominates the market. Analysis of oligopoly markets is complicated by the interconnected relationships among the producers. Whereas firms in a perfectly competitive market cannot influence markets, and a monopolist completely influences the production side of the market, the outcome in the oligopolist market depends on the firms' strategic behaviour. One extreme possibility is that the firms collude, either explicitly or implicitly, to act like a monopolist. This is called a cartel. But oligopolistic firms may also compete with one another, at least to some extent. The analysis of oligopolistic behaviour is complicated because oligopolies try to anticipate the behaviour of their competitors in order to raise their profits.

Mainstream banking in Canada can be described as an oligopoly: five or six very large banks control the lion's share of the market. The U.S. banking system, until recently,[9] was closer to that archetypical perfectly competitive structure (Allen, Engert, and Liu 2006, 3–4). The structure of fringe banking is mixed. With regard to pawnshops, there appears to be a more competitive market. Cheque cashing has been dominated by Money Mart, and the majority of the payday lending market is now supplied by two firms, Money Mart and Cash Store Financial. Thus, the payday lending industry appears to be more concentrated than is mainstream banking. Once again, natural barriers associated with an outlet-based network, and brand recognition, appear to be potential factors in preventing entry.

Mainstream Banks

The oligopolistic market structure of the Canadian retail banking sector has certain strengths and weaknesses. On the one hand, any imperfectly competitive market structure cannot ensure that firms' profits are restricted to what is adequate, and there is no certainty that firms are operating efficiently. On the other hand, large firms are in a position to take advantage of economies of scale.

Without competitive pressures there is no guarantee that firms will pursue the efficient allocation of resources (allocative efficiency) and efficient management (x-efficiency). In their analysis of Canadian banking, Allen and Liu found that x-inefficiency existed in banks and that its level was similar to the levels associated with U.S. banks (2007, 242). In comparing banks in Canada, the United States, Australia, and the United Kingdom, Fitzpatrick and McQuinn (2008) found limited differences among banks in this group, except for the UK banks, which were the least efficient.

Data on firm scale support the notion that mainstream bank operations experience economies of scale (Allen, Engert, and Liu 2006). The ranking of efficiency finds that larger banks are more cost-efficient than smaller banks (Allen and Liu 2007, 242) and that the largest five Canadian banks have obtained maximum efficiencies of scale (Kerton and Sen, n.d., 4). One study found that the economies of scale of Canadian banks are higher than those of U.S. bank holding corporations (Allen and Liu 2007, 242).[10]

At the local level, studies have examined whether competition is inhibited through imperfect market structures. One study found a negative and statistically significant relationship between the number of local competitors and the interest rates on small business loans (Mallet and Sen 2001).

Data on the efficiency and scale economies of the credit union sector are more limited. Credit unions are much smaller than the mainstream banks. The credit union sector does work within a federation of sorts. Particularly in Quebec, the caisses populaires operate within a network, the Desjardins Federation. In other provinces, credit unions operate through Credit Union Central, but the Central's role is more limited than that of the Federation. For instance the Desjardins Federation operates a 'solidarity' program (offering microcredit for business and consumption purposes) with partner caisses populaires throughout the province. A similarly sized program does not exist within the other provincial credit union centrals. One study found that the Quebec caisses populaires were more efficient than Ontario credit unions (Gueyie, Fisher, and Desrochers 2004).

Fringe Banks

Data on the efficiency of fringe banks are more limited than that for mainstream banks. One study undertaken for the Canadian Payday Loan Association in 2004 involved data from nineteen responding member firms, which held 474 of the then estimated 1,000 total outlets; the sample therefore represented just under one-half of the industry (Ernst and Young LLP 2004, 22).

The cost structures of payday lenders is different than those of mainstream banks. Payday lenders have relatively high operating costs. Operating costs refer to the costs required to run the business, including staff costs and the costs to run the outlets, but excluding loan capital costs and the cost of bad debt. By far the largest cost faced by a payday lender is its operating cost, estimated at three-quarters of its total costs (Ernst and Young LLP 2004, 23). Loan capital costs – the cost to the firm of financing the loans (either through borrowing or through allocating some of its capital for the purpose of a loan fund) – were estimated at 2.7% of total costs. Bad debt costs represented 21.1% of total costs (Ernst and Young LLP 2004, 29). Bad debt expense is the cost incurred by the firm when borrowers do not repay their loans in full. However, 21.1% is likely an overestimate. Robinson argued that as payday lenders have expanded their scale, they have been able to reduce the bad debt expenses. For instance, DFC's default rate ranged from 1.0% to 1.6% between 2003 and 2007 (Robinson 2007).

Another efficiency of which some payday lenders have taken advantage is economies of scope. For example, they can expand the scope of their operations by providing more financial services. A firm providing payday loans can add cheque cashing, bill payments, and money orders. These services build on the competencies of the staff and use the infrastructure available (retail location, electronic connections). Studies have found that, in general, multi-line fringe banks (fringe banks offering more than one financial service) are more efficient than the single-service fringe banks (Ernst and Young LLP 2004).

The efficiencies to be gained from economies of scale and scope are considerable. The cost per $100 payday loan varies from small firms ($21.22) to large firms ($15.35) and from mono-line firms ($20.17) to multi-line firms ($15.29) (Ernst and Young LLP 2004). Based on his analysis of the declining cost per payday loan with the increase in firm size, Robinson argued in the Manitoba Public Utilities Board hearing to cap payday loan fees that a base cap of $17 per $100 (for the first $250, plus 12% on the next $250, plus 10% on anything beyond that) would allow the most efficient payday lenders to operate and earn adequate profits.

Costs

Generally in economics, costs are divided into two types: fixed and variable. Fixed costs, also known as overhead costs, do not vary with the quantity that the firm produces. They include, for example, the costs of maintaining outlets and of servicing the debt incurred at the firm's outset. These do not vary with the firm's level of output. Variable costs are costs that vary with the amount that the firm produces. They include, for example, staff salaries and other inputs that vary as production levels change.

Another way to categorize costs is through operating costs – costs incurred in daily operations such as salaries and office administration – and other costs, such as capital costs, to finance branches and credit. It is generally argued that the operating costs for payday lenders are quite high and that these are fixed costs of their production. With small loan amounts and relatively minimal infrastructure requirements, fringe banks do not require a lot of capital investment. However, they do require relatively high levels of spending to pay staff and run the outlets. This is different from the running of a large diversified mainstream bank. The capital requirements of mainstream banks are much greater because they make large loans and major investments.

A final, important concept with reference to creditors such as banks and payday lenders is the concept of bad-debt expense. Lending money holds risks, particularly because some borrowers – for various reasons – are unwilling or unable to repay the debt in a timely fashion or at all. When the creditor decides that the loan will not be further serviced by the borrower, the remaining principal and interest charges become a bad-debt expense to the lender. (When faced with a lot of bad-debt expense, banks will often raise interest rates on their outstanding loans in order to raise their revenues and not experience declining profits.) Bad-debt expenses, as a share of total costs, are higher for payday lenders than for mainstream bankers (Robinson 2007). For instance, one study of payday lenders in Canada found that the bad-debt costs represented 21% of total costs (Ernst and Young LLP 2004, 29). As mentioned above, this is likely an overestimate of the majority of the industry today. A typical mainstream bank's bad debts are much smaller. For instance, RBC's loan loss allowance for 2009 for all of its operations (Canada and international) was $3.2 billion on retail and wholesale loans of $284.2 billion, representing 0.64% of the loan portfolio (RBC 2009a).

John Caskey pioneered studies of fringe banking in the United States in the 1990s, and his 1994 book included an analysis of the reason for the growth in the number of certain types of fringe banks. Caskey (1994) identified a number of factors that came together to explain the 1980s' cheque-cashing boom. These factors, discussed herein (in chapter 2), examined variables on the demand- and supply-side of the financial services market. Caskey argues that broad socio-economic changes, mainstream bank closures, and the application of service fees created a new opportunity for entrepreneurs: 'As check cashers' bright business signs began to spring up at key transit points in areas across the country, public awareness of the business grew. This growing awareness fed the imagination of many entrepreneurs, some of whom entered the business *de novo*, others of whom decided to expand their existing operations into regional chains' (110).

As generalizations go, it is probably fair to say that fringe banking, compared with mainstream banking or other businesses in many other sectors, is a labour-intensive operation. This means that a fringe bank requires relatively more staff per volume of sales compared with, say, a mainstream bank. Of course, the labour intensity varies across the type and the scale of fringe bank. The higher labour intensity of fringe banks is due to the relatively small size of the service provided (the size of the loan or of the cheque cashed) and the relatively less automated nature of the processing. Pawnbroking is an example, if an extreme case. A typical pawn loan based on a home product may range from $30 to $100. For this loan to be processed, the pawnbroker must examine the good, process the pawn ticket, and store the item. The appraisal of the good may take time and need to be done by a qualified appraiser. If the appraisal is too high and the customer decides to not redeem the item, the broker may not cover his costs with the sale of the unredeemed good. For the pawn ticket to be redeemed, the pawnbroker must process the payment and return the item. Therefore, for a loan of $30 to $100 the pawnbroker has invested quite a bit of time. The situation may be somewhat less labour intensive for the cheque casher and the payday lender. They do not have to worry about appraising or storing a good. However, they do process small-sum services; for example, they cash a $500 cheque or provide a $350 payday loan. In this sense, they too face a labour-intensive process (see box 4.1).

Box 4.1 An Example of the Labour Intensity of Payday Loans

To begin with, a teller 'has to tell [the client] how much it costs, how she will repay it (with a cheque dated seven days hence) and other conditions of the loan. He has to prepare the loan agreement. She takes out a loan for $100 repayable within seven days. The entire process takes 20 minutes. Suppose the clerk earns $12 per hour, including benefits. Suppose the loan charge is 1% of the face amount, or $1. If that rate is compounded for 52.14 weeks, it will come close to 60% per annum, which is the limit under the Criminal Code. The clerk's time alone costs the store $4, and so it loses three times the value of its revenue on this transaction, before allowing for any other costs (the bad debt rate alone is probably more than 1% of total loan volume) and assuming that the clerk has an uninterrupted stream of customers who all take out loans. Therefore, the clerk didn't charge her 1%, he charged her his store's standard fee of 20% of the principal, regardless of the time to maturity. In one week she will have to repay $120.

'This simple example demonstrates that standalone payday lenders cannot possibly charge interest rates that look anything like those we are accustomed to on more conventional loans, like credit cards and mortgages. The small size of the loan and the time to process it requires that payday lenders charge very high fees. It is possible that if conventional financial institutions would offer such loans, their much greater economies of scale and scope would allow them to charge far lower rates. But our question in this analysis has to be what might be a reasonable rate for the alternative financial institutions or fringe banks to charge.'

Source: Robinson (2007)

Another important cost element for fringe banks is their lack of automation. Some of their processing is not automated or the level of automation is lower compared with that of a mainstream bank. The pawnbroker is once again the extreme case. The appraisal of the item, the processing, and the redemption of the loan may all be done by hand, by the pawnbroker. Even submission of the item's description to the police for tracing may be done by hand (although in some jurisdictions this has been automated). The cheque casher and the payday lender once again do not face appraisal costs, but to be efficient they need to process hundreds of small-value cheques or dozens of payday loans each day. Some aspects of the process, such as verifying a person's identification, may be streamlined by having clients' photo identification placed on the bank's computer system. First-time customers require a large investment of time on the part of the teller.[11] Compare this to the way in which mainstream banks manage small loans. In fact, they don't. Mainstream banks have largely exited the small-loan market. Instead, they provide credit cards and lines. These products allow the approved client to continuously borrow small amounts of money up to the credit limit. Clients are approved through an automated process that relies on their credit score. Clients can keep their card, or possibly increase their credit limit, as long as their outstanding balance is limited and/or their credit score is kept up. These functions are automated so that a human has little role in the process.

Branch Networks

Mainstream Banks

Mainstream banks and their regulation have a long and important role in Canada's economic history. These banks have traditionally been called *chartered banks* in that they have received government charter. The first Bank Act was enacted in 1871 to regulate the activities of chartered banks (Siklos 2004). It has been modified many times since then, and in 1981 created the Schedule II banks, which allowed foreign bank subsidiaries to operate in Canada. The Bank Act's most recent major overhaul took place in 2001 with Bill C-8, which amended the act and created the Financial Consumer Agency of Canada. Siklos argues that over the years changes to the Bank Act have led to '(1) widening of the scope of chartered banking operations, and (2) concern over bank safety' (2004, 356).

While financial inclusion has not been a prime concern of the Bank Act, there is evidence that Bank Act revisions in 2001 were informed by the concerns about financial service access that had been raised in the MacKay Report (Task Force on the Future of the Canadian Financial Services Sector 1998b).[12] For instance, the report had sought to measure the number of people without a bank account and had identified the key obstacles to low-income people using a bank account, including the availability of bank branches, the affordability of accounts, the hold periods placed on cheque cashing, and the problems of personal identification.

An important issue for financial inclusion is the accessibility of the bank branch. Low-income people, compared to other people, are more likely to not have a car, to rely on public transportation, to not own a computer, to not have Internet hook-up, and to not have a telephone. This means that having a bricks-and-mortar bank branch close by is important. This section considers the total size of the mainstream bank branch networks.

The total number of mainstream bank branches – banks, trusts, and credit unions – has increased slightly over the twenty-five-year period ending in 2007. In 1982 there were 12,195 branches, and by 2007 this had increased to 14,871, representing a 22% increase (Canadian Payments Association 2008).[13] The number of bank branches increased through the period, from 7,323 in 1982 to 9,418 in 2007 (table 4.4). The number of trust company branches also increased, while the number of credit union branches declined. The banks' share of the total rose from 60% to just over 63%, the trusts' share rose slightly from 7% to just under 10%, and the credit unions' share dropped from 32% to 25%.

Of course, a branch is only one way to access one's bank. The telephone, Internet, ATMs, and point-of-sale terminals have dramatically changed retail banking in the last two decades. One indicator of this rapid change is the number of ATMs. The number of cash-dispensing ATMs rose from 12,808 in 1995 to 16,886 in 2008, representing a rise by almost one-third (Canadian Bankers Association 2009a).

Table 4.4
Numbers of mainstream bank branches by type

Year	Banks	Trusts	Credit unions	Other	Sub-total	Non-members	Banks as % of total	Trusts as % of total	Credit unions as % of total
1982	7,323	868	3,873	131	12,195	459	60.0%	7.1%	31.8%
1985	7,147	1,117	3,830	134	12,228	239	58.4%	9.1%	31.3%
1990	7,446	1,759	3,610	143	12,958	103	57.5%	13.6%	27.9%
1995	8,074	1,564	3,404	154	13,196	192	61.2%	11.9%	25.8%
2000	8,348	1,539	3,376	159	13,422	289	62.2%	11.5%	25.2%
2005	9,181	1,480	3,660	180	14,501	150	63.3%	10.2%	25.2%
2007	9,418	1,476	3,780	197	14,871	292	63.3%	9.9%	25.4%

Source: Canadian Payments Association

The large role of non-branch banking in Canada is demonstrated by international comparisons. As noted in the introduction, financial inclusion levels in Canada are quite high. Estimates suggest that 3% of adults are unbanked. What is interesting is that in terms of branch density – measured by the number of branches per 100,000 people – Canada ranks quite low, internationally speaking. According to one study, Canada ranked 105, out of 135 countries, with 23.7 branches per 100,000 people (Consultative Group to Assist the Poor 2009, 54–6). Countries with denser commercial bank networks included countries with a higher rate of financial inclusion than that of Canada, like Denmark with 46.7 banks per 100,000 people. Surprisingly, many countries that rank higher than Canada have lower levels of financial inclusion. Consider the United States with 9% of its adult population unbanked. It has 35.4 branches per 100,000 persons, or 11.7 more branches per 100,000 people than Canada has. Ireland has a much higher unbanked rate at 17% of its adult population, but it has 34.1 branches per 100,000, or 10.4 more branches per 100,000 people. Therefore, at the international level there is no simple correlation between branch density and financial inclusion. Regarding the distribution of the branch network among provinces, while density is not uniform across the country, there does not appear to be a regional bias (table 4.5).

Table 4.5
Density of mainstream bank networks by selected provinces

	1987	2005
Newfoundland and Labrador	3,710.7	2,857.8
Nova Scotia	2,026.0	2,386.5
New Brunswick	2,097.6	2,119.0
Ontario	2,036.8	2,163.1
Quebec	2,321.2	2,256.5
Manitoba	1,923.0	2,031.6
Alberta	1,932.8	2,313.5
Saskatchewan	1,330.9	1,401.4

Source: Canadian Payments Association and Statistics Canada

Fringe Banks

Data on fringe banks are hard to come by. This is partly explained by the limited amount of government regulation of this sector. Without regulation there are few official sources of data. Until the recent flurry of reforms, new laws, and regulations for payday lending, the only well-known regulation of fringe banks was the placing of a fee cap on income-tax-refund advancers and the licensing and monitoring of pawnbrokers. Besides the Criminal Rate of Interest, section 347 of the Criminal Code of Canada, which has not been used by government to regulate small lenders, there are no federal regulations related to fees and terms for pawnshop loans, cheque cashing, and rent-to-owns.

The reason for the limited government regulation with regard to fringe banks is not clear. The stigma associated with fringe banks may be a factor. From a political economy perspective (fringe banks serve low-income people, who are relatively powerless) it follows that government would not aggressively regulate fringe banks. Why would government work for effective regulation of fringe banks when they primarily serve the poor, a group that has little political clout? Stigma also comes from the exploitation thesis. Fringe bank opponents argue that fringe banks exploit the poor by charging high fees;[14] since fringe banks charge high fees, then they 'prey on' or exploit the poor. Government regulation of fringe banks might be criticized by fringe bank opponents as legitimizing exploitation (see box 4.2).

Box 4.2 Fringe Banks and Exploitation

Some people conclude that high fees for fringe bank services are evidence that fringe banks exploit their clients. They argue that since mainstream banks can charge lower fees for similar services, so can fringe banks. Thus they conclude that fringe banks are over-charging. While there may be other grounds for arguing that fringe banks are exploitative (for example, unfair disclosure of fees and rules, and encouragement of repetitive use of payday loans), the above argument is not solid. Fringe banks may charge higher fees, as already discussed, because they face higher costs. They rely on a small number of transaction services, and since they are not deposit takers, they cannot loan money at higher interest rates than they pay to depositors. However, if fringe banks are charging higher fees *and* earning massive profits, then the exploitation argument is stronger.

One final note on the exploitation thesis: even if it could be dem-onstrated that fringe banks are not earning massive profits, that they are observing fair disclosure of fees and rules, and that they are doing the best they can to keep their fees to a minimum, this does not mean that fringe bank consumers are not being exploited. There is something ethically troublesome about a situation where (1) low-income people are paying high fees for low-quality services and (2) middle-income people are paying low fees for higher-quality services. In this case, however, the victims (low-income people) are not exploited by their financial service provider; their exploitation has more to do with the lack of general support from social and eco-nomic institutions and an absence of appropriate financial services from mainstream banks. It is the 'system' that is a root cause of the exploitation.

There is a belief among many people, some government officials in-cluded, that pawnbrokers deliberately trade in stolen goods and are tied with criminal activity. In many provinces, pawnbrokers are re-quired to submit to the police a list of all pawned items, either daily or weekly. Some cities have a web-based system that requires immediate submission of these data. A major challenge in effectively monitoring for stolen goods is that monitoring systems rely on the serial numbers of the stolen goods, but for a lot of stolen property there is no record of the serial number. Owing to this perception, some government officials hesitate to regulate the pawnbroking industry.[15]

Another reason for the paucity of data on fringe banking is that these firms, like mainstream banks, value the privacy of their data. If they are not required to report these data, via regulation, to a government agency and if they are not publicly traded, they do not make the data of their costs and returns publicly available. Since there are few regulations and most fringe banks are small private operations – other than Money Mart and Cash Store Financial – the data on fringe banks are limited. Official data on the number of fringe banks are limited to Statistics Canada data that lump particular fringe banks in with other types of businesses. Unofficial sources of data are company websites, industry association databases, and telephone directories.

Statistics Canada data refer to fringe banks such as pawnshops, cheque cashers, and payday lenders, but they fall within broad business categories. These data are available within a six-digit category in the North American Industry Classification System (NAICS), previously under the Standard Industry Classification (SIC) system.[16] The establishments[17] in each business category are further categorized by their number of employees.[18] However, since the data for one type of fringe bank are lumped in with other (often quite different) businesses, and the definition of establishment is ambiguous, these data do not cast a lot of light on our topic.

Presented below are data coming from a combination of official and unofficial sources. They demonstrate that fringe banking is a significant and, in the case of payday lending, growing sector.

PAYDAY LENDERS AND CHEQUE CASHERS

Standard Industry Classification Data. The data for payday lenders and cheque cashers is probably one of the most accessible among the fringe banks because the industry association provides current data on outlets, the two largest firms are publicly traded, and there are categories for both types of firms in most commercial telephone directories. The standard industry codes are not much help, but some reference will be made to them here.

Starting with the most general data from the standard industry categories, two categories are of interest here: (1) NAICS 522291, 'Consumer Lending,' which includes firms that provide unsecured cash loans, such as payday lenders, finance companies, and mutual benefit associations[19]; and (2) NAICS 522390, 'Other Activities Related to

Credit Intermediation,' which covers firms not classified elsewhere that facilitate credit intermediation such as cheque cashing, money orders, and travellers' cheques.[20] There was no reference to payday lending under the older SIC system, but there was reference to cheque cashing.[21]

'Consumer Lending' establishment data demonstrate rapid growth during the period 1998–2007 (table 4.6). The number of establishments increased for every year except 2005, with a considerable 5.1% average annual growth over the ten-year period. The data do not allow more precise analysis of growth, but firms with 20–49 employees (a middle-size category) and 200–499 employees (a large-size category) experienced the most rapid rise with 30.9% and 20.4% annual growth, respectively. Finally, in 2001 the first establishment with 500 or more employees is recorded.

There is a major overlap between payday lenders and cheque cashers, probably so much overlap that we can say that there aren't payday lenders and cheque cashers but there are fringe banks that offer several services, and payday lending and cheque cashing are two important services that they offer. Nevertheless, there are some firms that offer one but not the other (for example, Financial Stop provides cheque cashing but not payday lending). There are standard industry

Table 4.6
NAICS 522291, 'Consumer Lending,' establishment counts

Year	Total	Change
1998	477	
1999	499	4.6%
2000	548	9.8
2001	603	10.0
2002	619	2.7
2003	640	3.4
2004	696	8.8
2005	694	−0.3
2006	697	0.4
2007	741	6.3
Average		5.1

classification data for cheque cashers. Cheque cashers are included within NAICS 52239, 'Other Activities Related to Credit Intermediation.' Establishment counts in this category demonstrate higher growth than do those in the 'Consumer Lending' categlory, rising from 141 establishments in 1998 to 448 establishments in 2007 and averaging 14.1% annual growth. However, the employee categories experiencing most growth included those with 1–4 and 5–9 employees (small sizes) and those with an indeterminate number of employees. Therefore, it is hard to say the extent to which the establishment growth reflects a more general growth.

The standard industry codes are very general and, in the case of cheque cashing under SIC, involve diverse firms. Therefore, any conclusions must be tentative. The data demonstrate considerable growth: 5.1% and 14.1% average annual growth over a ten-year period for 'Consumer Lending' and 'Other Activities Related to Credit Intermediation,' respectively. We can now draw on the unofficial data sources to provide another vantage on the industry.

Industry and Telephone Directory Data. The payday loan industry in Canada probably began in the mid 1990s and took off in the early 2000s. One of the big companies, National Money Mart Inc., has been around longer, but its core business used to be cheque cashing. Sometime in the 1990s, Money Mart, other cheque cashers, and new companies began to offer payday loans. In terms of outlet numbers, Money Mart grew consistently between 1997 and 2008, from 143 outlets to 480. Cash Store Financial Inc. began its operations around 2002 with 19 outlets and grew extremely quickly through 2009, when it had 450 outlets. These two firms control the lion's share of the payday loan industry. Combined, the number of outlets in Canada rose from 143 in 1997 to 911 in 2009 (table 4.7).

Determining the total number of outlets in Canada is complicated by the lack of authoritative data.[22] For the last few years the industry association, CPLA, collected data on the outlet numbers of its members and other identifiable payday lenders. These data show that the numbers increased from 1,367 in 2007 to 1,451 in 2009. Robinson (2006) estimated the number of outlets in 2005 to be 1,300. Two other estimates, one for 1997 and one for 2001, were inferred from data available in two Dollar Financial Group (now Corporation) 10-K reports to generate figure 4.1. The figure demonstrates the very rapid growth in the number of outlets from 2001 to 2005, from 380 outlets (estimated) to 1,300 outlets (estimated).

Table 4.7
Number of Money Mart and Cash Store Financial outlets, 1997–2009

Year	Money Mart	Cash Store Financial	Combined
1997	143	–	143
1998	156	–	156
1999	181	–	181
2000	220	–	220
2001	243	–	243
2002	254	19	273
2003	290	57	347
2004	311	108	419
2005	345	277	622
2006	370	338	708
2007	415	358	773
2008	480	400	880
2009	461	450	911

Source: Dollar Financial Group 10-K reports, 1997–2009; Cash Store Financial annual
reports, 2002–9; Robinson (2006); Canadian Payday Lenders Association.

Figure 4.1: Estimated number of payday-lender outlets in Canada, 1997–2009

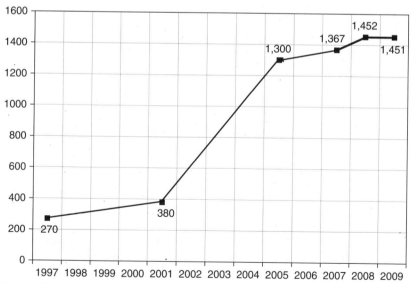

Source: See discussion in text.

Table 4.8
Number of payday-lender outlets in Canada, by province, per capita, and by CPLA
membership, 2007–9

Province/Territory	Total number of outlets			Population	Outlets/ 100,000 people (2009)	CPLA outlets as % of total outlets (2009)
	2007	2008	2009			
Ontario	687	766	731	13,069,182	5.6	35.4%
British Columbia	237	242	254	4,455,207	5.7	35.8%
Alberta	241	237	246	3,687,662	6.7	39.8%
Manitoba	71	74	89	1,221,964	7.3	44.9%
Saskatchewan	45	45	44	1,030,129	4.3	63.6%
Nova Scotia	29	34	32	938,183	3.4	25.0%
New Brunswick	35	27	27	749,468	3.6	29.6%
Newfoundland	15	20	20	508,925	3.9	10.0%
Prince Edward Island	4	4	4	140,985	2.8	25.0%
Northwest Territories (and Nunavut)	1	1	2	75,622	2.6	50.0%
Yukon	2	2	2	33,653	5.9	50.0%
Total	1,367	1,452	1,451	33,739,859	4.3	37.0%
CPLA outlets as % of total outlets	36.4%	36.9%	37.0%			

Source: Canadian Payday Loan Association 2009. Population data: CANSIM using
CHASS. 2007 and 2008 – Table 510001, 'Estimates of Population, by Age Group and
Sex for July 1, Canada, Provinces and Territories, Annually (Persons)'; 2009 data –
Table 3601, 'Estimates of Total Population, Canada, Provinces and Territories.'

From 2007 through 2009 the number of outlets increased marginally
from 1,367 in 2007 to 1,451 in 2009 (table 4.8). About one-half of the outlets are in Ontario.[23] After Ontario, British Columbia and Alberta have
the most outlets. Payday lending seems to be particularly popular in
Western Canada. On a per capita basis the highest number of payday
lender outlets is found in Manitoba, followed closely by other Western Canadian jurisdictions – Alberta, Yukon, and British Columbia –
and then Ontario. The lowest per capita rates of payday-lender outlets
were in Atlantic Canada. There are over twice the number of outlets
per 100,000 people in Manitoba compared with the number in Nova
Scotia – jurisdictions with similar absolute populations and close

median income levels: $56,400 for Nova Scotia and $58,700 for Manitoba (Statistics Canada website for 2006).

Many payday loan firms are members of CPLA, the industry's largest association. There are other associations, for instance the British Columbia Payday Loan Association. According to data provided by CPLA, 37% of the 1,451 outlets in 2009 were run by firms that were members and 63% belonged to companies that were not part of the industry association. The CPLA participation rate is higher in the Prairie provinces and Ontario and lower in Atlantic Canada.

PAWNSHOPS AND SECOND-HAND SHOPS

Standard Industry Classification Data. Standard industry classification data can be used to provide an initial insight into the pawnshop outlet numbers. Pawnshops are included in NAICS 522299, 'All Other Non-depository Credit Institutions,' which is not helpful for our purposes as it includes a broad and diverse group of services such as real estate credit and international trade financing. However, under the NAICS there is another classification that is useful for our purposes: NAICS 453310, 'Used Merchandise Stores.' Under the SIC system, pawnshops were included with used merchandise retailers in classification J6591, 'Second-Hand Merchandise Stores.'

Turning first to the older SIC data, two points of clarification are needed. From 1990 to 1994, the data excluded firms with no employees. There were no data for 1995 and 1996. It was only in 1997 that the data included firms with no employees, and this increased the number of establishments significantly, from 1,969 in 1994 to 3,042 in 1997. For uniformity purposes, the data for 1997 reported below exclude establishments with no employees (table 4.9). A second point of clarification is that, in some jurisdictions in Canada, second-hand stores offer the equivalent of pawn loans. Rather than being licensed as pawnshops, these stores offer what is sometimes referred to as a 'buy-back' option. The customer sells the item to the second-hand store but can buy it back, for a fee, within a certain period. Anecdotal evidence indicates that this is available in Ontario, owing to its more restrictive pawnbroking regulations (which require the loan to be for a one-year term), and in some larger chain second-hand shops.

With these qualifications in mind, the data below demonstrate, once again, substantial growth in establishments during the period 1990–7. The number of second-hand establishments increased significantly, in several employee-level categories ranging from 1–199, and on average by 8.5% annually.

Table 4.9
Number of second-hand-merchandise establishments (SIC J6591),
including pawnshops

Year	Total*	Growth (%)**
1990	1,343	
1991	1,382	2.9
1992	1,428	3.3
1993	1,423	−0.4
1994	1,494	5.0
1995	n/a	
1996	n/a	
1997	1,969	31.8 (from 1994)
Average		8.5

*For uniformity of the data, the numbers of businesses with no employees
were excluded. These data were only available for 1997. If these data
were included, then there were 3,042 establishments in 1997.
**Since data for 1995 and 1996 are unavailable, the percent change for
1997 was determined by using 1994 as the base year.

In 1998, with the implementation of NAICS, data for used merchandise stores were separated from that for pawnbrokers. The data show arise in the total number and in the number of large establishments (100–199 and 200–299) from 1998 to the early or mid 2000s. By 2007, however, the total number of establishments had dropped to the 1999 level.

Industry and Telephone Directory Data. City telephone directories provide another source of data for pawnshops. Such data were collected in fourteen Canadian cities in 2006. Since some pawn loans or equivalent buy-back plans are not included in these data, the numbers of outlets presented here are underestimated.

The largest-sized cities have the most pawnshops, including Edmonton, Vancouver, Montreal, Calgary, Ottawa-Hull, and Winnipeg. As with payday lenders, there are more pawnshops per capita in Western Canada than elsewhere (table 4.10). Saskatoon, Edmonton, Winnipeg, Victoria, and Calgary are among the top six ranked cities. Outside of the west, only Saint John is among the top group, ranking number

Table 4.10
Numbers of pawnshops in selected Canadian cities, ranked by number of pawnshops per capita, 2006

	Pawnshops*	Population	Pawnshops per capita
Saskatoon	24	225,927	10.6
Saint John	12	122,678	9.8
Edmonton	65	937,845	6.9
Winnipeg	32	671,274	4.8
Victoria	15	311,902	4.8
Calgary	43	951,395	4.5
Ottawa-Hull	40	1,063,664	3.8
Regina	7	192,800	3.6
Halifax	12	359,183	3.3
Montreal	59	3,426,350	1.7
Quebec City	11	682,757	1.6
Vancouver	64	1,986,965	3.2
St John's	1	172,918	0.6
Toronto	24	4,682,897	0.5
Total	409		

Source: Buckland 2006b
*Data taken from 'Pawn' category in Yellow Pages website.

two. According to one pawnbroker, the low number of pawnshops in Ontario cities has to do with the provincial regulation requiring pawn loans to be one year in duration. According to the same source, these regulations have led second-hand retailers to become active in lending.

Conclusion

As rich countries' incomes rise, very often a rising share of their agricultural and manufacturing needs is met through imports. If the General Agreement on Trade in Services is to have its way, then the same will apply to financial services, although financial services are not traded at present like food and wares. Thus, banking, along with other components of the information economy, plays an important role in the economies of the global North. In fact, mainstream banks are among the largest corporations in Canada, they are very profitable, and they have even been able to weather the recent financial and economic crisis. It is not surprising that mainstream banks, with little public debate, are able to operate as oligopolies in the face of the competition-efficiency tension. Without high levels of competition (what economists call *perfect competition*) we cannot be assured that they are effectively contributing to the common good. In this case, regulation is called for. One important principle of regulation is that low-income people have fair and adequate access to quality financial services from mainstream banks. Their large size gives us greater hope that they can take advantage of economies of scale, but even on that count we cannot be sure that mainstream banks embrace these economies.

Inner-city banking is a unique phenomenon as we find large numbers of fringe bank outlets operating with a few remaining mainstream bank branches. Like mainstream banks, fringe banks operate within a competition-efficiency milieu (in the case of payday loans), but with even greater concentration. The costs they face to provide a lot of tiny loans are high, and they surely pass these costs on to the consumer.

While the number of mainstream banks in Canada has grown slightly in the last twenty years, the number of payday lenders and other fringe banks has risen precipitously. Many, but not all, of these fringe banks are located in lower-income neighbourhoods in the inner city and suburbs. The limited data available find that mainstream banks have closed branches in the low-income neighbourhoods and opened them in better-off neighbourhoods. Western Canada, as a region, has a greater concentration of some fringe banks.

Clearly, the result of this situation is two-tier or multi-tier banking, where low-income people and neighbourhoods are more likely to rely on expensive and limited fringe banks. Other people and neighbourhoods are able to take advantage of the services of mainstream banks.

5 Working for Financial Inclusion

There may be a variety of reasons to reform banking such as improving efficiency, boosting competition, and promoting financial inclusion. The point of this chapter is to argue that banking is important for poor people and that banking could be changed – radically or more moderately – to make it more accessible for them. In order for financial exclusion to be overcome, changes must be made to bank practice and government policy. Financial institutions must design and provide appropriate banking services for low-income people. This chapter begins with this supposition, asks what type of services is most useful, and then considers the possible bank structures and policy reforms that could promote this.

The chapter first contrasts the visions of what banking could be, categorized here as radical changes, reform, and status quo. It then picks up from the discussion in the introduction about government policy and considers ways in which relevant government policy in Canada might be reformed to promote financial inclusion. Most notably, this could be achieved by ramping up basic banking regulations, extending government services, and unifying financial consumer protection. Drawing in part on the lessons in chapter 2, it then considers the changes to banking that could make it more accessible and useful for low-income people. Finally, the chapter examines some currently available projects that address financial inclusion to some extent, including community banking projects, asset-building projects, financial literacy projects, and microcredit.

Rethinking Banking in the Light of Financial Exclusion

Putting First Things First: Poverty and Exclusion

Before examining the different visions for bank reform, it is important to consider the cart-and-horse issue. It might be argued from a poverty and community perspective that the most effective way to reduce financial exclusion is to reduce poverty. If poor people had adequate income through decent employment or income support, they would be more likely to want to – and indeed need to – use the developmental services of a mainstream bank. With a higher and more stable income, a person might consider saving for larger items including retirement. This would create an incentive for the person to get a mainstream bank account.

Improvements in income security could come through reduced unemployment and growth in higher-wage jobs. Welfare reform could support people better with decent income and encourage those who are able to move to employment. Changes like these could assist many poor people and would create incentives for them to shift into mainstream banking. However, poverty is not likely to be overcome as long as the rates of unemployment and of reliance on social assistance are high, low-end wages and social assistance levels are low, and social assistance is inflexible. Moreover, financial exclusion itself can foster poverty. Therefore, it would be useful to promote financial inclusion with the important caveat that efforts to foster inclusion in financial services should not be done in such a way as to undermine inclusion in other areas. If working towards the one goal does undermine the other goal, then the trade-offs must be carefully and democratically considered.

Contrasting Visions for Banking

One can imagine a variety of ways to approach the financial-exclusion challenge. Drawing on the traditions of social science, a broad set of categories includes radical restructuring, reformation, and status quo. The reformist and status quo approaches have extensive appeal in contemporary politics and are associated with reform neoliberal and neoconservative approaches, respectively. Today there is not much political capital for a state-directed radical restructuring approach. The collapse of the socialist economic model has left radical economics lacking a state-based model. New directions for radical restructuring today include community rooting and restructuring for environmental sustainability. The former issue relates to the topic of this book and will be addressed in this chapter. The latter issue, strengthening the environmental sensitivity of banking, while important, is beyond the scope of this study.

The status quo, neoconservative approach argues that the existing bank structure is the best. Government tinkering with bank reform will only foster inefficiency. Let the market do its magic, and new technologies will help to address any current gaps. This is an interesting perspective, but two concerns about it will be raised: market structure and the relationship between economy and society. First, with respect to market structure and as discussed in chapter 4, banking in Canada is oligopolistic. Consequently, we cannot be assured of efficiency or of this structure effectively contributing to the common good. Since there are no a priori grounds to assume that this market structure is effective, proponents of the status quo must look elsewhere for evidence. One route is productivity studies. As discussed in chapter 4, Canadian banks are about as productive as are banks in other Anglo-American countries (except the United Kingdom). This does not preclude the existence of x-inefficiency, which may be a general characteristic of banks throughout this region.

Another option for status quo proponents is that, from a common-sense perspective, it appears that the five big banks are competing with one another. The discussion runs something like this: 'Sure, banks are – relative to other Canadian companies – big, but there are several of them, and as far as we can tell, they compete with one another. How do we know they compete with one another? Well, they spend a lot of money on advertising, and anyway the banks assure us that they're competing with one another. By international standards Canadian banks are small. If anything, they need to get bigger in order to compete with the big United States and EU banks.' This argument seems reasonable: there are five or six large banks and many more small banks and credit unions; therefore, there must be some level of competition among these companies. But to ensure theoretically the optimal outcome, there needs to be more; there needs to be evidence that banks are 'price takers,' that they cannot influence the price of their products, and that they earn only average (normal) profit levels. Furthermore, advertising is not evidence of perfect competition; it is evidence of something called *monopolistic competition*, another form of imperfect competition. Now, this is not to say that banks are exploiting Canadians; it is simply to say that we do not have the theoretical grounds to assume that they are not. Therefore, mainstream bank operations must be scrutinized and regulated in order to ensure that the common good is achieved. Oligopoly, monopoly, and monopolistic competition – the more noted versions of imperfect competition – can laden the supplier with heavy profits at the expense of the consumer and manipulate the consumer through advertising, to name a couple of noted problems that imperfect markets can create.

Another point raised by status quo proponents is that business, and the economy more generally, is separate from society. Thus, business should do what it does best: generate profits. Society should do what it does best: look after people. Unfortunately this view does not see that business is a product of society and itself shapes society. Business people are part of a society; they are raised in families, educated in schools, and live in neighbourhoods. Thus, their views are influenced by the social processes. Moreover, businesses, *through* advertising, and business strategies, influence society. For instance, by the shifting off-shore of low-end manufacturing, low-wage jobs are lost, leading to un-employment among low-skilled people.

Two possible, radical approaches to bank change include a community-based approach and an environment-based approach. But simply insert-ing an interest in community or the environment does not imply radical change. Indeed, much of the emphasis in the last quarter-century in South-ern countries under the auspices of development, and in Northern coun-tries under the auspices of social change, has involved community-based moderate reforms. Radical change suggests an immoderate 'flipping' of valuations whereby community or environmental interests drive bank provision.

Community-based change involves empowering groups of people through access to greater resources, and strengthening their capacity to work together to participate in achieving self-defined goals. Radical community-based change involves a major decentralization of power from national and international to local levels, moving the community closer to self-sufficiency (Loxley 2007; Shragge 1993). This means a dramatic shift of production, distribution, and decision making to the local level. With reference to financial services, it demands a radical movement of transactions and developmental financial services from banks to community. Mechanisms that allow communities to produce, exchange, borrow, and save without relying on banks are examples of this. Some tangible examples include local barter systems, and local credit or savings schemes. The local exchange trading system (LETS) is an example of a local barter system. It facilitates the trading of goods and services without the use of money. LETS offers a barter fund and system of accounts that allow people to trade with their neighbour instead of relying on the market. A carpenter looking for assistance with her income tax return could find an accountant who would provide the service. Rather than paying for the service, the carpenter offers her carpentry skills to others in the system. Contributions are accounted in the system as assets, and utilization is accounted as a liability for each participant.

Savings and credit societies are another way in which local people can 'opt out' of market-based systems. Examples include the ROSCA (rotating savings and credit association), which pools funds from a group of individuals and distributes each pot around the group, and the ASCRA (accumulating savings and credit association), which pools funds and loans these out to members on specified terms. These schemes are found throughout the South but are not common in Canada.

The LETS and ROSCA schemes have the potential to be used by many people to a limited extent (involving a marginal change in their lives) and by some people to a great extent (a more radical change). The consequences of relying exclusively on these community-based systems would increase a person's transactions costs: the time and effort needed to attend to daily needs. For instance, with a LET system, instead of selling one's labour and paying for one's apartment with cash, one spends more time in finding someone who needs one's labour and who is selling something one needs. With a ROSCA system, one might receive the pot at an inconvenient time, when it is not useful. For some people, the time and effort required to work within and to support a community-based system may be an end in itself. In this case, the additional transactions costs associated with a community system are not costs but are, in fact, benefits. These people are likely to embrace the LETS and the ROSCAs for some or much of their financial services. For other people these transactions costs may be seen as just that, costs. They might not be willing to voluntarily engage in these systems.

Another direction that a radical restructuring of banking might take relates to the environment. Evidence has mounted that economic growth is damaging the environment. Economic growth has been financed by the growing use of the sink-and-source functions of the earth's resources. The accumulation of pollutants in the environment (land, air, and sea), the degradation of forests and agricultural land, the loss of natural and agricultural biodiversity, and global warming are some of the major environmental challenges we face today. Economic policy in most countries is rooted in neoclassical economic theory, which finds that a market-based approach to economic and social improvement will only lead to marginal environmental problems (called *externalities*), but the evidence is that pollution and resource depletion are not marginal externalities but are central and internal environmental challenges to the planet.

Banking's role in the economy was discussed in chapter 4. Economics has argued that banking's role is not the prime driver, not a part, of the 'real' economy but is a stimulant of economic activity. However, the discussion of financialization in chapter 1 points to an expanding role of financial markets and financial thinking in the economy today compared with twenty years ago. Thus banks and financialization have taken an important part in stimulating economic growth and are thereby connected with environmental disruption.

One popular alternative to economic growth as a means to social improvement is steady-state economy. The steady-state economy is one that strives to maintain zero economic growth in order to reduce throughput and environmental troubles (Daly 1991). Daly and Cobb (1989) have argued that steady-state economy can be consistent with a society that is rooted in vibrant community. Rather than society being forced to conform to the needs of the economy, the needs of society should drive the economic structure.

What would banking look like within a steady-state economy? Banks would be required in order to facilitate economic transactions, but they would not need to foster economic growth. With a zero-growth goal, banks would no longer need to generate high profits but would be concerned only with covering their operating costs. Banks would not need to pay high dividends to shareholders or interest to depositors, and they would not need to charge high interest rates to borrowers. Of course, banks would still need to cover their costs and could do so through fees and/or an interest differential between loans and deposits.

Some have sought to blend the community-based and environmental approaches with regard to banking. For instance, according to the concept of patient capital, depositors interested in supporting certain types of environmentally sensitive activity (for example, providing capital for renewable energy investment) would accept a lower return than that available in the market. This would allow people and communities that are committed to the investment's goal to pool their funds in order to achieve their goal. However, since the focus of this book is financial exclusion, this discussion has only skimmed the surface of the bank restructuring necessary for environmental sustainability.

The Role of Financial Literacy

There is no doubt that people from all income backgrounds have financial literacy needs. Financial literacy helps people to meet their financial and life goals. The understanding of household budgeting, expenditure control, future planning, and effective decision making about investments can assist people from a range of backgrounds. Although this study is not about the ways in which financial literacy – or education in general – improves or constrains one's well-being, banks have a role in financial literacy, and therefore a couple of comments are justified.

The precise literacy requirements for people from different income backgrounds and with different income goals will vary. A low-income person relying on social assistance and *seeking* to build up assets to gain employment and ultimately personal retirement savings may not be too different from a middle-income person seeking a voluntary simple lifestyle. Their financial literacy requirements may be quite similar: household planning, effective use of basic credit and savings devices, and retirement savings. But the literacy requirements for a low-income person who is unable to build up assets to gain employment are different. The literacy requirements for the upper-income person with millions in assets are different again.

Outside of formal education, literacy is built and maintained in nonformal and informal settings. For people relying on mainstream banks for their financial services, one source of literacy is the bank. Generally, mainstream banks provide a variety of services that can be used by a client to foster her or his financial literacy. These resources include printed materials that compare financial services, including accounts, investments, and mortgages; web-based planning tools for budgeting, investments, retirement, and estates; and financial planners who are able to assist a person with an overall plan and the use of various financial planning tools.

Fringe banks, on the other hand, offer none of these services. Moreover, partly due to poor regulation, even basic tasks such as comparative shopping for the lowest fees for a fringe bank service are not easily done. Thus, banking at a mainstream bank provides the client with the opportunity to build her or his financial literacy. Meanwhile the fringe bank client must look elsewhere for that opportunity. To the extent that we rely on daily activities – work, shopping, time with friends and family, and banking – for learning, then two-tier banking acts as one more barrier to low-income people achieving a better life. One banking system that recognizes different needs is better.

Reformist Approaches to Banking

A reformist approach to banking rejects that radical change is necessary but finds that the status quo is not acceptable either. In the liberal tradition, it conceptualizes social improvement as the result of incremental changes that build one upon the other. With regard to banking, it sees large corporate banks as legitimate actors as long as they operate in such a way as to promote the common good. Banks are important facilitators of economic activity, but their activities must be harnessed for the benefit of society. The state is in the best position to do this.

Arguments for state intervention come from several angles: public good, market failure, and the common good perspective. Let us first examine the public-good argument. Arguably, mainstream banks provide a public good – recall that this is defined in economics as a good that is not excludable (people can be excluded from consuming it through the charging of a price; this is not possible for instance with the air that we breathe) and not subtractable (one person's consumption subtracts from what is available for another person's consumption). While banking services meet the first condition, they do not meet the second. In fact, the reverse is the case: by including more people within the banking system it is possible to improve everyone's transactions and credit efficiencies, thereby boosting the entire economy.

As discussed above, proponents of state action argue that in order to minimize the damage that banks can cause to the economy and society – owing to their oligopolistic market structure – government regulation is justified. An addendum to this argument relates to the particular challenges faced by low-income people of integrating with the market. A pro-poor reformist approach might find that financial exclusion, particularly in light of high bank profits, is a market failure that must be addressed. The state has a role to play in fostering a bank structure or bank behaviour that minimizes this social harm. Civil society, most notably community organizations working with excluded people, would have an important role to play in addressing financial exclusion.

A final argument for government intervention in mainstream banking is from the common good perspective, discussed in chapter 2. It is related to the public good concept but is broader in scope. Rather than justifying government economic action on the basis of the existence of public goods, it justifies its action based on the benefits to a society and an economy from equity. By common good, it is meant that some poor people fall outside the market system, and they would be better off if supports were in place to assist them in taking advantage of these services. Society as a whole will benefit indirectly by a lowering of poverty and its correlated problems. In a contemporary Northern country everyone needs access to a bank account. Getting a job, paying for goods and services, receiving government entitlements – all hinge on having a bank account. Moreover, a market economy is rocked by the boom-bust cycle that puts people out of work. These macroeconomic cycles place people in periods of employment and unemployment, for which access to financial services is important. Finally, everyone faces life-cycle expenses – birth, education, death – and for many people these expenses cannot be met from current income. For all these reasons, financial inclusion is a must for all Canadians.

Interestingly, banks themselves can benefit from a large and growing customer base. More customers mean more services and, holding service fees constant, this means higher bank revenue. Therefore, it is in the private interests of banks to expand their client base. For both of these reasons, the public and the private good, it makes sense to bring the roughly one million unbanked adults into the banking system, if they want. And the state has a responsibility to ensure that this can happen.

Carbo, Gardener, and Molyneux (2005) identify several state approaches to banking in Northern countries today, all of which might be termed reformist: affirmative action, mediation, legislation, and provider. These approaches are not mutually exclusive and are examined below.

The affirmative-action approach is one in which the state seeks to ensure provision of banking services to marginalized groups. This is done by providing incentives to banks to take affirmative action in order to meet the financial service needs of underbanked people. Thethirty-year-old U.S. Community Reinvestment Act (CRA) is an example of this. Here, banks that can demonstrate investment in poorer neighbourhoods receive credits that can be used to gain other regulatory advantages such as allowing bank mergers and chapter applications. Evidence is based on three tests: that credit is allocated to all households in the working area including low- and moderate-income households, that there are investments allocated for community development, and that retail services are available to all households in the bank's operating region including low- and moderate-income households. Proponents of the CRA claim that this system has funnelled billions of dollars into marginalized communities. Opponents claim it has created greater economic inefficiencies.

State mediation occurs when the state uses its moral suasion capacity to encourage banks to set and report on certain goals. For instance, the UK government, in order to reduce financial exclusion, threatened banks with mandating the provision of universal banking (Carbo, Gardener, and Molyneux 2005, 108). This placed pressure on the banks, which then agreed to work on a basic bank account and a strategy to promote financial inclusion. The French government also used its mediating skills to encourage banks to establish basic banking services, but in 1998 it also enacted the anti-exclusion law that 'gives any person residing in France the right to open a deposit account' (Carbo, Gardener, and Molyneux 2005, 108). This law established a detailed list of twelve points that must be met by banks in their product design. Canada, Portugal, and Sweden used legislation to promote basic banking.

States are sometimes influenced by religion, as is the case in some Islamic republics. Rooted in Koranic injunction, Islam disallows interest being charged on credit. As a result, Islamic banks do not charge interest, and some Islamic countries such as Pakistan disallow banks from doing so (Hassan and Lewis 2007). This is not, however, an effort to stall productive investment but a way to restrict exploitative usury. Rather than paying one interest rate on deposits and charging a higher interest rate on loans, a bank following Islamic principles uses various means of profit and loss sharing.

> In banning *riba* [interest charged on credit], Islam seeks to establish a society based upon fairness and justice (Holy Qur'an 2:239). A loan provides the lender with a fixed return irrespective of the outcome of the borrower's venture. It is much fairer to have a sharing of profits and losses. Fairness in this context has two dimensions: the supplier of capital possesses a right to reward, but this reward should be commensurate

with the risk and effort involved and thus be governed by the return on the individual project for which funds are supplied (Presley, 1988). Hence what is forbidden in Islam is the predetermined return. The sharing of profit is legitimate and the acceptability of that practice has provided the foundation for the development and implementation of Islamic banking. (Hassan and Lewis 2007, 47)

States sometimes provide banking services, usually through a state agency such as the postal corporation. Finally, states sometimes engage in research and development on new financial service products. For instance, the U.S. Federal Deposit Insurance Corporation has piloted a research project with banks to determine the feasibility of banks' offering small loans that could compete with payday loans (FDIC 2010). This research demonstrated that banks could offer loan products similar to payday loans but generally in a loss-leader situation.

Government Policy

Government policy sets the stage in which banking is provided and livelihoods are generated. As discussed earlier, both international and domestic opinion and pressure rule out some types of policy changes in the short run. Radical changes, by definition, are not in the offing in the immediate future. This does not preclude individuals and groups from opting out of mainstream banking through local economy and finance systems. However, in the short run, reform is more likely, and pro-poor reform must compete with other voices. To be effective in influencing policy, the pro-poor reform voice needs to be clear, reasoned and, to the extent that this is possible, unified. At the risk of being repetitive, probably one of the best ways to overcome financial exclusion is to address poverty. Policies that promote poverty eradication are important ones for achieving financial inclusion. Beyond those types of policies, this section addresses three categories of policy reform: federal banking regulations, consumer protection, and federal government services.

A critical part of regulating for financial inclusion is the development of holistic policy, beginning with the identification of financial exclusion as a social problem. It requires the acknowledgment that many low-income people are not fully served by mainstream banks and that they rely on fringe and informal financial service providers for some or all of their needs. It requires the regulation of mainstream, fringe, and, to the extent possible, informal financial service providers. This will require cooperation among different levels of government, particularly federal and provincial or territorial.

Federal Banking Regulations

Banks and trust companies are regulated by the federal government, while credit unions and caisses populaires, for now, are regulated by the provincial governments. This section is concerned primarily with the federal-level regulation of banks and trusts. However, similar types of regulations could be developed at the provincial level for credit unions and caisses populaires.

The principal point in this section is that the federal Access to Basic Banking Services Regulations, which resulted from the 1998 MacKay Report, introduced into federal regulation the idea of consumer rights to basic banking. That was useful; however, it did not go far enough. Moreover, there are two principal weaknesses of the regulations: the requirements are inadequate, and the enforcement is weak.

RAMPING UP THE BASIC BANKING REQUIREMENTS
The Access to Basic Banking Services Regulations require that federally regulated banks, upon proof of a person's identity, open an account for that person and cash a federal government cheque of less than $1,500, for free. This seems reasonable, but bank behaviour can undermine any benefits to the unbanked from these regulations, and banks can ignore the regulations.

Expansion of the Basic Banking Concept. Even if banks follow the Access to Basic Banking Services Regulations, bank behaviour can actually undermine the requirements in a number of ways. A major factor in bank choice has to do with access: is the location convenient, and is it open at convenient times? Basic banking requirements may call for banks to open accounts, but if mainstream banks close branches in inner-city locations, low-income people are less likely to use their services. Design is another important ingredient in bank choice. Mainstream banks currently maintain a three- to seven-day hold on cheques. Fringe banks do not place a hold on cheques. Banks may be willing to immediately cash federal government cheques free, but they will not do so for most provincial government cheques. Bank accounts and cheque cashing are important basic banking services, but there are others. Simple development services such as small loans and asset-building programs are not available at mainstream banks. Small loans are available at pawnshops and payday lenders, at high costs to the consumer, but savings schemes are not available. Finally, the shopping experience is an important factor that has been identified in neighbourhood surveys and mystery shopping. Once again, mainstream banks may offer account opening, but if they do not do so in a polite and respectful manner, then this weighs against using them. To address financial inclusion, government and banks must expand the concept of basic banking.

Enforcement. Another problem with banking access rules is that they are easily ignored. Without effective enforcement of regulations there is little use for an expanded concept. There would only be a growing list of regulations that are ignored.

Presently basic banking regulations are enforced by the Financial Consumer Agency of Canada in two ways. First, a financial consumer who is unable to resolve a problem with a bank can make a formal complaint upon which the FCAC commissioner will act. However, a complaint system is only useful if people (1) know about the service and the regulations and (2) know about the complaint mechanism. It is unlikely that an unbanked person is going to be aware of basic banking regulations, not to mention the complaint process. Second, the FCAC undertakes mystery shopping (on an irregular basis) to determine bank observance of various requirements, including basic banking. Some critics of the FCAC have argued that it has not acted on the results of the mystery shopping (Conacher 2007). Part of the challenge in responding to mystery shopping results is that the method involves an element of deception on the part of the shoppers and thus creates a somewhat artificial experience.

Another challenge for the FCAC in enforcing the regulations is that its funding comes from the banks that it regulates. This may create a basic conflict of interest. Enforcing regulations could undermine the viability of the organizations that fund the agency. That probably would not affect the FCAC's finances, but it might affect the willingness of banks to collaborate with it.

In order to improve the effectiveness of enforcement, the FCAC must be able to test that banks are meeting the requirements of expanded basic banking. The point of basic banking is that people have better access to banks, not just that they can open an account. Thus, expanding the basic banking concept is critical. In addition, the FCAC must be given new tools for evaluating bank operations.[1] In addition to mystery shopping, evaluation methods could include customer surveys. Most important for financial inclusion, the FCAC must have the means to test banks' treatment of non-customers, possibly through neighbourhood surveys and national surveys that deliberately represent low-income people.

A final change needed at the FCAC is ensuring that research results lead to effective enforcement. This might be achieved if, rather than being funded by the organizations that it is expected to regulate, all or part of the FCAC were funded from general government revenues so that it did not face a potential conflict of interest. Also, the FCAC commissioner could be given more power to penalize offenders, including publicizing the results of the agency's surveys and research.

Another way in which the FCAC can have an impact on financial exclusion is through citizen education about banking, financial services, and finances. The FCAC does have a mandate to educate consumers about financial services but needs to find ways to inform low-income and financially excluded people. Efforts at financial education must reach everyone, including poor people, who are less likely to have a computer and access to the Internet. Financial literacy is something that happens for many adults through daily activities: working, managing a home, and banking. Thus, the FCAC must find ways to extend its curriculum into people's daily lives. This might be done through a general public education process using existing institutions such as schools and banks. The curriculum for financial education should expand to include an understanding of Canada's banking system and the ways in which financial services affect one's household finances.

To address basic banking through provincially regulated credit unions, the FCAC should have partnerships with the provincial agencies that are responsible for enforcement there.

Financial Inclusion Fund. As discussed above, there are different means by which the government could foster financial inclusion. Carbo, Gardener, and Molyneux (2005) categorize the approaches as affirmative action, mediator, legislator, and provider. Perhaps fitting within the affirmative-action and legislator categories, the federal government might enact a tax on banks that would be used to fund financial inclusion efforts. The 'basic banking' tax could be a fixed proportion of profit or revenue (for example, 1% of their revenue) or it might be a tax with a sliding scale that is higher for those banks with less evidence of financial inclusion efforts. Resources collected from the tax could be used to fund a special 'basic-banking' bank (for example, a state bank or a postal bank) or the funds could be available to banks that demonstrate they are providing basic banking services.

Consumer Protection

Consumer protection regulations are presently the main way in which consumers are protected from fringe bank abuse. Fair business practices are also involved. The Canadian federal system lodges consumer protection and fair business practices at the provincial level. This means that fourteen different jurisdictions develop regulations. Through the Consumer Measures Committee these governments seek to coordinate the regulations.

FAIR DISCLOSURE AND USURY CEILINGS

In Canada, payday loan regulations are based on two principles: the fair disclosure of fees and a cap on payday loan fees. Common sense would support the notion of fair disclosure: how can a consumer look after his or her interests in a purchase without knowing its price? Neoclassical economic theory supports this common-sense view; it requires that the consumer be well informed for its models to work. Credit can be a particularly complicated service, and some fringe banks take advantage of that fact by creating all sorts of fees and ancillary services (for example, debit cards). Thus, common sense and theory support the idea that credit schemes such as payday loans should be simplified and all fees brought together into a common format (for example, APR) so that, at the very minimum, people can compare fringe bank fees. That fair disclosure is part of the payday loan regulations is a good step. It will be important to monitor, enforce, evaluate, and revise these regulations.

A more controversial aspect of payday lending regulation is usury ceilings. Usury caps have an interesting history. During the Middle Ages usury was outlawed in some European countries. Today some Islamic countries and banks that follow Islamic rules disallow charging interest on loans. There is a tendency for more reservation about employing usury ceilings in Anglo-American countries, in that they are seen to be akin to minimum wages and to act as obstacles to a well-functioning market (Anderloni et al. 2008). Usury ceilings are more common in continental Western Europe, particularly France, Belgium, and Germany.[2] The United States, perhaps the premier market economy, has given the role of applying payday loan rate caps over to the state level; as a result, one finds a patchwork quilt of usury ceilings across states, including several states with rate caps below levels found in Canada.

The interest-cap debate has played out in Canada through the payday loan regulations. In Manitoba, payday loan industry proponents argued either for ceilings that were so high that only payday lenders with ridiculously high fees would face a price correction, or for no ceiling at all. A consumer coalition (in which the author participated) advocated an 'efficient-scale' cap that was designed to allow the most efficient payday lenders (that is, Money Mart and Advance America, a U.S. firm that was opening National Cash Advance branches in Canada at the time) to continue to operate. The base cap was set at $17 per $100 loaned, which is below the caps set by other provinces. Other provincial caps include Ontario at $21 per $100 loaned, British Columbia at $23 per $100 loaned, and Nova Scotia at $31 per $100 loaned.

MORE ORGANIZED REGULATIONS

The Consumer Measures Committee is a provincial, territorial, and federal committee that works at consumer regulations across the country. The committee can meet, research, and agree on regulations that are suitable for a particular area, but it is up to the provinces and the territories to enact legislation and to regulate. This can be a challenging process. Take, for instance, payday lending regulations. As discussed in the introduction, the creation and enacting of fourteen sets of laws – instead of one federal law – is a time-consuming process. Payday lenders have their roots in Canada in the late 1990s and increased dramatically in numbers in the mid 2000s. Today the CPLA estimates that two million Canadians have used payday loans. However, at the time of writing in 2010, only four provinces had regulations in place. Meanwhile payday loan consumers in some provinces continue to operate in an unregulated environment.

One alternative is for the federal government to return to its role as regulator of small loans. This role began more than one hundred years ago, in 1906, with the Money Lenders Act and was replaced in 1939 by the Small Loans Act (Smyth 2001). The latter act was repealed when section 347 of the Criminal Code of Canada was established. It is not clear why the federal government handed over its jurisdiction to regulate payday lenders to the provinces. It is not immediately obvious how small consumer loans are a consumer protection issue as opposed to a finance issue, which would be a federal government responsibility. Certainly, for a hundred years the federal government understood small loans to be the latter.

Another option is for the federal government to establish separate regulations for payday lenders, akin to what it did with income-tax-refund advancers (discussed in the introduction).

Regardless of the option pursued, it is important that regulations be unified and implemented in a timely fashion. The advantage of federal regulations is that only one level of government is involved.

PLUGGING HOLES IN FRINGE BANKING

Even if payday loan regulations were in force across the country, which they are not, there remains a major hole in the regulation of other fringe banks. There are no regulations about credit associated with other fringe banks such as pawnshops and rent-to-owns. This means that the unbanked consumer who relies on these fringe banks has little security. An obvious extension is to apply these regulations (the concept of a cap and fair disclosure) to the services of other fringe banks, including pawn loans and rent-to-own loans.

Additional Government Supports

In addition to regulation, the federal and provincial governments could support efforts at financial inclusion in other ways. Some possibilities include the extension of indemnification agreements to provincial and municipal cheques, and the use of loan guarantees.

CHEQUE-CASHING INDEMNIFICATION

The federal government has an agreement with federally regulated banks to indemnify them for losses they incur in connection with federal government cheques valued up to $1,500. This allows banks to forgo the hold period and provides the client with immediate cash at no charge. This same form of indemnification could be undertaken by provincial and municipal governments for similar types of entitlement cheques.

LOAN GUARANTEES

The federal government provides loan guarantees to a variety of organizations for a variety of purposes. Loan guarantees take away the credit risk from the lender and place it on the government. This reduces the risk, and consequently the costs, to the lender. Potentially, loan guarantees make borrowing to marginal groups more remunerative. One challenge of loan guarantees is that they create problematic incentives, termed *moral hazard* in economics. The lenders may have the incentive to lend to risky (as opposed to simply credit-less) borrowers. To avoid the creation of problematic incentives, the lender that receives the guarantees must continue to follow its own safe and sound lending practices.

Examples of loan guarantees include the federal government's Western Economic Diversification Loan and Investment Program.[3] This program provides guarantees to credit unions that have microcredit programs. However, such a program supports producer, not consumer, loans. France's Social Cohesion Fund is a loan guarantee program that provides guarantees for consumer loans. Its mandate is to provide credit to underbanked people in order to improve employment and promote social cohesion (Gloukoviezoff 2007, 5). A total of €73,000,000 will be available over five years to cooperative banks, the postal bank, municipal pawnbrokers, and some credit card issuers.

It is possible that loan guarantees – perhaps funded through the basic banking tax discussed earlier – could be used to promote small loans to low-income people.

Bank Reforms

If one accepts the reformist agenda for building financial inclusion, then financial institutions are central actors. How can existing mainstream banks be reformed to foster financial inclusion? Two issues are raised in this section: reforms to bank services and reforms to bank structure.

Recognition of the Financially Excluded

Canada is a country made up of many different people, and there is not one archetypical (that is, 'average' or middle-income) Canadian. There are many (for example, low-income people) who do not fit a middle-income archetype. By the use of language that attempts to apply to all Canadians, some Canadians are left out. An important first step in promoting financial inclusion is for banks to develop a more effective language to illustrate that they provide services to people from a variety of social and economic backgrounds. Carbo, Gardener, and Molyneux (2007, 23) identified this as a problem of the banking model that was followed by many banks in the North: 'The so-called "shareholder value model" pursued by financial sector firms appears to emphasise increasingly the "standard customer" in more profitable markets segments. Marginal customers may become ever more excluded. For example, as financial services firms "desert" particular geographic localities and customer segments, information for assessing respective risk is reduced; asymmetric information problems worsen.'

Variety of Basic Banking Needs

Recognizing that all Canadians' financial service needs are not the same and, specifically, that many low-income Canadians have particular financial service needs is an important first step in financial inclusion. The next step is to identify these services. To do so, this section draws on the access, fees, product design, services, and staff culture ideas presented in chapter 3. The concept involves raising the benefits and reducing the costs, thereby raising the net benefit to becoming banked as compared to relying on fringe banks.

ACCESS

Accessibility is an important issue in promoting financial inclusion. Bank services need to be accessible in terms of physical location and operating hours. Electronic access (via debit cards, ATMs, telephone, and the Internet) can be useful, but bricks-and-mortar bank branches are critical. The trouble is that mainstream banks have pulled many branches out of inner-city neighbourhoods, presumably because they have found these branches to be marginally or not at all profitable. The resulting gap has helped to drive the rising number of fringe banks. There is a need for more mainstream bank branches in these locations, but new branches are not likely to be, at least in the near future, as lucrative as the existing branches. Thus, there needs to be means to address these bricks-and-mortar gaps: first, to identify financially excluded regions and, second, to promote the establishment of bank branches there.

Identifying underserved regions might be done through a mapping process. This was used by the UK government to reduce financial exclusion.[4] It mapped the financial institutions (credit unions and community development credit unions) that it planned to support with funds through the Growth Fund and overlaid the maps with deprivation indicators. The result was an identification of financial institutions that were centrally placed to affect regional poverty and reduce financial exclusion.

Once the underserved regions have been identified, the next task is to bring in mainstream bank branches. This could be done in a variety of ways. For instance, the regions might be divided among the large banks and the interested credit unions. Alternatively, to establish a branch in an underserved area, interested financial institutions might apply for funding from the previously discussed financial inclusion fund (financed from a tax of bank revenue).

FEES

For reasonably comparable financial services, mainstream bank fees are lower than fringe bank fees. However, as discussed in chapter 3, other benefits and costs come into play in comparing and choosing financial services. These issues were previously discussed and include a variety of economic (such as the distance to the bank) and social (a sense of respect from bank staff) costs. The success of fringe banks demonstrates that some people are willing to pay more for services that are convenient and, in the case of cheque cashing (but not payday lending), with fees that come up front. The lesson is to keep fees simple, low, and, to the extent possible, up front. At minimum, banks must make efforts to explain to new bank clients how they are charged and how they can keep additional charges to a minimum.

SERVICES DESIGN

In some cases, fringe banks have been successful because they have designed financial services that are attractive to low-income people. By addressing some of these design features in their own products, mainstream financial institutions could build financial inclusion. Two design features are particularly problematic: personal identification requirements and hold periods for cheque cashing.

Personal ID is an obstacle for some low-income people who do nothave adequate ID and/or cannot afford to get it. Mainstream banks could draw a lesson from fringe banks by providing a form of personal ID for interested patrons. Some fringe banks use their own ID system in which the client's photo and salient information are on their computer system. Several community banking projects (Pigeon Park Savings, Cash and Save, and Community Financial Services Centre) have implemented an ID system.

A cheque-hold policy acts as an obstacle for people to use mainstream banks, leading some to use fringe banks or informal financial service providers. If the payment comes from a government agency or a business with direct deposit access, then direct deposit is a good option. This assumes that a person has a bank account, and the likelihood of this will be higher if banks are more proactive about promoting financial inclusion. Another solution is for other levels of government to make indemnification arrangements with banks.

ADDITIONAL SERVICES

Research has found that poor people need the full set of banking services such as savings and credit. Low-income people do save, and one major limitation to saving is a lack of appropriate savings devices. Instead of making large deposits that amount to larger sums, poor people save small amounts that amount to small total sums. The placement of small savings like this at mainstream banks has few benefits to low-income savers (and, without addressing the expanded basic banking issues, there are many obstacles). Middle-income Canadians, by contrast, are motivated to save (but often do not, as evidenced by the low savings rates) by accessing higher-return savings and investments such as mutual funds and by accessing government asset-building programs such as the Registered Retirement Savings Program or the Registered Education Savings Program.

For low-income people to have incentives to save, savings services need to be designed that are useful for them. Offered here are some examples of goal-oriented savings, but more general savings schemes may also be useful. Goal-oriented savings are savings that are deliberately associated with a particular goal. Identification of particular goals can boost a person's motivation to save. In the Canadian context, the entitlement implications have to be ironed out so that personal savings do not undermine current and future entitlements. Research has found that high returns are not necessary for inducing savings. In some cases, people are even willing to pay for useful savings systems. The key is that the schemes are useful: convenient and accepting of small deposits. Banks might experiment with schemes that allow convenient deposit of small sums on a regular basis. Layaway plans have been referred to positively by some respondents in neighbourhood surveys. Individual development accounts also offer a route to goal-oriented savings. Currently these are available through participating non-profit organizations in various locations across the country (see below).

In addition to building savings, low-income people – like everyone else – require access to appropriate credit from time to time. Appropriate credit here is defined as credit that assists people to meet life-cycle and crisis needs without fostering unsustainable debt loads. Unlike loans to middle-income people, these loans need to be small, and flexible repayment is important. A small loan is characteristically needed by low-income people because it fits within their general spending. The flexible repayment is needed because, unlike middle-income people, when low-income people face unexpected crises, the loan repayment may come at the price of basics such as a meal, diapers, or medication. What are the forms in which credit might be delivered? Consider some popular loan schemes presently used by low-income people, such as pawn loans, payday loans, and rent-to-own contracts. In the first two cases a small sum is loaned for a short period of time, collateralized by either a consumer good or a pay cheque. Flexibility is achieved through the use (and expensive consequences) of extensions, repeats, or rollovers. Rent-to-own contracts are like layaway plans (and thus are similar to individual development accounts) but in reverse, in that the consumer gets the good before it has been paid for.

Mainstream banks do not offer small loans; instead they offer credit lines and cards. A credit card is a useful tool for certain purposes. It provides the client with continuous access to credit up to a limit, assuming it is adequately serviced. It has also allowed for the automation of the credit checks and monitoring, which has facilitated the proliferation of credit. However, there are limitations to the credit card: it is an unfocused form of credit (it can be used for many things at a time and over time), and it does not involve a pattern of disciplined repayment. Therefore, credit cards are not always appropriate when a person is looking for a focused small loan with an attached repayment process. It would be useful if banks would reintroduce the small loan. One source of innovation in this area is the work by several credit unions and banks in the United States and Australia, particularly in light of the payday loan growth (see box 5.1 below and reference to the FDIC's Small-Dollar Loan Pilot Program above). In some cases these loan schemes have themselves been profitable, and in other cases banks have seen the business case for them as loss leaders to attract new clients who will eventually use other, more lucrative bank products. It may be that these small loans can be successfully offered at APRs that are higher than the rates associated with other mainstream bank products. Internationally, microfinance institutions have become very prominent and often charge interest rates in the 20% to 30% APR range. This interest rate may seem high compared with the cost of mainstream credit products, but it is considerably lower than the interest rates charged at pawnshops, payday lenders, and rent-to-own stores.

Box 5.1 Bank Partnerships – Australia Example

The National Australia Bank (NAB) is one of the largest banks in Australia and an active player in micro-lending. It recently pledged A$130 million in capital. With partners, it is involved in three types of small-loan programs: No Interest Loan Schemes, Small Loans Pilot Project, and StepUP Loans.

With the Good Shepherd Youth and Family Services, NAB developed the No Interest Loan Schemes in 1981, which, in partnership with community organizations, offer small loans (ranging from A$800 to A$1,200) to low-income people throughout Australia. NAB provides loan capital, state governments provide the funds for operations, and the loan agreement is with the community organization. They currently offer 5,500 loans per year but plan to increase this to 6,500 in 2009 and to 14,000 in 2012.

The StepUp Loan scheme builds on the experiences with No Interest Loan Schemes and seeks to utilize a no-interest loan as a way to help unbanked people move into mainstream banking. Begun in 2004, the program offers small consumer loans and insurance and currently offers loans in twenty-one locations in six Australian states. NAB provides the loan capital and works with Good Shepherd, which works with the clients. The loan agreement is with the bank. Loan sizes range from A$800 to A$3,000 and average A$2,700; there were 599 outstanding loans, valued at A$1.46 million, at the end of 2007.

NAB put A$1 million as loan capital and partnered with Money Fast in 2008 in their Small Loans Pilot Project. The goal of the program is to offer small loans (the average size in the first quarter of

the second year of operations was A\$3,357) at a middle-range in-
terest rate (28.25% per year) within a program that is self-financing.
The self-financing goal was already achieved in the second year of
operations.

Sources: No Interest Loan Schemes: National Australia Bank (n.d.),
'No Interest Loan Schemes' StepUP Loans: National Australia Bank
(n.d.), 'StepUP Loans'
Small Loans Pilot Project: National Australia Bank (n.d.), 'NAB
Small Loans Pilot Project'

In addition to accessing credit, people need to be able to demonstrate that they are creditworthy. By doing so, through credit reporting, they can access greater credit in the future. This is sustainable
where the household's economic situation is improving. Other products that might improve access to appropriate credit include secured
credit cards. These are credit cards with a limit set according to the
amount of funds that the client has deposited in a secure account. This
form of credit card can assist a person in building his or her credit rating, but since it requires the person to have the credit limit in the form
of savings, it does not solve the liquidity problem.

THE SHOPPING EXPERIENCE
National and neighbourhood surveys and mystery shopping, as discussed in chapter 2, have demonstrated that low-income clients may
find banking at mainstream banks challenging. While tellers may or
may not be respectful, they may have relatively less interest and eagerness in low-income clients compared with middle- or upper-income
clients. This may also affect the time that they spend with these clients
and the information that they provide. Even advertising basic banking
services would be a positive step to make people aware of the availability of these services. The development of a best-practices guide
might also be a step in the right direction. The guide could assist interested financial institutions in better serving low-income clients (for
example see Carlson 2005).

NEW TECHNOLOGIES
New information and communication technologies are no doubt important factors to consider in addressing financial exclusion. The new

financial service technologies such as ATMs and Internet banking reduce bank costs and raise the potential of delivering financial services universally. No doubt the more recent financial service technologies such as chip cards can offer even more cost reductions to banks. For basic banking access, these technologies must be accessible to low-income people. Internet-based access for people without a computer is not helpful. Banks must carefully consider the assets and needs of thelow-income client. Moreover, there is evidence that bricks-and-mortar branches are still important to low-income clients, partly because some low-income people – like many people – still prefer the in-person transaction.

Bank Structure

Reforming banks to support financial inclusion requires changes at mission and structural levels. What is presented here are some possible means to improving banks' performance of financial inclusion. However, this is only a discussion of some options, and it does not analyse the structural issues in depth.

THE COMMUNITY FOCUS

One imaginable way for banking to address financial exclusion is by creating a stronger link to various communities, including unbanked communities. Credit unions and non-profit pawnshops are commonly seen as means to strengthen financial services to unbanked people. Sometimes state-based banks have been mandated to provide services to underbanked people.

An important issue to clarify when considering community focus and financial inclusion is that they are not the same thing. Community organizations are not automatically concerned with poverty and issues such as financial exclusion. A chamber of commerce might be considered a community organization (of businesses), but it is not primarily interested in the well-being of low-income people. To build financial inclusion, what is needed is a greater focus on the communities of financially excluded people.

In continental Europe the state and cooperatives are more active in banking, compared with the United States and the United Kingdom. In some cases the state is involved in the delivery of banking services through postal banks (France and even the United Kingdom). These models are in a state of flux. Until the U.S. sub-prime mortgage crisis there was pressure on these countries to follow the U.S. model of liberalization (Carbo, Gardener, and Molyneux 2007). However, following the crisis, confidence in the U.S. banking system as a model has declined. The consequences of these changes for the state-run banks are not clear. Nevertheless, theirs is a model that should be considered by the Canadian government. A state-run bank that specifically fosters financial inclusion and is financed through, say, the financial inclusion tax is one model to consider.

Also, in the United States and continental Europe one finds pawnshops that operate within a non-profit mandate, providing small loans at fees that are lower than those at commercial pawnshops. The European public pawnshops have a long tradition, stretching back to the seventeenth century, as a response to the lack of alternative credit opportunities for those who relied on commercial pawnbrokers. These services offer pawn loans like commercial brokers do, but at a lower interest rate and on terms that are more beneficial to the client.[5] Views about pawnshops are conflicted. On the one hand, the terms for the loan are generally not as good as those at a commercial bank, and there is no credit-record building. A French commentator noted: 'But [*prêt sur gage* / the pawn loan] can not really be considered as a proper answer to financial exclusion as first, they are not available in every town, and second, they are obliged to request an item (usually jewelry) as a basis for the loan' (Gloukoviezoff 2007, 4). On the other hand, the pawn loan provides small loans to many people who would otherwise be unable to access a loan. The improved terms of the non-profit pawnshop offer slightly more benefits to the customer.

Canada does have experience with state-based banks, mostly in the provision of loans to business. Canadian state-based banks include the Business Development Bank of Canada and the Farm Credit Corporation. The Business Development Bank of Canada is a Crown corporation that provides loans for small and medium-sized business. The Farm Credit Corporation provides loans for farming. Ironically, the only state-based bank for consumer services is in the province of Alberta, through the Alberta Treasury Branch. The Alberta Treasury Branch provides retail banking throughout the province and has its roots in a government response to the depression that affected communities in the 1930s. Since Canada Post has off-loaded most of its outlets, it makes the postal system an unlikely means for the state to deliver banking services. Nor is there a tradition of public or non-profit pawnshops in Canada.

More likely to address financial exclusion in Canada than a state bank or a public pawnshop are the existing credit union or caisse populaire systems. Compared with the United States and the United Kingdom, Canada has a relatively large credit union system in relation to commercial banking. That is interesting, considering one root of the credit union concept – and the cooperative notion more generally – is the United Kingdom in the work of Robert Owen. However, credit unions in the United Kingdom are relatively small, and the sector represents a small share of the UK adult population. In 2008 there were just over 652,000 UK members, which represented 1.6% of the economically active population (World Council of Credit Unions 2010). The sector's total assets amounted to US$857 million. Meanwhile credit unions in the United States had 89,900,000 members, which represented a 43.7% penetration rate. Credit union assets in the United States amounted to US$185.1 billion, which represented 6.5% of all commercial bank (and credit union) assets (World Council of Credit Unions 2010; U.S. Federal Reserve Board 2010). Canada's credit union members were 10,900,000, which represented 47.3% of the economically active population. Their assets amounted to US$185 billion, or 8.8% of all bank assets. Thus, Canadian credit unions have participation rates that are 3.6 percentage points higher than those in the United States and almost thirty times those in the United Kingdom. The Canadian credit union system assets as a share of total financial institution assets are 1.35 times larger than in the United States. And Canadian credit union assets are more than two hundred times larger than those of the UK credit union system. Thus the Canadian credit union system has significant capacity compared with the systems in the United States and particularly with the system in the United Kingdom.

In the United States there are a variety of types of credit unions including the *community development* credit union, a type of credit union that is particularly focused on addressing financial inclusion among low-income populations. In recent years the UK government has seen the enhancement of credit unions as a key means to addressing financial inclusion. For the six-year period between 2005 and 2011 it committed to spending $80 million for capital and administration of the Growth Fund. This is a fund intended to finance loans to underbanked people from credit unions and community development financial institutions.

However, credit unions themselves face challenges in addressing financial inclusion. On the one hand, akin to cooperatives, they have their impetus in a democratic form of governance. This democratic ideal might be the source of including people who have been excluded. On the other hand, credit unions are owned by their members and accountable to them. The membership may be narrowly or broadly defined. For instance, sometimes membership is 'close bond,' meaning that only people from a certain occupation, ethnicity, or religious affiliation can be members. In this case it is more difficult for the credit union to address the needs of the financially excluded if they do not fit the membership criteria.

Exactly how these conflicting ideals – a broad democratic vision versus a narrower community vision – are addressed in practice is an important question. A Woodstock Institute study examined the way in which credit unions fared relative to banks in the United States regarding community reinvestment. It found that credit unions did not do better than banks in serving unbanked people (Jacob, Bush and Immergluck 2002). But another study found that community development banks did better than regular banks did in serving the underserved (Bush and Smith 2003). There is also evidence that in the United States credit unions have been quite active in seeking to provide affordable small-sum loans in response to the growth of payday lenders. Work by the Credit Union National Association (CUNA) and the National Federation of Community Development Credit Unions is the evidence of this. CUNA completed a major report that described ten different payday loan alternative products offered at different member credit unions: 'This payday loan implementation guide is intended to help credit unions develop solutions that are appropriate for the credit unions and its members. It is not a turn-key answer, but some turn-key products are featured as examples' (Pierce 2008a).

The National Federation of Community Development Credit Unions completed a study of payday loan alternative projects with its members, called 'The Alternatives to Payday Lending Program (APPLE).' It involved six case studies of payday loan alternatives at community development credit unions (Williams 2007). The report included descriptions of the programs and is one of the few reports to provide a detailed analysis of their costs: 'However, even including charge-offs, it is clear that the affordable PDLs [payday loans] are profitable for each credit union. This is particularly notable given the innovative nature of these loan products. Given more experience to refine underwriting standards and reduce loan costs, it is possible that each credit union has the capacity to increase gross margin percentages even more' (Williams 2007, 14).

U.S. banks, particularly through the FDIC's Small Loans Pilot Project, are also developing small-loan alternatives, but considering the relative sizes of these two types of financial institutions (that is, banks and credit unions), it appears that credit unions are more active in seeking to address this credit gap.

A final piece of evidence that credit unions are important players in addressing financial inclusion is a report examining a group of community banking projects in Canada. It found that credit unions were more active than were banks: three of the four projects had a credit union as the financial partner (discussed below) (Buckland 2008a). The point here is that there is evidence – if somewhat mixed – that credit unions do play and can play an important role in addressing financial exclusion.

A challenge for the credit union sector is that, outside of Quebec, credit unions are autonomous and relatively small. This makes it more difficult for them to compete with large banks. In Quebec the caisses populaires work within a more federated system and, when combined, form one of the largest financial institutions in Canada. Credit unions in English-speaking Canada do not work within this type of federation; their actions are more autonomous. This means that their small size can create inefficiencies that put them at a disadvantage relative to the big banks. However, many credit unions are going through a process of merger and acquisition at present. Mergers and acquisitions are one means to foster scale economies. The use of associations and federations is another means. If products, services, and delivery systems could be developed within the auspices of a credit union association, it might be possible to deliver them through a number of credit unions. Perhaps credit unions and caisses populaires could strengthen their cooperation. In addition, the credit union system might draw on lessons from the Desjardins Group regarding federation. If credit unions were able to join in a federation, they might be better able to take advantage of efficiencies.

The federal government is discussing the creation of legislation for national credit unions. The creation of regulations allowing credit unions to operate nationally has the potential for them to take advantage of scale economies. The implications for their financial inclusion efforts are, however, not clear.

This is not to argue that credit unions should be the sole, or even the primary, means by which financial inclusion is pursued. Their resources are limited, and the resources of the big banks are much larger. Owing to their relative size and protected status, mainstream banks have a greater responsibility than do credit unions to work for financial inclusion.

CORPORATE SOCIAL RESPONSIBILITY

From a reformist perspective, banks – some of the economy's largest companies – need to be leaders in corporate social responsibility. This is a movement that recognizes the social and environmental (among other) responsibilities that corporations have.

The notion of corporate social responsibility could be a means to engage financial institutions in financial inclusion. To succeed, shareholders need to be educated about the need for a double, triple, or multiple bottom line for good corporate governance. This could be achieved through a shift in mission statements from a singular pursuit of profit to a set of goals that include building financial inclusion. This type of internal commitment may be an effective means to develop strategies and operations for reducing financial exclusion.

Currently, federally regulated banks in Canada generate annual public-accountability statements, but these are statements about the public contributions – such as employment and charity – that they have made within their singular profit focus; they are not a means to evaluate and improve upon their social outcomes. A clear statement about financial inclusion in the company's mission, with accompanying tangible goals, and effective reporting could facilitate a financial institution's engagement of this issue.

RELATIONS AND PARTNERSHIPS

A final structural approach to building financial inclusion is financial institutions' partnering with other organizations that have useful expertise or resources. Banks have relations with many organizations, but partnerships that advance basic banking are less frequent. More partnerships could be made with government, other banks, and community organizations. This section is focused on the ways in which banks do and can work with civil society organizations to foster financial inclusion. These partnerships could assist banks – which have the ultimate responsibility to provide the services – to meet the needs of unbanked people more effectively.

Banks have relationships with government regarding some of their basic banking services. For instance, the federal government offers banks indemnification for certain types of cheques. It also provides loan guarantees for certain types of producer loans. These types of partnerships could be expanded in areas that build financial inclusion. For instance, provincial and municipal governments could provide indemnification agreements with banks for cheques from these governments. Loan guarantees could be made available for small consumer loans to the underbanked.

Canadian mainstream banks have relationships with fringe banks in a number of ways. For instance, mainstream banks have invested in fringe banks (ACORN Canada 2007), and fringe banks use mainstream banks as sources of credit and cheque clearing (Buckland et al. 2003). Other examples of mainstream-fringe bank partnerships have taken place in Australia and the United States. A small loan program in Australia is funded by the National Australia Bank, and loans are delivered through a fringe bank. This type of partnership between mainstream and fringe banks has been common in the United States and much criticized because it allows banks to ignore state usury caps. Owing to the reality of two-tier banking, relations between mainstream and fringe banks must be examined carefully.

A key argument in this book is that civil society can play an important role in assisting banks to address financial exclusion. Financial exclusion is a complex phenomenon that is linked with poverty. Consequently, the causes of financial exclusion are tied to the causes of poverty. Thus, financial inclusion must address the causes of poverty. Part of the solution is to ensure that financially excluded people can participate in institutions that positively affect their lives. Community organizations play an important role in fostering this type of participation.

At present, most mainstream banks do not have the capacity or the interest to work with, and provide services for, low-income people and communities. Mainstream banks generally lack the capacity to work with low-income people because their principal focus is on working with middle- and upper-income people. These latter groups have been the mainstay of banks' business. With the closure of inner-city branches, the discontinuance of offering small loans, and the general move upmarket (towards higher-end investments such as mutual funds and mortgages), banks have developed an expertise with middle- and upper-income people and not with low-income people. The result has been a gap in the provision of financial services for low-income people, a gap that fringe banks have sought to fill. A second reason that banks have difficulty working with low-income people relates to their structure. As for-profit organizations they are driven by shareholder interests, which are about increasing profit. Generally speaking, low-income people are not seen as a source of (at least short-run) profit. Of course, this is a short-sighted strategy because low-income people, with interest, agency, and assistance, can become middle- or upper-income people. A bank with a longer time frame could see this, but most corporations, including banks, have a short-term perspective. The consequences are that banks do not have the experience or interest in working effectively with low-income people.

This presents the opening for the involvement of community organizations. By definition, community organizations are of the local people and seek to foster their participation. Community organizations working with low-income communities are in a strategically important position for banks concerned with financial inclusion. Community organizations can represent low-income people and/or be able to bring low-income people into a process of needs identification, project implementation, and evaluation. Of course, community organizations are a diverse group, and they face many challenges. They often struggle with funding, their claims to legitimacy can be complicated, and they struggle with capacity building (Edwards and Hulme 1996). They are also small in size relative to financial institutions, which raises an important concern about asymmetric power. Nevertheless, community organizations can provide mainstream banks with an important link into a financially excluded neighbourhood.

Civil society organizations can and do play an important role in addressing financial inclusion. This is because of the recognition today of the importance of peoples' participation in the institutions that shape their lives. Community organizations are important civil society actors for addressing this goal. Civil society is also important because it can be a force to ensure that the interests of low-income people are considered in issues related to the common good. This type of role may be played by community organizations and/or by larger non-profit organizations.

Community Banking Projects. A very visible way in which banks have partnered with community organizations has been in community banking projects (Buckland 2008a). These are special banking projects that are tailored to meet the needs of particular communities and people. Sometimes they are separate standing operations, and sometimes they are a way to test new products, which can then be used by existing institutions. Community banking projects are common in the United States, the United Kingdom, and Australia.

The projects identified in the Canadian field research are Pigeon Park Savings (PPS, Vancouver), the Community Financial Services Centre (CFSC, Winnipeg), Cash and Save (Toronto), and the Fonds d'entraide Desjardins (Mutual Assistance Fund) of the Desjardins Fédération (Quebec). These projects were identified in earlier research (see Buckland et al. 2003) as projects that were designed with the goal of addressing financial exclusion in some way.

After the projects are described, the remainder of this section considers the learnings from the project experiences, including the importance of innovation, financial challenges, and the issue of cross-cultural dialogue. Comments will be limited to PPS, CFSC, and Cash and Save – the 'outlet based' projects involving one or two outlets that offer some combination of financial services. The Desjardins Fédération's Mutual Assistance Fund is probably the most different from the other three in that it is not rooted in one branch or location (or two) but is a program for all interested caisses populaires in Quebec. Detailed information about each project's partners are found in the appendix.

Cash and Save is a service centre of the Royal Bank of Canada. The name is intended to highlight its focus on low-fee cheque cashing. It has two outlets located in inner-city Toronto neighbourhoods: 1385 Queen Street West in Parkdale and 310 Gerrard Street East in Regent Park. The Parkdale outlet was opened in October 2002, and the Regent Park outlet one year later. The outlets are open to anyone for the purpose of basic financial services including cheque cashing, bill payments, money transfers, and money orders. With the client's provision of adequate personal identification on the first visit, the identification is placed on the computer system so that the client is not required to bring it for future visits. The fee for cashing a cheque was initially 1.25% of the cheque's face value (minimum $4), but by 2007 it had been raised to 1.99% of the cheque's value plus $0.99 (for payroll cheques with a maximum value of $1,500 and personal cheques with a maximum value of $300), still below the fees found at most cheque cashers. As per federal regulations, Cash and Save charges no fees to cash federal government cheques up to $1,500. Money transfers are made through another company (Moneygram), and Cash and Save adds no further fees. Fees for other services include $1.25 for bill payments and $2.49 for money orders up to $1,000. Currency exchange fees are $1.99 for amounts up to $1,000.

The Parkdale outlet is compact, with 400 square feet of office space. This creates a very intimate space that, on busy days, can lead to line-ups that run outside the outlet. Each outlet has a minimum of two staff including one on-site supervisor. Cash and Save deliberately seeks to employ neighbourhood residents and encourages them to pursue training in order to gain promotion in their regular branch network. Financial sustainability is a key goal of the Cash and Save business model. However, one informant indicated that RBC does not expect Cash and Save to generate the level of profits that other RBC units generate.

Pigeon Park Savings opened its doors in March 2004 and is located in the centre of Vancouver's Downtown Eastside, at 92 East Hastings Street (on the southwest corner of Hastings and Columbia Streets). The name comes from a nearby park, Pigeon Park, a gathering place for many area residents. Pigeon Park Savings is a project of Portland Hotel Community Services Society (PHS) and Vancity Credit Union. It is a single outlet that is open to anyone and primarily serves neighbourhood residents. Pigeon Park Savings offers a simple account that includes unlimited transactions (either in person or at the ATM), counter cheques, bill payments, direct deposits, and money transfers for a $5 monthly flat fee. The fee to cash a cheque for non-members is $1.99 for amounts up to $1,000 and $2.99 for amounts over $1,000. It also offers a $20 overdraft for members experiencing special needs. The overdraft comes at no charge and requires the member to apply to the manager. Pigeon Park Savings will also provide members, for no additional charge, an additional account that can be used for savings. The outlet is large with 5,475 square feet of space that includes a large back room, ample space for teller kiosks, and a large reception area. First-time clients drawing welfare benefits are able to use photocopied personal identification that has been verified by their welfare office. In fall 2007, Pigeon Park Savings had 4,200 members, but this was projected to rise to between 4,500 and 5,000. The atmosphere of the branch is intended to be open and respectful of neighbourhood residents. There is no security guard; staff members are first of all PHS program workers, and then they are trained as tellers.

Pigeon Park Savings is a program of PHS and a branch of Vancity Credit Union. PHS provides the staff members who manage and provide teller services, while Vancity contributes backroom processing, a computer system, and technical support. Vancity has also financially supported the Pigeon Park Savings' operations since its inception. One of the five PHS co-directors was based in the outlet during the first three years of operations to assist with program implementation. The full-time staff include a manager, an assistant manager, and a teller. The current staff members have all worked previously with PHS, and they live in the neighbourhood.

The Community Financial Services Centre is a pilot project of North End Community Renewal Corporation (NECRC), a community agency, and was developed and implemented with Assiniboine Credit Union (ACU). The CFSC is located in Winnipeg's North End, at 888 Main Street; a former Canadian Imperial Bank of Commerce branch, it has approximately 400 square feet of space that it rents from Mt Carmel Clinic. It accepts clients who are referred to it by community partner agencies. The project offers a number of financial services to the working- and welfare-poor and assists them in developing a relationship with a mainstream bank. Services include free CFSC photo identification, access to an ACU account, assistance in applying for direct deposit, free on-site cheque depositing and cheque cashing at ACU branches with no holds,[6] and one-on-one financial counselling (optional) including assistance in creating a credit history. In addition, the CFSC plans to offer group-based financial management training in the future. The ACU member can select a basic savings or chequing account with thirty free transactions per month. For the pilot project period ACU provides the $5 membership-share fee and waives the $4.75 monthly chequing-account fee.

As of June 2008 the CFSC had 153 clients issued with its ID cards (risen from 80 in the fall of 2007), had facilitated the opening of 136 bank accounts (133 at ACU and 3 at another bank), had completed 79 one-on-one counselling sessions, had assisted in creating 8 credit histories, and had issued 21 loans. It has a full-time manager and one staff member and plans to hire an additional staff member.

The Desjardins Fédération's Fonds d'entraide Desjardins (Mutual Assistance Fund) is one of several solidarity products that Desjardins offers. Others include Microcrédit Desjardins aux enterprises (loans for small business) and Créavenir Desjardins (loans for young people). The Mutual Assistance Fund was formed after the appointment of a new president in 2000, when Desjardins revised its mission statement by strengthening its commitment to solidarity and set aside $500,000 as capital for the fund.

The idea behind the Mutual Assistance Fund is the provision of assistance to people who are experiencing financial difficulties, through financial counselling and access to small emergency loans of $500 to $1,000. The loans are provided at a low or no interest rate to people who are otherwise unable to access credit. The project involves the federation, a local caisse populaire, and a credit-counselling agency. The federation and the local caisse provide the capital and contribute to the financial counsellor's salary. The local caisse agrees to maintain the loan fund by replenishing any loan losses. The credit-counselling agency refers clients to the program, does pre-lending counselling, and monitors repayment. As of December 2007, approximately $1.3 million had been loaned, in 2,421 loans with an average loan size of $549 and a repayment rate of 89%. The typical borrower is between twenty-five and fifty-four years of age, often a female relying on social assistance and with an annual income of less than $10,000. The Mutual Assistance Fund was operating in twenty-eight locations, involving 299 out of 536 caisses populaires, across fifteen of the total seventeen regions of Quebec.

In the three outlet-based cases, the outlet is not marketed as a branch of the partner financial institution, but there are links in each case. The link to a regular RBC branch with Cash and Save occurs when clients express interest in a bank account and the staff provide them with a 'warm referral'; that is, they arrange an appointment with a local RBC branch so that the client can set up an account. Informants claimed that few Cash and Save customers requested the referral, likely because of the preference for the close location and the transaction services provided by Cash and Save. With Pigeon Park Savings, members can access their account through Interac and Exchange ATMs, which they do regularly. With respect to the Community Financial Service Centre, members who have opened accounts with Assiniboine Credit Union are able to access any ACU branch or ATM.

In terms of orientation to the public, Cash and Save and Pigeon Park Savings are open to anyone, while the Community Financial Services Centre and the Desjardins Mutual Assistance Fund are available on a referral basis.

There are several organizations involved in the design and, in some cases, the operations of these financial service projects. Indeed, one of the key lessons from this research is that community banking projects are necessarily complex and therefore involve operations in a field where no one organization has sufficient expertise. As a result they require input from a number of types of organizations. The key types of organizations involved in these projects are community organizations, financial institutions, and research or consulting firms. Community organizations provide a number of critically important inputs including knowledge of and connection to the neighbourhood and its residents. This knowledge and these networks can combine to provide relationships and legitimacy that can be used to develop and support the projects. Financial institutions bring the expertise about delivering financial services. For Cash and Save and the Community Financial Services Centre a research component was also critical in the business planning.

Innovation. In three outlet-based projects it was clear that there had been considerable innovation involved in their development. As described in an earlier section, it is argued that mainstream banks in Canada have not made a significant effort to address the financial service needs of low-income people. Thus, identifying key services and packaging these into a viable business model was a challenge. This challenge required innovation.

In the case of Pigeon Park Savings, respondents described it as a 'new tier,' a 'junior credit union,' a 'Red Green'[7] or 'duct-tape' design, suggesting a credit union with a more basic set of services, perhaps akin to a Credit Union Service Organization (CUSO) in the United States. The design of the project was done largely by Vancity Credit Union with input from PHS staff about resident financial service needs. The design was intended to provide basic credit union services – including an account, teller service, and ATM service – while simplifying the project's information systems and minimizing costs. To facilitate these goals, the branch required a new and simplified computer system that was separate from the Vancity system, and basic office furnishings. PHS would provide staff, and Vancity would provide basic teller training. A key design challenge was that the project would need to meet the heavy anti-money-laundering regulations and personal identification requirements faced by banks and credit unions. With the support of Vancity, Pigeon Park Savings was able to establish ID requirements that met regulatory requirements and overcame the personal ID hurdle that many unbanked people face. An example of this was the use of photocopied personal ID that had been verified by the member's welfare office.

The Cash and Save is owned by the Royal Bank of Canada (RBC), but it was the result of collaboration with a non-profit organization, StChristopher House, and a consulting company, Bain and Company.

The role of Bain and Company was identified as critical by several respondents to developing the business case for Cash and Save. Working with RBC and St Christopher House, Bain started by identifying the financial service needs of Parkdale residents and found that they were the set of services offered by a cheque casher. Bain argued that it was this set of services that was needed by area residents, not the set available in a typical mainstream bank branch. Bain then researched the infrastructure required to deliver these services and assisted in the development of a full business plan. The model offered cheque cashing as a core service at a fee that was lower than that offered elsewhere, within a business that was to be, financially, completely reliant on fees. Respondents indicated that lending was initially included in the Cash and Save business plan, but the decision was made to not offer it initially; until now it has not been added and likely will not be added.

The Community Financial Services Centre design has its roots in a community-university research project, through the Winnipeg Inner-City Research Alliance. In the final report, based on a survey of residents, a basic account, timely cheque cashing, access to small loans, and personal identification were identified as the key needs for neighbourhood residents (Buckland et al. 2003). The report also noted the residents' desire to have a mainstream bank or credit union account. In addition to revealing financial service needs, the report included a feasibility assessment of a few different financial service models including a non-profit pawnshop and a cheque casher (Buckland et al., 2003). The feasibility study indicated that such a centre would be feasible if government and private support were available. It argued that this support was justified by the fact that a centre would reduce social costs (for example, the costs of stolen cash and income lost to fringe bank fees). The Canadian Imperial Bank of Commerce later funded a full business plan for the centre that retained many of the features found in the feasibility report.

Unique Financial Challenges. All of the community banking projects face unique financial challenges, unlike those of a typical bank. They relate to the type of financial services that are provided and the resulting revenue and costs. Generally the services involve small sums and few, if any, deposits that can generate interest income. This means that staff time for each transaction is high relative to the fee for the service. Cashing a $200 cheque, processing a $100 withdrawal, or completing the paper work for a $50 loan may involve less staff time than doing the equivalent processing for a much larger-value transaction, but not in proportion to the value. Processing a $50 loan does notinvolve one-hundredth of the time required to process a $5,000 loan.The consequences of these factors are that complete financial self-reliance – that is, the ability to cover their costs through revenue generated by services – of these projects is unlikely. This fact creates a particular challenge for the community banking projects.

RBC's goal is that Cash and Save be financially viable, that is, to cover at minimum its costs through fee revenue. However, RBC informants have indicated that profit expectations for Cash and Save are lower than those for other operations. While RBC would not provide specifics about Cash and Save's present profitability, it was able to say that it is not meeting expected financial goals.[8] How RBC plans to achieve the financial goal is not clear; one RBC respondent said that the bank is still in the evaluation and 'pause position.'

According to respondents, an improved financial position might be achieved by expanding services into lending (drawing efficiency through economies of scope) or replicating Cash and Save (adding efficiency through economies of scale). As previously mentioned, RBC has no plans to introduce payday loans to Cash and Save. As for replication, while this would allow the bank to experience economies of scale, the extent of such efficiency is not known. Moreover, there are obstacles preventing replication of Cash and Save.[9] Most pressing, RBC has announced that it will open a full RBC branch in Regent Park. If this is the case, it is hard to imagine the Regent Park Cash and Save continuing. There would be no economies of scale to offset the high fixed costs with only one Cash and Save.

Pigeon Park Savings, offering a set of basic credit union services, faces its own financial challenges. Like Cash and Save, it offers financial services involving small sums that require a significant amount of staff time, and it was, until recently, seeking to become financially reliant on only its fee revenues. The Pigeon Park Savings building is provided by Vancouver Coastal Health at no rental charge. Although there was a point in time when the government was considering selling the building, access to physical space is not considered a major challenge. Both partners agree that a major goal for Pigeon Park Savings is that it become financially self-sufficient. In covering staff salaries and other operating costs, Pigeon Park Savings is currently losing approximately $100,000 each year. Since its inception these operating losses have been covered by Vancity Credit Union.

More recently, it is felt that Pigeon Park Savings will need to generate revenue from non-fee sources such as donations. However, there is
concern that relying too much on an external subsidy might make the
project vulnerable. As one informant said, 'a project is only as sustainable as its subsidy.' When this point was raised by respondents, it was
usually made in connection with the challenges and ultimate closure
of Four Corners Savings Association, located one block away. Respondents generally felt that Four Corners was an expensive operation that
relied excessively on government subsidies. Accordingly, this reliance
was the catalyst to Four Corners' ultimate downfall: when a new government came to power in 2001, political support and more funding for
the association was not forthcoming.

Pigeon Park Savings relies heavily on members' account service fees
to fund its operations. Key informants argued that the project could at-
tain financial self-sufficiency by relying on growing service fees. With
the rapid rise in membership over the past three years, Pigeon Park
Savings has substantially increased its revenues (table 5.1), but it has
also faced continuously rising operating costs. As membership has
grown so have the line-ups at Pigeon Park Savings. On the day that
income-assistance cheques are issued, up to ten tellers are required.
What this has meant is that the (approximate) annualized operating losses dipped during the period from 2005 to early 2006 but then
jumped in late 2006, to $100,000 per year.

Estimates of the number of members needed to achieve breakeven
are 4,400 to 5,500. It is not clear whether these estimates are based on
a formula that includes higher staff costs as membership rises. Until
the financial viability of Pigeon Park Savings has been demonstrated,
management does not plan to introduce new services. In fact, the
long-run viability of Pigeon Park Savings is still uncertain.

The goal of complete financial self-sufficiency at Pigeon Park Savings
seems to be rooted in at least two sources. First, there is a reluctance
to look to government for support. Respondents felt that the closure
of Four Corners Savings Association was due to dependence on unreliable government subsidies. Government funding is unreliable, it is
argued, because when new political parties come to power, they in-
evitably shift government spending priorities. That the closure of Four
Corners was a key catalyst for Pigeon Park Savings seems to have left
a powerful imprint on PPS stakeholders in terms of the need to achieve
financial self-sufficiency. A second factor behind the goal of financial
self-sufficiencymay be the fact that PPS is a branch of Vancity Credit

Table 5.1
Pigeon Park Savings' membership numbers and approximate
annual operating loss, 2005–2007

	Membership	Approximate operating loss per year $, annualized
March 2005	0	–
June 2005	1,800	60,000
August 2006	3,600	36,000
December 2006	3,900	100,000
June 2007	4,200	n/a

Union, a for-profit business. By definition, for-profit companies see financial self-reliance as a prerequisite for a viable organization. RBC has similar expectations about its Cash and Save.

The Community Financial Services Centre has its own particular challenges. As a pilot project, its client base is much smaller than that of Pigeon Park Savings, and its reliance on public funds much greater. In fact, the centre is presently able to generate no fee revenue. In the feasibility study, public funding was justified in that a centre would contribute to the common good by lowering the rates of lost cheques through the use of direct deposit; by reducing the loss of members' income that occurs through fringe bank fees; by transiting clients into mainstream banking; and by reducing the likelihood of clients being reliant on welfare programs. Since it was contributing to the common good – and, by definition, could not charge for this service – the centre could not be financially self-sufficient and would need to rely on outside funding.

The Winnipeg Partnership Agreement – a tripartite municipal, provincial, and federal government program – has been the major funder of CFSC, providing $300,000 for the first three years of its operations. The Winnipeg Foundation provided $50,000 in grants. While Assiniboine Credit Union (ACU) provides no direct cash support, it does cover some project expenses (for example, evaluations) and provides in-kind support including staff time; it pays membership fees and waives monthly account fees. External financial support for the CFSC is over $100,000 per year, which is similar to the level of support that Pigeon Park Savings receives from Vancity.

The financial data on the projects are limited. The Cash and Save might be close to breaking even, but that might not be sufficient for RBC. Both CFSC and PPS operations require non-fee support. PPS currently fills its financial gap with support from Vancity, while the CFSC relies primarily on support from government. PPS generates significant revenue from its service fees, which CFSC does not. PPS also has a larger number of clients than the CFSC has. However, the CFSC has more of a developmental emphasis than PPS does, including services such credit building, financial counselling, and supporting its clients in their development of a regularized relationship with a mainstream bank. A simple cost-per-client calculation would show that PPS's costs are lower than the CFSC's are, but their mandates are different. PPS seeks to provide basic financial services to neighbourhood residents. The CFSC seeks to assist clients in transitioning to a bank relationship. Each model is important and offers significant insights into financial inclusion. Since the CFSC has no fee revenue, it is particularly reliant on external support.

Cross-Cultural Dialogue. Dialogue across 'cultures' was identified as another factor associated with the community banking projects. By *culture*, we refer not to the foundational concept of worldview but to differences in attitudes and experiences across different socio-economic groups within a society. For instance, different groups living within the same society may have different attitudes about, and experiences with, life goals, finances, and financial services. In some cases, these differences may become an obstacle to different groups in trusting one another, communicating, and working together. For these groups to work together, cross-cultural dialogue is necessary.

The most obvious cross-cultural tension identified by respondents was between banks and inner-city residents. As these two groups have such different cultures, they do not often communicate and sometimes have feelings of distrust towards each other. Key informants referred to a level of distrust among some inner-city residents towards banks. Respondents also reported that with some financial institution staff there was distrust towards, and suspicion of, inner-city residents. One respondent described the corporate culture of the financial institution as one in which low-income people were seen to have caused their own poverty. Thus, building trust and better communication was essential in developing successful community banking projects.

Several respondents noted that the projects required the building of cross-cultural dialogue and trust. PHS, the North End Community Renewal Corporation (NECRC), St Christopher House, and the various budget-counselling agencies involved with the Desjardins project all had staff who played important 'bridging' roles. PHS was respected by Vancity Credit Union as an organization working with and for Vancouver's Downtown Eastside residents. In fact, one Vancity Credit Union respondent claimed that the credit union would not work in the Downtown Eastside on its own but only in partnership with a community agency. St Christopher House's role in Cash and Save was critical for promoting understanding within RBC of the unique challenges of Parkdale residents, although its role seems to have declined after the design phase. In Winnipeg several community organizations, within the auspices of the NECRC, played an important role in the development of the Community Financial Services Centre.

Conclusions about Community Banking Projects. The banking conditions in inner cities in Canada are quickly changing. Cheque cashers, instant-tax-refund advancers, and payday lenders are growing in numbers, and these outlets are spilling into the suburbs. Inner-city-based community organizations, banks, and credit unions have noted this development, and some have sought to address it through special community banking projects. We have identified four of these projects, Pigeon Park Savings, Cash and Save, the Community Financial Services Centre, and the Desjardins Mutual Assistance Fund. Three of these projects are located in one or two inner cities and offer a set of financial services to neighbourhood residents. The Desjardins program works with low-income people throughout the province of Quebec. Each project is the result of partnerships, most importantly between a community organization, a financial institution, and a research or consulting agency.

One key conclusion from this research is that community banking projects are expensive and are not likely to become self-sufficient. Cash and Save is probably (we do not know for sure) the closest to financial self-sufficiency, but it offers the most basic set of services, devoid of savings, credit repair or credit building, or financial literacy. Why these projects need to become completely self-sufficient is unclear. They can and do contribute to the common good. By reducing transaction fees and theft and helping some unbanked people into a relationship with a mainstream bank, they may provide a positive benefit to society. Since low-income people, by definition, cannot fully pay for this service, community banking projects cannot collect sufficient fees. This is akin to the public transit challenge where buses reduce noise, gasoline use, and carbon emissions, but they cannot charge a fee to cover their costs. However, governments invest in public transit because there is a net benefit to society. While this justifies some external support for these projects, it does not imply that these projects must be entirely reliant on external support.

Another conclusion from this research is that having partnerships and building relationships across types of organizations is important. Without partnerships such as the Royal Bank of Canada and St Christopher House, the Community Financial Services Centre and Assiniboine Credit Union, and PHS Community Services Society and Vancity Credit Union, these projects would likely not exist. Relationships between key community and financial institution leaders are important. While some community organizations may vilify mainstream banks, and some banks may criticize community organizations, these organizations need each other in order to succeed in the work of financial inclusion. How can organizations from such different backgrounds be brought together in greater numbers and on a more regular basis? One way is to develop a common language and seek to understand common and conflicting interests, understandings, and values. Networks and associations that operate at the local and national level could usefully support this type of relationship. Building networks beyond one's industry association is beneficial for success in this field. Another way to bring people together is through participation in the boards of each other's organization. Financial institutions in particular might consider dedicating senior staff to board work on local social organizations and inviting community representatives onto their boards.

The role of government in these projects needs to be clarified, both in terms of public policy and funding. Considering the strong public-good case that can be made for these types of projects, there is a rationale for government support. However, some stakeholders are concerned, perhaps excessively, that government funding is unreliable. Clearer government policy about its own funding of public-good projects would help. Moreover, federal policy on the responsibilities of financial institutions in this field is weak. The Access to Basic Banking Services Regulations are not sufficient to encourage more bank engagement with the issue. Since banks receive certain government protection, they must be required to provide their services more extensively.

Finally, the small number of community banking projects in Canada reflects a shortage of resources and interest. This suggests that mainstream banks are largely disinterested in having unbanked and underbanked people as customers. This has likely helped to fuel the growth of fringe bank services and numbers. Financial inclusion efforts require innovation, partnerships, and a culture shift, and they are financially challenging. They also make an important contribution to meeting a social and economic need of many low-income Canadians.

Asset Building and Financial Education. There are a variety of other programs in which civil society organizations are involved, sometimes in partnership with banks, that relate to financial inclusion. Credit counselling in Canada is offered by both non-profit and for-profit organizations and generally seeks to assist persons with unsustainable debt. Ideally the credit counselling program can use a personal debt crisis as a moment of learning about financial literacy. Producer microcredit schemes are commonly offered to small businesses, and civil society organizations may be working with financial institutions to deliver such programs. With the Task Force on Financial Literacy recommending more financial education, this area is likely to be a growth sector.

In terms of their impact on financial exclusion, individual development accounts directed at low-income households offer considerable potential. Matched savings schemes draw people into a relationship with a bank through the savings account, they assist clients in attaining a savings goal, and they often provide participants with financial management training (Robson and Nares 2006). To the extent that financial exclusion is caused by deep-rooted structural problems, asset-building is limited in its impact, however. Indeed, financial exclusion may constrain some people from participating in asset-building programs. If individual development accounts were offered in combination with financial inclusion efforts, some of these obstacles might be overcome. To more effectively address financial inclusion, asset-building programs must recognize and address the obstacles of the welfare wall that low-income people face.

Advocacy. Another approach to financial inclusion is through advocacy for better government and bank policy and practice. In Canada most advocates for bank change are reform oriented. For instance, the Canadian Community Reinvestment Coalition has critiqued the enforcement of the Access to Basic Banking Services Regulations and has called for, among other things, community reinvestment regulations as in the United States and a different type of financial consumer agency to replace the current Financial Consumer Agency of Canada. ACORN Canada, an organization with its roots in the United States, has actively criticized the payday loan industry, arguing that it charges usurious fees and facilitates the creation of a second-tier of banking. The Public Interest Advocacy Centre engages in a number of consumer issues including banking and in particular has surveyed payday loan users and examined ATM fees. Regarding payday loans, it has called for reforms such as the fair disclosure of fees.

One might find it odd to suggest that banks could partner with civil society advocates when these advocates sometimes criticize banks, but in fact there may be common interests between these actors. For instance, some bank economics departments such as the TD Canada Economics Group have analysed the role of income-support programs in Canada and concluded that reform is needed in order for low-income people to be able to move out of poverty. Reforming income support could facilitate financial inclusion and improve the well-being of many low-income Canadians. Through other efforts such as community banking projects and asset-building, banks have demonstrated an interest in issues beyond the financial 'bottom line.' Some credit unions such as Desjardins, Vancity, and Assiniboine have made major commitments to social responsibility and social goals.

Conclusion

In the more immediate future, reforms could be introduced to banking that would reduce financial exclusion. These reforms involve expanding the concept of basic banking, strengthening the federal and provincial regulations that affect mainstream and fringe banks, and financial institutions' identifying financial exclusion as an issue and deliberately addressing it. Civil society organizations can support this effort, and the role of government is important.

6 Conclusion

Summary of Cross-Cutting Themes

The Financial Exclusion–Poverty Relationship

A central theme in this book is the relationship between financial exclusion and poverty, a relationship that is supported by three important pieces of evidence. First, studies from the United States and the United Kingdom, to name just two countries, have identified this link. National surveys in Canada, such as Statistics Canada's Survey of Financial Security, are a second source of data that evidences this relationship. Finally, field work completed in three inner cities, which informed chapter 3, has found that low-income people have a complex relationship with fringe and mainstream banks. This is not to say that some non-poor – middle- and upper-income – people are not financially excluded. Surely there are people in that situation. Perhaps language and culture barriers prevent newcomer Canadians from getting a bank account. Perhaps some other middle-income people prefer anonymity, for various reasons, in their financial dealings. But these issues are outside of the scope of this study. Moreover, this study has concentrated on the inner-city poor, not on the suburban poor or the rural poor. These people will face banking barriers as well. The rural poor's situation might be quite different from the inner-city poor's, while the suburban poor's situation may have some similarities.

That the financial exclusion–poverty relationship exists surprises few people. Indeed the relationship seems to be a sub-case of the classic study by Caplovitz, *The Poor Pay More*, about the low-income experience with expensive retailers. Poor people who live in poor neighbourhoods face small retail operations having goods that are priced higher than those found at a supermarket, department store, or big-box outlet. Other parts of the inner-city economy are equally constraining on local development. This has been documented in the community economic development literature: few and poorly paid local jobs and the export of local surplus. This result is obvious. Is it very important? Two-tier retailing is not a big deal, so why is two-tier banking?

Two-tier banking is of particular concern if we accept that banking, compared with other retailers, plays a special role in our economy. Banking is different than other retail services, on a number of levels. First, banking faces special regulations that favour the big domestic banks. They are protected from extreme foreign competition. However, that protection may reduce competition and therefore reduce service provision to certain population groups such as low-income people. From a consumer perspective, being limited to expensive local stores may be acceptable, but being limited to only local fringe banks affects not only one's short-term prospects but also one's long-term prospects. Not being able to access developmental services is particularly limiting to one's long-term options. If one cannot develop a credit record, how can one get a credit card, let alone a mortgage or retirement savings? Two-tier banking can be highly problematic for poor people.

Another way to look at the question of two-tier banking is to ask about the origin of fringe banks. Where did the need for fringe banks originate? One possibility is that a lot of transactions that take place in fringe banks today used to be handled by informal financial services. Where in the past people would rely on cheque cashing and small loans from a corner store and pawnshops and on a loan from a friend or family member and would transfer money to relatives, fringe banks and fringe bank chains have developed a business model that allows them to take advantage of scale efficiencies and to take over more and more of this activity. In this scenario, fringe banks may be seen as a step up from informal financial services and a step towards mainstream banking. Alternatively, mainstream banks' branch closures, their cessation of offering small loans, and just generally their moving upmarket under the shareholder-value pressure may have created holes in the provision of banking services that fringe banks have plugged. Under this scenario, the plug – fringe banks – does not offer a step towards mainstream financial services; rather, it offers services that stall a financially excluded person's march to inclusion because of fringe bank expenses and problematic business practices.

Where does the truth lie? Without more data on fringe bank customers and the state of the informal financial sector, it is difficult to say
definitively. Most likely, there is some strength in both of the above
explanations. Fringe banks have grown by attracting people who previously relied on mainstream banks and people who previously relied on
informal financial services.

Institutions Matter

This study finds that institutions matter. It also finds that institutions
are a product of the social reality in which they operate. Institutions
of inner-city banking are the result of a 'bottom-up' informal process
where residents choose, in the face of few options, to relate with certain banks, employers, and government agencies. Additionally, some
residents and small businesses, through bottom-up means, provide informal financial services. Simultaneously, institutions are manifested
by the 'top-down' formal processes of big banks. The result of all these
processes is that inner cities are filled with fringe bank outlets and
fewer mainstream bank branches. It is the interaction of informal and
formal processes of residents, banks, and governments that generates
inner-city banking.

One definition of institutions is that they are the rules and norms
for behaviour and trust. Rules and norms around inner-city banking
range from very informal to very formal, and they affect suppliers and
consumers. These rules and norms are driven and affected by, among
others, consumers, bankers, and government policy. Informal manifestation of rules and norms includes consumer knowledge of mainstream
and fringe bank fees and services.

As we have seen, inner-city residents have a complex set of rules and
norms regarding inner-city banks. For instance, they make decisions
about financial service choice that consider not just the direct financial
service fee but also the indirect economic costs (for example, transportation to the bank) and social costs (for example, respectful treatment
by the teller). Other identified rules include, with regard to cheque
cashing, preference for cash and payment up front, and with regard
to small loans, preference, at least sometimes, for a one-time loan and
repayment cycle (versus a credit card). Whereas middle-income people
may normally assume that mainstream banks are *the* financial service
provider, normative behaviour among inner-city residents is to shop
around at different types of banks. Many inner-city residents will shop

around at informal, fringe, and mainstream financial services. In this sense, they have a broader set of institutions to draw on for their financial services. However, the problem they face is that informal and fringe banks do not provide developmental services, and mainstream banks do not offer enough appropriate developmental services.

The informal manifestation of rules and norms on the supplier side might be the friend offering a loan or a corner store cashing a cheque for a customer who is buying some of its goods. Informality is evidenced in such things as a variable fee, or the rules (such as reciprocating the loan in the future) not being explicitly stated. Yet inner-city residents clearly rely on these types of services because they trust certain family members, friends, or local retailers. Manifestations that are more formal are, with respectively higher levels of formality, fringe banks and mainstream banks. Not all fringe banks post their fees using fair disclosure rules, but some do. Fringe banks also have rules about personal identification requirements and loan duration, for example. But it is at the mainstream banks that one finds the greatest formalization of rules regarding service use, which are manifested most clearly by pamphlets and posters with details about the types and characteristics of their services. However, basic banking products and issues – low-fee accounts, personal identification requirements, cheque-cashing policies – are generally not as formalized as other bank products. Moreover, inner-city residents do not necessarily choose the most formal service. In some cases the least formal is chosen. In other cases a semi-formal service is used.

Government policy affects the level of formality of institutions as well as the rules and norms. Informal policy would be policy that is non-existent or ad hoc, for instance government policy regarding pawnshops. Here municipal governments regulate the sale of second-hand items for the purpose of reducing the trade in stolen property, but there is no regulation regarding interest or fees charged. The regulation of payday lenders is an example of semi-formal (but moving towards formal) regulation, while mainstream banking is formally regulated.

For inner-city financial service institutions to become more supportive of inner-city residents, a shift is needed. The shift is one that engages the different actors – residents, bankers, and government – to imagine, design, and implement new rules and norms for citizen and for banker. These new rules and norms could affect both citizen and banker. They would lead inner-city residents, as they continue to address daily financial struggles, to be able to consider the longer-term and to think about the relevance of developmental financial services. This would be assisted by government policy, for example, that promoted asset-building for low-income people. It might be manifested by mainstream banks that listened to the local residents and designed services that were appropriate for them.

More than the Market Is Required

Markets are useful for certain tasks, but the results of this study show that markets cannot be left to themselves to resolve financial (and other types of) exclusion. Efforts must be made to ensure that financial services are provided to excluded people. This likely will not happen without the influence of financially excluded communities and a pro-poor state.

Theoretically, markets are useful ways to provide certain types of goods and services. Abstracting from issues such as class, gender, and ethnicity, economic theory finds that the most effective type of goods that markets can provide is private goods: goods that are excludable and subtractable. Goods that are not characterized by these features include goods that are subtractable but not excludable (that is, common pool resources), those that are excludable but not subtractable (that is, club goods), and those that are neither (that is, public goods) (Todaro and Smith 2006). If banking is seen to have a public-good element that it is not entirely excludable and subtractable – and there is a strong case for this – then relying strictly on markets is insufficient. While banking may be somewhat excludable (for example, through a branch-location strategy, the promotion of basic banking, and service orientation to low-income people), it is not subtractable or, more to the point, additive. That is, if financially excluded people had access to appropriate banking, they, their banks, and the rest of the economy would be better off. This is because having a bank account and other basic financial services presents the unbanked with options to improve their financial position. If their position is improved, so is the bank's because they will use more of the bank's services. As the newly banked and banks' bottom lines improve, the economy is stimulated and government revenues rise (and expenses decline).

Particular types of markets offer different types of benefits and costs. On the one hand, we hear a lot about the way in which competitive markets can address so many problems. Fine, but what is meant by a *competitive* market? If we mean the neoclassical archetype of *perfect* competition, we will have difficulty fitting Canadian banking into this definition. Certainly there are several banks, but the top five mainstream banks dominate the industry. So how can we be sure that they are effectively competing to meet the common good? Theoretically speaking, we cannot be sure. Also, perfect competition implies that there are many small producers. However, in many industries larger producers can experience greater efficiencies. So it is not clear that small is always beautiful. If it is large that is necessary, then what follows is the need for accountability, and in the case of financial exclusion this accountability needs to be to the financially excluded. It can be facilitated through relationships with community organizations and pro-poor government policy.

Thus far, the points have underscored the limitations of the market, assuming that society is simply an amalgam of individuals. But this is a limiting assumption. In fact, much lies between the individual and the state. There are classes, genders, and ethnicities represented in Canada, and there are tensions in society along these lines. In the same way that gender bias is ultimately rooted in patriarchy, one might argue that financial exclusion is rooted in the control of banking on the part of a certain class or set of classes. This is evidenced in the expression *shareholder value*, that corporate interests are equated with the interests of the corporation's, mostly well-off, shareholders.

Even Adam Smith – often described as the father of a market-based economy, and author of *The Wealth of Nations* – understood the limitations of the marketplace. He argued in his book *The Theory of Moral Sentiments* that ethics must underscore the efforts of the butcher, the brewer, and the baker. Smith (1759) notes: 'The wise and virtuous man is at all times willing that his own private interest should be sacrificed to the public interest of his own particular order or society. He is at all times willing, too, that the interest of this order or society should be sacrificed to the greater interest of the state or sovereignty, of which it is only a subordinate part' (Smith 2001, part VI, section II, chapter 3).

Future Directions

Gaps in the Research

Several gaps in the data have been identified through this research. They include a lack of quantitative national-level data on financial exclusion, a lack of quantitative data on bank branch locations over time, and a lack of national-level data on low-income people. This research has relied heavily on mixed-method surveys that help to diagnose particular problems, but what is needed are national-level surveys that can take these results and quantify the problems nationally.

Gaps in Policy and Practice

As discussed in chapter 4, the major gap in banking that fosters financial exclusion has been the lack of careful reflection on the banking needs of low-income people. This reflection starts with banks accepting that there is not one 'average' Canadian with the same financial service needs. In fact, there are many different groups in society, and to address financial exclusion it is important for banks to identify and understand better the needs of low-income people. In summary, these needs can be met by making banking accessible, ensuring reasonable fees that are simple to understand and preferably up front, designing services that are rooted in an understanding of that group's reality including services beyond an account, and providing service that is respectful and helpful.

Ideally, these basic banking needs would be met through the initiative of mainstream banks, but that is unlikely. What is more likely is that carefully constructed government regulation would seek to enhance bank accountability to low-income citizens. This might be done through expanded basic banking regulations and consumer protection and the generation of supportive resources.

Appendix: The Importance of Partnerships in Community Banking Project

In all four community banking projects (Cash and Save, Pigeon Park Savings, Community Financial Services Centre, and the Mutual Assistance Fund), partnerships, at one or more stages, were a key input. Addressing the financial service needs of low-income Canadians is complex, and not any one type of organization has significant experience in this area. Mainstream banks have tended to focus more on the financial services appropriate for middle- and upper-income Canadians. Arguably, this means that they often do not fully understand the financial needs and banking interests of low-income Canadians. To develop community banking projects, mainstream banks require the assistance of organizations that have an understanding of these needs.

For their part, community organizations have seen that access to banking is an obstacle for many of their clients, but they lack the technical expertise to address the issue. Some non-profit organizations engage in quasi-financial services such as advice on completing tax returns, provision of asset-building programs, and assistance in opening a bank account, but it is rare for them to directly provide financial services. Thus, some community organizations and financial institutions have complementary expertise, and when this is combined with a common interest in addressing financial inclusion, pragmatic solutions can result.

Cash and Save is the product of important partnerships with a financial institution (Royal Bank of Canada), a community organization (St Christopher House), and a consulting company (Bain and Company). St Christopher House had identified financial exclusion as an issue for neighbourhood residents. When an RBC branch was closed in

Parkdale, a relationship began between St Christopher House and RBC that led to the establishment of two term positions to examine the problem. RBC funded the positions, a community developer and a community banker, and one of them was housed at St Christopher House. According to one survey respondent, these two organizations had different assignments: RBC was to 'deliver the bank,' and St Christopher House was to 'deliver the neighbourhood,' to the discussion of how to foster financial inclusion. This was not a confrontational relationship between an advocacy-style community agency and an aggressive for-profit corporation; it was a relationship between two organizations with a common set of interests. The participation of Bain and Company, a financial consulting agency, led to another component in the partnership. While RBC's competencies were in a standard set of banking services, the bank did not feel that it had the expertise to identify or provide financial services for low-income people. Bain had the competence and was willing to contribute human resources. It was motivated by a concern about financial exclusion and an interest in developing a business relationship with RBC. The research phase included representatives from the three organizations – RBC, St Christopher House, and Bain and Company – visiting community banking projects in the United States.

Pigeon Park Savings relies on an important relationship between PHS and Vancity Credit Union. It is a project of PHS and a branch of Vancity. PHS manages daily 'front-room' operations (client services) with a manager. As in all Vancity branches, daily transactions are tallied and reconciled by the staff, and this information is sent to Vancity for the 'back-room' work, including the clearing of cheques. One staff member at Vancity Credit Union has as part of her job description to act as a liaison with Pigeon Park Savings. This delegation of responsibilities partly explains the better balance sheet of Pigeon Park Savings compared with that of Four Corners Savings Association, in that Four Corners was responsible for performing both front-room and back-room work. Initially an advisory board was struck to provide input into the design of Pigeon Park Savings, but this group no longer functions. Pigeon Park Savings does not have its own board but operates as a project of PHS.

According to respondents, even before the development of Pigeon Park Savings, both partners valued the work of the other. PHS staff value Vancity's banking expertise, that Pigeon Park Savings is considered a Vancity branch, and that the Pigeon Park Savings ATM card can be used at other credit unions and retailers (via point-of-service out-lets). Vancity Credit Union also trains PHS staff on the teller functions and provides a 'bare-bones' computer system for the tellers. Vancity values the role that PHS plays in terms of daily retail operations, and the relationship that PHS has with residents. A Vancity respondent claimed that Pigeon Park Savings must be driven by the community and that a Vancity Credit Union branch could not survive in the Down-town Eastside.

The Community Financial Services Centre currently involves rela-tionships among a community organization, a credit union, and a gov-ernment funding program. The roots of the CFSC go back to the work of the Alternative Financial Services Coalition (AFSC) and some of its members, namely North End Stella Community Ministry of the United Church of Canada, SEED Winnipeg, Mennonite Central Committee, and Assiniboine Credit Union. The CFSC is now officially a project of North End Community Renewal Corporation (NECRC). It relies on a number of community agencies for client referral. The Canadian Impe-rial Bank of Commerce helped to fund the initial business plan, do-nated its former Main Street and Selkirk Avenue branch office to Mt Carmel Clinic, and maintains an ATM on the site. NECRC and Assini-boine Credit Union developed and implemented the operating model, with roles and responsibilities set out in a formal agreement. The Win-nipeg Partnership Agreement, a tripartite fund, is the key funding or-ganization.

The Desjardins Mutual Assistance Fund project involves a three-way partnership. The project was initiated by Desjardins Fédération by setting aside capital funds in 2000. The federation makes agreements with local caisses that each will contribute equal amounts towards the loan capital and will contribute to the salary of the financial counsellor. A budget-counselling agency is responsible for the client selection, loan dispersal, and repayment.

Once the projects got going, working relationships among the part-nerships changed. Once Cash and Save had opened its doors, RBC implemented the project. Bain and Company's involvement ended, and St Christopher House continued in the role of community consul-tant. In fact, St Christopher House's input in the project declined,[1] pre-sumably because RBC saw community consultation as something that had taken place at the beginning of the project. Yonge Street Mission acted as the community consultant for the Cash and Save in Regent Park. PHS and Vancity Credit Union regularly communicate regarding

Pigeon Park Savings operations. PHS staff provide teller services, and Vancity provides back-room processing. Senior staff at both organizations maintain significant interest and communication on the project. A similar situation exists for the Community Financial Services Centre, where the staff at the centre, NECRC, and Assiniboine Credit Union stay in regular communication. The Desjardins program relies on the ongoing relationship that it has with the local caisse populaire and a budget-counselling agency.

Notes

1 The Context of Financial Exclusion in Canada

1 This includes all units as well as what Statistics Canada refers to as *economic families* – those with more than one member – and *unattached individuals*.

2 The Gini coefficient is defined as the area between the Lorenz curve – which plots the share of income or assets received by different population groups (for example, quintiles or deciles) – and the line of perfect equality, divided by the area below the line of perfect equality. A Gini coefficient of zero represents perfect equality (each population group receives an equal amount of income), and a coefficient of one represents perfect inequality (the richest population group receives all the income).

3 These figures are calculated from Statistics Canada data in Statistics Canada (n.d., *Table 3800009*).

4 These figures are calculated from Statistics Canada data in Statistics Canada (n.d., Table 384).

5 These figures are calculated from Statistics Canada data in Statistics Canada (n.d., *Table 2030015*).

6 Statistics Canada, for one, claims that response rates to its surveys are higher among all income categories than are the rates for private surveys because Canadians are more willing to participate in a government agency survey. Moreover, StatsCan has partly overcome the under-coverage problem by linking its survey data with tax-return data, for which there is a high return (Picot 2009).

7 For a general discussion of the challenges of using different methods to accurately represent low-income people see Frenette, Green, and Picot (2007).

8 Data limitations of the survey meant that bank exclusion was indicated by whether the respondent had a non-zero bank account (banked) or not (having either a bank account with a zero balance or no bank account at all).

9 Respondents were asked if they had used a pawnshop within the last year.

10 Respondents were asked if they had used a payday loan within the last three years.

11 Statistics Canada has completed a new survey, the Canadian Financial Capability Survey, implemented in 2009; see Statistics Canada (2009).

12 In a recent budget the federal government announced that it is considering creating federal legislation for credit unions that would allow them to operate nationally.

13 For a comparison of regulations affecting different types of banks in Canada see Office of the Superintendent of Financial Institutions Canada (2010b).

14 For more details see Department of Finance Canada (2002).

15 The top eight banks are BMO Financial Group, Canadian Western Bank, Canadian Imperial Bank of Commerce (CIBC), Laurentian Bank of Canada, National Bank of Canada, RBC Financial Group, Scotiabank, TD Bank Financial Group.

16 These figures have been taken from Statistics Canada (n.d., *Table 282*).

17 In many Southern nations informal financial services are more elaborate than in Canadian inner cities. Both credit and savings services are available through, for instance, rotating credit societies (sometimes referred to as rotating savings and credit associations [ROSCAs])
and accumulating savings societies (sometimes referred to as accumulating savings and credit associations [ASCRAs]).

18 A similar but not as extensive process was also undertaken with respect to capping the fees for cashing government cheques.

19 DFC is the parent company of Dollar Financial Group (DFG), and from 2007 only DFC's 10-K reports were available. It is likely that the net income position of DFC is worse than that of DFG because of debt it incurred in, for example, the purchase of Canadian franchises of Money Mart (Robinson 2009).

20 Membership in the Consumer Measures Committee and a list of provincial and territorial departments responsible for consumer affairs can be found at the website for the Consumer Measures Committee, http://cmcweb.ca/eic/site/cmc-cmc.nsf/eng/h_fe00018.html.

21 Much of this section is taken from Buckland (2008b).

22 Bill C-8, 'An Act to Establish the Financial Consumer Agency of Canada and to Amend Certain Acts in Relation to Financial Institutions,' of 2001 (FCA Act) (Government of Canada 2002).

23 For this section see Financial Consumer Agency of Canada (2008).

24 In a subsequent meeting between bank officials and area leaders the bank did agree to leave its ATM at the location, to sell the building to a local non-profit organization for one dollar, and to help fund a business plan for a community banking project.

25 For information about the voluntary codes see Financial Consumer Agency of Canada (2009).

26 See Department of Justice, Canada (2010).

27 See Canada Revenue Agency (2009).

28 Annual percentage rate (linear) is the most common method of converting fees for loans of different time periods into an equivalent interest rate on an annual basis. APR does not include daily compounding and is calculated as follows: APR = (loan fees / loan principal) (365/12). Effective annual rate (EAR) is another method of converting loan fees into an annual form. It does involve annual compounding and therefore generally leads to much higher rates. The formula for EAR is as follows: EAR = [((loan principal + loan fees) / loan principal)$^{(365/T)}$ – 1][100%].

29 See Government of Ontario (n.d.).

30 See City of Toronto (n.d.).

31 The Doing Business in Winnipeg By-Law was updated in 2008; see City of Winnipeg (2008).

32 For more information see Winnipeg Police Service (2007).

33 The Consumer Measures Committee (Alternative Consumer Credit Working Group) has developed a method to convert small-loan fees into an annual percentage rate (APR). All fees (relating to interest, administration, and cheque cashing, for example) would be lumped together and then annualized. This would be appropriate for payday lenders, rent-to-own firms, and pawnshops.

34 The Canadian Payday Loan Association website maintains an archive of important government decisions regarding payday lending regulations. See Canadian Payday Loan Association 2010.

35 For general information on payday loan regulations in Alberta, see Service Alberta (2010).

36 For general information on payday loan regulations in British Columbia see British Columbia Ministry of Public Safety and Solicitor General (n.d.); for details on regulations see Consumer Protection BC (n.d.).

37 For general information on payday loan regulations in Nova Scotia see Service Nova Scotia and Municipal Relations (2010); for details on the rate cap decision of the Nova Scotia Utility and Review Board see Nova Scotia Utility and Review Board (2010).

38 For general information on payday loan regulation in Ontario and links to rate cap information see Ontario Ministry of Consumer Services (2010).

39 For information on the Saskatchewan regulations see Government of Saskatchewan (2009); for the relevant Saskatchewan act see Government of Saskatchewan (n.d.).

40 For Manitoba payday loan regulations see Government of Manitoba (n.d.); for recommendations from the Manitoba Public Utilities Board see Manitoba Public Utilities Board (n.d.).

41 For issues relating to cheque-cashing fees in Manitoba see Buckland (2006b); for issues relating to cheque-cashing fees in Ontario see Law Commission of Ontario (2009).

42 See for instance a study exploring the consequences of bank mergers on rural areas in British Columbia, Bowles (2000).

43 For a general discussion of the Competition Bureau's process of reviewing bank-merger applications see Competition Bureau Canada (1998).

44 Competition Bureau Canada (1999).

45 See Hillmer (2011).

46 If the foreign bank chooses to open a branch, it is either (as in the case of a lending branch) not permitted to take deposits or (as in the case of a full-service branch) permitted to take deposits greater than $150,000.

47 Department of Finance Canada (2001).

48 Here welfare programs refer to programs that provide financial assistance to an unemployed person who is without access to employment insurance or sufficient retirement income. Welfare income is a provincial responsibility variously referred to as employment and income assistance, income assistance, Ontario Works, etc. Another important program is the Guaranteed Income Supplement, which is administered by the federal government and provides income to those low-income senior citizens who receive Old Age Security. The National Child Benefit is another important federal program.

49 In the case of the Guaranteed Income Supplement (GIS), retirement income from personal savings reduces future GIS payments.

50 In Manitoba, Employment and Income Assistance (EIA) recipients must exhaust their savings before entering the program. Once in the program, their savings are limited, and, in some cases, the welfare clients with

whom we spoke understood that any savings they accumulated would
lead to a reduction in welfare benefits (Buckland et al. 2003, 40).
51 In Manitoba, EIA clients can either open an account for direct deposit of
benefits or receive them by cheque. Alberta is piloting a program where
welfare payments are loaded onto a debit card.
52 Financial Services Authority (2000).
53 By the end of the nineteenth century there were a total of 915 outlets across
Canada: 508 in Ontario, 157 in Quebec, 60 in Nova Scotia, 47 in New Bruns-
wick, 49 in Manitoba, 54 in British Columbia, 10 in Prince Edward Island,
and 30 in the Territories (McGuiness 1976, 13).

2 Theories about Financial Exclusion

1 This can be evidenced by a review of the current set of development
economics textbooks such as Perkins et al. (2001) or by an examination of
the policies of influential development organizations such as the World
Bank.
2 Of course, the large difference in the interest rate of a payday loan to that
of equivalent loans from mainstream sources (for example, a credit card
or a line of credit) casts doubt on this simple analysis, but once again the
neoclassical analysis would conclude that usury ceilings were at fault.
3 The federal government spends approximately $22 billion annually on
various programs that support asset building, and the 'overwhelming
majority' of this benefits middle- and upper-income Canadians (Robson
and Nares 2006, 30).
4 More recent studies, using similar methods, found similar results to those
of Caplovitz, for instance in examining retail service locations in Baltimore
(Job Opportunities Task Force 2007) and in twelve major U.S. cities (The
Brookings Institution 2006).
5 Key Canadian studies that examine some aspect of financial exclusion
include Ramsay (2000, 2001), Robinson (2006), Aitken (2006), Buckland
and Martin (2005), Buckland and Dong (2008), Simpson and Buckland
(2009), research undertaken for Manitoba Public Utilities Board (for
example, Buckland et al. 2007), and studies sponsored by the Public Interest Advocacy Centre (Lott and Grant 2002) and ACORN Canada (Stratcom
Strategic Communications 2005).
6 Robinson does not use these words but alludes to assymetric information:
'Since the available evidence shows that competition on rates is not
happening, the customers are not well-informed and in a good position

to exercise the best choices and there seem to be excess profits available,
I conclude that Canada should regulate the rates that payday lenders can
charge, as well as other aspects of the business' (2006, 7).

3 Choosing Banking Services When the Options Are Limited

1 2006 census data for these neighbourhoods are available in different for-
mats. Each city provides selective descriptive statistics by neighbourhood
that have been taken from the Statistics Canada census. The neighbourhoods or neighbourhood clusters most relevant to this study are South Parkdale (a portion of the Parkdale-Roncesvalles area), Toronto (City of Toronto
2007); Strathcona (including the Downtown Eastside and some adjoining
area), Vancouver (City of Vancouver, n.d.); and Point Douglas South (a portion of the North End), Winnipeg (City of Winnipeg, n.d.). More extensive
census data are available directly from Statistics Canada by census tract
(Statistics Canada 2006). The most relevant census tracts for each neighbourhood are 5350004.00 for a portion of Parkdale, Toronto; 9330059.06 for a portion of Vancouver's DTES; and 6020043.00 for a portion of Winnipeg's
North End. To access 2006 census data by census tract, see Statistics Canada
(2006).
2 Gastown features tourist attractions such as upmarket shops and
restaurants.
3 The response rate on this question for Vancouver respondents was very low –
only one out of five answered – therefore, we do not report on the share of
respondents both having a mainstream account and using fringe banks.
4 Many respondents referred to sticking to a budget, which was the only
option for several respondents who had virtually no access to credit (except
for pawnshop credit). They referred to various forms of budgeting including
a formal written budget and an informal mental budget. An example of the
latter was described by one respondent who received two cheques per month
and allocated one of them to rent and the other to food and remaining needs.
This is an example of a simple and effective budget. Some respondents were
exclusively focused on daily living, but others reported they set life goals that
involved some savings. Goals included family reunification (for example,
regaining custody of a child), small consumer goods (computer, musical instruments), and the education or training necessary to become independent
of social assistance. Savings were achieved through storing money at home,
delaying submission of income tax returns (when a refund was anticipated),
and using periodic benefits such as child tax benefits to purchase larger
items. For a complete discussion of this see Buckland (2010).

5 The survey was mixed method in that it included quantitative questions (that is, questions involving numerical or coded answers) and qualitative questions. The survey included questions about the types of financial services that people used and the reasons that respondents used certain financial services, questions about their current financial situation, and questions about their socio-economic situation. In total, eighty-three respondents participated, with roughly equal representation for each site: Parkdale (Toronto), DTES (Vancouver), and inner-city (including North End) Winnipeg. The survey used for this method is similar to an earlier survey used just in Winnipeg's North End (Buckland and Martin 2005).

6 A financial-life-history (henceforth *the history*) method is the other method drawn on in these results. It included fifteen participants in total located in Parkdale (Toronto), DTES (Vancouver), and inner-city (including North End) Winnipeg. It provides the basis for the examination of the dynamic factors affecting financial service choice. A full discussion of this method can be found in Buckland, Fikkert, and Eagan (2010).

7 Quantitative and qualitative data were analysed in the survey, but primarily a qualitative analysis was made of the financial life histories. For details on the field and analytical methods see Buckland, Fikkert, and Eagan (2010) and Buckland and Martin (2005). For the survey, descriptive statistics were generated by a statistical program for numbered and coded responses. The percentages reported below are based on the 'valid per cent'; that is, they were determined using the total number of participants responding to that question. Qualitative content analysis of relevant data was used to analyse the open-ended questions. This was done by reading all the responses several times and then placing them into different categories such as 'personal identification' or 'cheque-cashing hold policy.' Then a framework was developed with the categories, involving the hierarchical relationships between them.

8 Mixed-method research is aligned with a poverty and community-based approach and is necessary when national level data are unavailable. This approach identifies class, gender, and location (among others) as factors that constrain certain groups' social and economic well-being (Kirby, Greaves, and Reid 2006; Berg 2009). In particular, it sees the lack of power and voice among low-income people as an important barrier to well-being. One way in which power and voice are addressed involves using qualitative research methods. These methods place less emphasis on the reliability found in a randomly designed, statistically significant survey and place more emphasis on the voice of the respondent (Babbie 2002). Emphasizing the voice of the respondent allows her to describe, define, and analyse the

problems and solutions that she values. There is now a large volume of literature on mixed research methods (Tashakkori and Teddle 2003) that demonstrates the usefulness of mixed methods for certain purposes, such as problem identification and theory building.

9 For instance, Money Mart takes a photograph and personal information from a client, both of which are kept on file for the client's return.

10 J.D. Power and Associates now use a customer service satisfaction survey.

11 This paragraph draws on Buckland (2008b, 9).

4 The Business of Inner-City Banking

1 Orthodox or liberal approaches (such as Lewis and Chenery) to economic development tend to highlight the compatibility of the interests of different social groups. Non-orthodox theorists (such as Marx, neomarxist, and dependency theorists) found the orthodox analysis limited because it ignored important social conflicts.

2 For the purpose of this analysis, countries are divided into two groups, Northern and Southern. Northern, sometimes referred to as *developed*, nations include rich countries of the northern hemisphere plus new entrants from places such as East Asia and Latin America. Southern, sometimes referred to as *developing*, nations refer to poor countries in Africa, South Asia, and parts of Latin America.

3 This real-unreal dichotomy is an interesting categorization scheme for some purposes. It is reminiscent of the classical economics treatment of labour inputs versus non-labour inputs (capital and land) to production. The labour theory of value posited that labour alone was the source of economic value. Land and capital were able to generate value only with the application of labour. On their own, capital and land were not useful, and therefore labour was the true or 'real' source of value. In the case of banking, the real-unreal dichotomy finds that banking can only generate economic value through supporting the producing sectors of the economy such as industry and agriculture; therefore, banking is not a 'real' sector.

4 Testing this theory would be difficult because even publicly traded companies do not provide data on the profitability of different branches.

5 A list of CPLA members and their outlet locations can be found on the CPLA website, http://www.cpla-acps.ca/english/aboutmemberslist.php.

6 This is such an important element of neoclassical economics that, in fact, the discipline is usually defined in this way; that is, economics is the study of the allocation of scarce resources.

7 An important barrier to perfect competition, albeit understated in neoclassical economics, is the self-interest of firms that prefer imperfect competition, which allows them some level of control over the markets.

8 Farm input markets, however, are often imperfectly competitive. Fertilizer, seed, and mechanical inputs are often supplied by sectors that are oligopolistic.

9 The sub-prime mortgage crisis and the collapse of some U.S. banks have led to a greater concentration within retail banking in the United States (Caskey, personal communication, 2010).

10 In the United States, regulations restrict banks from offering branch services outside one state, but bank holding companies are able to do so.

11 The fact that payday lenders rely on repeat borrowers has been the source of a critique of payday lenders. It has been argued that payday lenders rely on such borrowers because compared with first-time borrowers they requires less processing time. Some have argued that this creates an incentive for payday lenders to encourage excessive, repetitive borrowing (see Stegman and Farris 2003). In Canada, data to test this claim are not available; however, from the Survey of Financial Security, data demonstrated that repeat borrowing was more common among low-income payday loan clients (Buckland et al. 2007).

12 See Task Force on the Future of the Canadian Financial Services Sector (1998).

13 These data refer to branches of the banks that are members of the Canadian Payments Association (CPA). CPA members include direct clearers (those that are able to directly clear payments through their settlement account with the Bank of Canada) and indirect clearers (those that rely on direct clearers to clear payments). The data reported here exclude non-members. In 2007, non-members represented 2% of the total number of branches, and thus they represent a small share of mainstream bank branches.

14 It does not follow that high fees imply exploitation. High fees may simply reflect high costs. For businesses to exploit consumers they require some type of market power, such as monopoly power, in order to generate high profits or they mislead their clients through complex fees and contracts.

15 Many people believe that there is a close relationship between pawnbrokers and organized crime. I have heard many anecdotes, but I have seen few statistics to support or refute this theory. One government official told me that they would not enforce any regulations on pawnshops because the government agents were afraid to enter the pawnshops and be victimized. A police officer involved in monitoring pawnshops told me that one pawnbroker was closely connected with organized crime.

16 For data on business units prepared by Statistics Canada, NAICS replaced the SIC system in 1998 (Statistics Canada 2007b). In terms of fringe banks, the new system involves a major change in data classification that makes a comparison of data between the two systems difficult.

17 An establishment is the smallest production entity for which a firm provides both cost and return data. Since each firm makes the determination of which is the smallest entity, establishment data varies across firms. For financial service firms this means that some establishments might be branches, and other establishments might be regional divisions (Horn 2009). Statistics Canada defines an establishment as follows: 'A statistical establishment is the production entity or the smallest grouping of production entities which: (a) Produces a homogeneous set of goods or services; (b) Does not cross provincial boundaries; and (c) Provides data on the value of output together with the cost of principal intermediate inputs used along with the cost and quantity of labor resources used to produce the output. For example, a plant in the manufacturing industry which provides accounting information regarding the value of shipments (sales),direct costs and labor costs is considered a single establishment. However, two stores in the retail industry may be considered one establishment if the accounting information, described in item (c) above, is not available separately, but is combined at a higher level' (Statistics Canada 2007a).

18 Data for establishments are categorized by the number of employees: 1–4, 5–9, 10–19, 20–49, 50–99, 100–199, 200–499, 500 or more, and indeterminate.

19 'This Canadian industry comprises establishments primarily engaged in providing unsecured cash loans to consumers. However, some cash lending activities may be secured by a chattel mortgage enabling the lender to take possession of the chattel in case of default. Examples of establishments in this Canadian industry are consumer loan companies, personal finance companies and small loan companies. Example Activities: Mutual benefit associations (loan association); Personal credit institutions; Personal loan companies' (Statistics Canada 2007b).

20 'This industry comprises establishments, not classified to any other industry, primarily engaged in facilitating credit intermediation, such as cheque-cashing, money order issuance, traveller's cheque issuance and servicing loans originated by others. Exclusion(s): foreign currency exchange dealers (52313, Commodity Contracts Dealing). Example Activities: Cheque cashing services; Money order issuance services; Travellers' cheque issuance services' (Statistics Canada 2007b).

21 This is a broad category indeed. Under SIC, cheque-cashing firms were included in R999, 'Other Services n.e.c.,' which includes a diverse set of

services such as Research and Development in the Social Sciences and Humanities, and Internet Publishing and Broadcasting. This category apparently included the establishment that funded some of the research for this book!

22 Data for 1999 and 2005 from telephone directories are available on the number of payday lender outlets in three cities: Metropolitan Toronto, Vancouver (proper), and Winnipeg. The number of outlets more than doubled in Toronto, rising from 41 to 96; they increased from 24 to 38 in Vancouver and increased seven-fold in Winnipeg, from 6 to 43 (Simpson and Buckland 2009).

23 Money Mart lists thirty-five outlets in Quebec, but since it does not provide payday loans there, these figures are not included in the payday loan data.

5 Working for Financial Inclusion

1 In the 4 March 2010 federal budget the government said that the FCAC would be given the resources to engage in research on financial consumer issues: 'The Government is proposing to give the Financial Consumer Agency of Canada (FCAC) new responsibilities that leverage its existing role and marketplace proximity. The FCAC will increase its field testing and stakeholder engagement to provide valuable and timely information to the Government on financial consumer trends and emerging issues. This will also allow the Government to improve the effectiveness of regulatory initiatives, while ensuring that these initiatives are more responsive to the needs of financial consumers' (Flaherty 2010).

2 In fact, one can find an interesting debate about the British system (which has no rate caps) and the German system (which has rate caps): 'It has also been suggested that the interest rate ceilings in Germany and France have led to higher levels of unregulated lending than in the United Kingdom, where there is no ceiling' (Anderloni et al. 2008). This point has been challenged by others.

3 See Western Economic Diversification Canada (2009).

4 For more information see United Kingdom HM Treasury, n.d.

5 Generally, if the pawned item is forfeited and sold for a price exceeding the principal and interest of the loan, the difference is given to the customer.

6 Special arrangements to deposit and cash cheques are available to clients who are ACU members, and apply to cheques from government agencies and referring community organizations up to a value of $1,500.

7 Referring to a Canadian television comedy that parodied home improvement and do-it-yourself.

8 A similar situation existed in 2003 when another RBC official was interviewed about Cash and Save's profitability (Buckland et al. 2003).

9 One respondent indicated that Cash and Save has gained some bad publicity for RBC from some media outlets that associate Cash and Save with other fringe banks. Replicating Cash and Save may increase this bad press.

Appendix: The Importance of Partnerships

1 This was evidenced by the fact that non-RBC informants were not able to comment much on the current situation for Cash and Save.

References

ACORN Canada. 2004. *Protecting Canadians' Interest: Reining in the Payday Lending Industry.* Vancouver: ACORN Canada.

– 2007. *A Conflict of Interest: How Canada's Largest Banks Support Predatory Lending.* Ottawa: ACORN Canada.

Advance America 2009. *Advance America 10-K Report.*

Agarwal, Sumit. 1997. 'Bargaining' and Gender Relations: Within and Beyond the Household. *Feminist Economics* 3, no. 1:1–51.

Aitken, Rob. 2006. Capital at Its Fringes. *New Political Economy* 11, no. 4:470–98.

Allen, Jason, Walter Engert, and Ying Liu. 2006. *Are Canadian Banks Efficient? A Canada–U.S. Comparison.* Bank of Canada, Working Papers.

Allen, Jason, and Ying Liu. 2005. *Efficiency and Economies of Scale of Large Canadian Banks.* Bank of Canada, Working Papers.

– 2007. Efficiency and Economies of Scale of Large Canadian Banks. *Canadian Journal of Economics* 40, no. 1:225–44.

Anderloni, Luisa, Bernard Bayot, Piotr Bledowski, Malgorzata Iwanicz-Drozdowska, and Elaine Kempson. 2008. *Financial Services Provision and Prevention of Financial Exclusion.* Brussels: Directorate-General for Employment, Social Affairs and Equal Opportunities, European Commission.

Anderloni, Luisa, Maria D. Braga, and Emanuele M. Carluccio, eds. 2007. *New Frontiers in Banking Services: Emerging Needs and Tailored Products for Untapped Markets.* Berlin and New York: Springer.

Anielski, Mark. 2007. *The Economics of Happiness: Building Genuine Wealth.* Gabriola Island, Canada: New Society Publishers.

Arrowsmith, Stephen, and Jean Pignal. 2010. *Initial Findings from the 2009 Canadian Financial Capability Survey.* Draft. Ottawa: Statistics Canada.

Association coopérative d'économie familiale du Centre de Montréal (ACEF
Centre). 1996. *The Highs and Lows of Access to Banking Services in Canada.* Report prepared for Industry Canada. Montreal: ACEF Centre.

Atkinson, Adele, Stephen McKay, Sharon Collard, and Elaine Kempson. 2007.
Levels of Financial Capability in the UK. *Public Money and Management* 27,
no. 1:29–36.

Ayres, Ian. 1991. Fair Driving: Gender and Race Discrimination in Retail Car
Negotiations. *Harvard Law Review* 104, no. 4:817–72.

Babbie, Earl 2002. *The Basics of Social Research.* 2nd. ed. Belmont, CA: Wadsworth Thomson Learning.

Bailey, Simon. 2006. *Why Financial Capability Matters.* Ottawa: Policy Research
Initiative.

Bair, Sheila. 2005. *Low Cost Payday Loans: Opportunities and Obstacles.* Baltimore, MD: Annie E. Casey Foundation.

Bank of Canada. 2008. *Financial System Review.* December. Ottawa: Bank of
Canada.

– 2009. *Financial System Review.* December. Ottawa: Bank of Canada.

Bank of Montreal. 2008. *2008 Corporate Responsibility Report and Public Accountability Statement.* Toronto: Bank of Montreal.

– 2009a. *Annual Report 2008.* Toronto: Bank of Montreal.

– 2009b. *Corporate Responsibility Report and Public Accountability Statement.* Toronto: Bank of Montreal.

Bannock, Graham, R.E. Baxter, and Ray Rees. 1982. *The Penguin Dictionary of
Economics,* 2nd. ed. London: Penguin.

Barr, Michael S. 2004. *Banking the Poor: Policies to Bring Low-Income Americans
into the Financial Mainstream.* Washington, DC: Brookings Institution.

– 2005a. An Inclusive, Progressive National Savings and Financial Services
Policy. *Harvard Law and Policy Review* 1, no. 1:161–84.

– 2005b. *Studying Low-Income Financial Services Behaviour.* Washington, DC:
Federal Reserve System.

– 2009. Financial Services, Savings, and Borrowing among Low- and Moderate-Income Households: Evidence from the Detroit Area Household Financial Services Survey. In *Insufficient Funds: Savings, Assets, Credit, and Banking
among Low-Income Households.* Edited by R.M. Blank and Michael Barr. New
York: Russell Sage.

Beck, Thorsten, Asli Demirguc-Kunt, and Maria Soledad Martinez Peria. 2005.
Reaching Out: Access to and Use of Banking Services across Countries.

– 2006. *Banking Services for Everyone? Barriers to Bank Access and Use around the
World.* Washington, DC: World Bank.

Benartzi, Shlomo, and Richard H. Thaler. 2004. Save More Tomorrow: Using Behavioral Economics to Increase Employee Saving. *Journal of Political Economy* 112, no. 1, part 2:S164–S187.

– 2007. Heuristics and Biases in Retirement Savings Behavior. *Journal of Economic Perspectives* 21, no. 3:81–104.

Berg, Bruce I. 2007. *Qualitative Research Methods for the Social Sciences.* 6th ed. Boston: Pearson Education.

– 2009. *Qualitative Research Methods for the Social Sciences.* 7th ed. Boston: Allyn and Bacon.

Berkes, Fikret. 2004. Rethinking Community-Based Conservation. *Conservation Biology* 18, no. 3:621–30.

Bertrand, Marianne, Dean Karlan, Sendhil Mullainathan, Eldar Shafir, and Jonathan Zinman. 2005. *What's Psychology Worth? A Field Experiment in the Consumer Credit Market.* NBER research paper no. 11892. Cambridge, MA: National Bureau of Economic Research.

Bertrand, Marianne, Sendhil Mullainathan, and Eldar Shafir. 2004. A Behavioral-Economics View of Poverty. *The American Economic Review* 94, no. 2, Papers and Proceedings of the One Hundred Sixteenth Annual Meeting of the American Economic Association, San Diego, CA, 3–5 January 2004: 419–23.

Beverly, Sondra G., and Emily K. Burkhalter. 2005. Improving the Financial Literacy and Practices of Youths. *Children and Schools* 27, no. 2:121–4.

Beverly, Sondra G., Amanda Moore McBride, and Mark Schreiner. 2003. A Framework of Asset-Accumulation Stages and Strategies. *Journal of Family and Economic Issues* 24, no. 2:143–56.

Beverly, Sondra G., and Michael Sherraden. 1999. Institutional Determinants of Saving: Implications for Low-Income Households and Public Policy. *The Journal of Socio-Economics* 28, 457–73.

Beverly, Sondra G., Jennifer Tescher, and Jennifer L. Romich. 2004. Linking Tax Refunds and Low-Cost Bank Accounts: Early Lessons for Program Design and Evaluation. *Journal of Consumer Affairs* 38, no. 2:332–41.

Beverly, Sondra G., Jennifer Tescher, Jennifer L. Romich, and David Marzahl. 2005. Linking Tax Refunds and Low-Cost Bank Accounts to Bank the Unbanked. In *Inclusion in the American Dream: Assets, Poverty, and Public Policy,* edited by Michael Sherraden. Oxford and New York: Oxford University Press.

Blank, R.M., and Michael Barr, eds. 2009. *Insufficient Funds: Savings, Assets, Credit, and Banking among Low-Income Households.* New York: Russell Sage.

Bordo, Michael D., Hugh Rockoff, and Angela Redish. 1996. *A Comparison of the United States and Canadian Banking Systems in the Twentieth Century:*

Stability vs. Efficiency? National Bureau of Economic Research, Working Papers 4546.

Bostic, R.W. 2002. Trends in Equal Access to Credit Products. In *The Impact of Public Policy on Consumer Credit*, edited by T.A. Durkin and M.E. Staten. London: Kluwer.

Bouman, F.J.A., and R. Houtman. 1988. Pawnbroking as an Instrument of Rural Banking in the Third World. *Economic Development and Cultural Change* 37, 69–89.

Bowles, Paul. 2000. Assessing the Impact of Proposed Bank Mergers on Rural Communities: A Case Study of British Columbia. *Social Indicators Research* 51, 17–40.

British Columbia Ministry of Public Safety and Solicitor General. n.d. Consultations on Policy and Legislation. Accessed 16 March 2010. http://www.pssg.gov.bc.ca/legislation/closed.htm#feb15.

Broadway, Michael J., and Gillian Jesty. 1998. Are Canadian Inner Cities Becoming More Dissimilar? An Analysis of Urban Deprivation Indicators. *Urban Studies* 35, no. 9:1423–38.

Brookings Institution. 2006. *From Poverty, Opportunity: Putting the Market to Work for Lower Income Families.* Washington, DC: Brookings Institution.

Brown, Jason, Nancy Higgitt, Susan Wingert, Miller Christine, and Larry Morrissette. 2005. Challenges Faced by Aboriginal Youth in the Inner City. *Canadian Journal of Urban Research* 14, no. 1:81.

Brown, Mick, Pat Conaty, and Ed Mayo. 2003. *Life Saving: Community Development Credit Unions.* London: New Economics Foundation.

Buckland, Jerry. 2005. *Fringe Banking in Winnipeg's North End.* Winnipeg and Ottawa: Canadian Centre for Policy Alternatives.

– 2006a. An Examination of Asset-Building as a Means to Foster Financial Inclusion: The Case of Individual Development Accounts. In *Wealth and Well-Being / Ownership and Opportunity: New Directions in Social Policy for Canada*, edited by Jennifer Robson and Peter Nares. Toronto: Social and Enterprise Development Innovations (SEDI).

– 2006b. *Social and Economic Factors to Consider in Setting Government Cheque Cashing Fees in Manitoba.*

– 2008a. Community Banking Projects for Low-Income Canadians: A Report Examining Four Projects to Promote Financial Inclusion. October 29. Available at SSRN: http://ssrn.com/abstract=1585804.

– 2008b. *Strengthening Banking in Inner Cities: Practices and Policies to Promote Financial Inclusion for Low-Income Canadians.* Winnipeg and Ottawa: Canadian Centre for Policy Alternatives.

– 2010. Are Low-income Canadians Financially Literate? Placing Financial
Literacy in the Context of Personal and Structural Constraints. *Adult Education Quarterly* 60, no. 4:357–76.

Buckland, Jerry, Marilyn Brennan, and Antonia Fikkert. 2010. *Are Poor People
Poorly Served by Canadian Banks? Testing Consumer Treatment Using Mystery
Shopping.* Institute of Urban Studies, University of Winnipeg, Research and
Working Paper no. 48. http://financial-exclusion.uwinnipeg.ca/.

Buckland, Jerry, Tom Carter, Wayne Simpson, Anita Friesen, and John Osborne.
2007. *Serving or Exploiting People Facing a Short-Term Credit Crunch? A Study
of Consumer Aspects of Payday Lending in Manitoba.* Report for the November
2007 Public Utilities Board Hearing to Cap Payday Loan Fees, Winnipeg, MB.

Buckland, Jerry, and Xiao-Yuan Dong. 2008. Banking on the Margins in Canada. *Economic Development Quarterly* 22, no. 3:252–63.

Buckland, Jerry, Antonia Fikkert, and Rick Eagan. 2010. Barriers to Improved
Capability for Low-income Canadians. *Journal of Interdisciplinary Economics*
22, no. 4:357–90.

Buckland, Jerry, Blair Hamilton, and Brendan Reimer. 2006. Community-
Based Models to Address the Decline of Inner-City Banking. *Canadian Journal of Urban Research*, 15: 109–28.

Buckland, Jerry, and Thibault Martin. 2005. Two-Tier Banking: The Rise of
Fringe Banks in Winnipeg's Inner City. *Canadian Journal of Urban Research* 14,
no. 1:158–81.

Buckland, Jerry, Thibault Martin, Nancy Barbour, Amelia Curran, Rana Mc-
Donald, and Brendan Reimer. 2003. *The Rise of Fringe Financial Services in
Winnipeg's North End: Client Experiences, Firm Legitimacy and Community-
Based Alternatives.* Winnipeg, MB: Winnipeg Inner City Research Alliance.

Buckland, Jerry, Chris Robinson, Wayne Simpson, and Marilyn Brennan. 2007.
*The Supply-Side of Payday Lending in Manitoba: Response to Interveners' Re-
ports.* Report for the November 2007 Public Utilities Board Hearing to Cap
Payday Loan Fees. Winnipeg, MB.

Buckland, Jerry, and Wayne Simpson. 2008. *Analysis of Credit Constraint and
Financial Exclusion with Canadian Microdata.*

Burgoyne, Carole B. 2008. Introduction: Special Issue on the Household Economy. *Journal of Socio-economics* 37, no. 2:455–7.

Burkey, Mark L., and Scott P. Simkins. 2004. Factors Affecting the Location of
Payday Lending and Traditional Banking Services in North Carolina. *Review
of Regional Studies* 34, no. 2:191–205.

Bush, Malcolm, and Geoff Smith. 2003. Community Development Banks
Substantially Outscore Other Banks in Serving Low-Income Minority

Communities: Implications for the Federal Budget and the Community Reinvestment Act. *Reinvestment Alert,* no. 19. Chicago: Woodstock Institute.

Caisses Desjardins du Québec. 2010. Vision, Mission, Values, and Priorities. Accessed 12 February 2010. http://www.desjardins.com/en/a_propos/qui-nous-sommes/mission.jsp.

Calder, Lendol. 2002. The Evolution of Consumer Credit in the United States. In *The Impact of Public Policy on Consumer Credit,* edited by Thomas A. Durkin and Michael E. Staten. Boston: Kluwer.

Canada Revenue Agency. 2009. Guide for Discounters. Accessed 12 February 2010. http://www.cra-arc.gc.ca/E/pub/tg/t4163/.

Canadian Bankers Association. 2009a. *Number of Cash Dispensing ABMs.* Toronto: Canadian Bankers Association.

– 2009b. *Fast Facts – The Canadian Banking System.* Toronto: Canadian Bankers Association.

Canadian Payday Loan Association. 2005. *Understanding Consumers of Canada's Payday Loans Industry.* Hamilton, ON: CPLA.

– 2009. Database on the Number of Payday Loan Outlets in Canada, by Province and Company, CPLA Member and Non-member. Hamilton, ON: CPLA.

– 2010a. Government Legislation. Accessed 16 March 2010. http://www.cpla-acps.ca/english/medialegislation.php.

– 2010b. Website. Accessed 22 March 2010. http://www.cpla-acps.ca/english/home.php.

Canadian Payments Association. 2008. Distribution of Branches. Ottawa: Canadian Payments Association.

Caplovitz, David. 1967. *The Poor Pay More: Consumer Practices of Low-Income Families.* New York: Free Press.

Carbo, Santiago, Edward P.M. Gardener, and Philip Molyneux. 2005. *Financial Exclusion.* New York: Palgrave MacMillan.

– 2007. Financial Exclusion in Europe. *Public Money and Management* 27, no.1:21.

Carbo, Santiago, Edward P.M. Gardener, and J. Williams. 2002. Efficiency in Banking: Empirical Evidence from the Savings Banks Sector. *Manchester School* 70, no. 2:204–28.

Carlson, Neil F. 2005. Making Financial Services Work for Everyone. A Report from a Convening Held at the Ford Foundation on Financial Services for Low-Income Customers. Chicago: Center of Financial Services Innovation.

Cash Canada. n.d. Website. Accessed 16 December 2009. http://cashcanada.com/.

Cash Canada Group Ltd. 2008. Management Discussion and Analysis for the Three and Nine Month Periods ended October 31, 2008 (Form 51–102F1). Edmonton, AB: Cash Canada Group.

Cash Converters. n.d. Website. Accessed 16 December 2009. http://www.cashconverters.ca/store_locations.htm.

Cash Converters International Ltd. 2008. Financial Report for the Half-Year Ended 31 December 2008. Perth, Australia.

Cash Money. n.d. Website. Accessed 16 Dec. 2009. http://www.cashmoney.ca/about-us.aspx.

Cash Store Financial. 2009. *Annual Report 2008*. Edmonton, AB: Cash Store Financial.

Caskey, John P. 1991. Pawnbroking in America: The Economics of a Forgotten Credit Market. *Journal of Money, Credit and Banking* 23, 85–99.

– 1994. *Fringe Banking: Check-Cashing Outlets, Pawnshops, and the Poor.* New York: Russell Sage Foundation.

– 2002. *The Economics of Payday Lending.* Madison, WI: Filene Research Institute.

– 2003. *Fringe Banking a Decade Later.* Swarthmore, PA: Swarthmore College.

– 2005a. Fringe Banking and the Rise of Payday Lending. In *Credit Markets for the Poor,* edited by Patrick Bolton and Howard Rosenthal. New York: Russell Sage Foundation.

– 2005b. Reaching Out to the Unbanked. In *Inclusion in the American Dream: Assets, Poverty, and Public Policy,* edited by Michael Sherraden. Oxford and New York: Oxford University Press.

– 2008. *Bringing Unbanked Households into the Banking System.* Washington, DC: Brookings Institute.

– 2010. Personal communication.

Caskey, John, and David B. Humphrey. 1999. *Credit Unions and Asset Accumulation by Lower-Income Households.* Madison, WI: Filene Research Institute.

Certified General Accountants Association of Canada. 2007. *Where Does the Money Go: The Increasing Reliance on Household Debt in Canada.* Burnaby, BC: Certified General Accountants Association of Canada.

Cheron, Emmanuel J., Helene Boidin, and Naoufel Daghfous. 1999. Basic Financial Services Needs of Low-Income Individuals: A Comparative Study in Canada. *International Journal of Bank Marketing* 17, no. 2:49–60.

CIBC (Canadian Imperial Bank of Commerce). 2009a. *Annual Report 2008*. Toronto: CIBC.

– 2009b. *Public Accountability Statement 2008.* Toronto: CIBC.

City of Toronto. Social Development, Finance and Administrative Division. 2007. Neighbourhood Profile Sheets. Accessed 3 June 2009. http://www.toronto.ca/demographics/cns_profiles/cns85.htm.

– n.d. Chapter 545: Toronto Municipal Code. Accessed 16 March 2010. http://www.toronto.ca/legdocs/municode/1184_545.pdf.

City of Vancouver. n.d. Community Web Pages. Accessed 3 June 2009. http://vancouver.ca/community_profiles/strathcona/index.htm.

City of Winnipeg. 2008. Doing Business in Winnipeg By-Law. Accessed 16March 2010. http://www.winnipeg.ca/clkdmis/DocExt/ViewDoc.asp?DocumentTypeId=1andDocId=4222.

– n.d. 2006 Census: Neighbourhood Cluster Profiles. Accessed 3 June 2009. http://winnipeg.ca/census/2006/Clusters/.

Collard, Sharon. 2007. Toward Financial Inclusion in the UK: Progress and Challenges. *Public Money and Management* 1, no. 2:13–120.

Collard, Sharon, and Elaine Kempson. 2005. *Affordable Credit: The Way Forward.* York, UK: Joseph Rowntree Foundation.

Collard, Sharon, Elaine Kempson, and C. Whyley. 2001. *Tackling Financial Exclusion: An Area-Based Approach.* Bristol, UK: Policy Press.

Collins, Daryl, Jonathon Morduch, Stuart Rutherford, and Orlanda Ruthven. 2009. *Portfolios of the Poor: How the World's Poor Live on $2 a Day.* Princeton and Oxford: Princeton University Press.

Commonwealth Business Council, and Visa. 2004. *Payment Solutions for Modernising Economies.* London: Commonwealth Business Council.

Competition Bureau Canada. 1998. The Competition Bureau and Bank Mergers. Accessed 16 March 2010. http://www.bureaudelaconcurrence.gc.ca/eic/site/cb-bc.nsf/eng/00825.html cont.

– 1999. Annual Report of the Commissioner of Competition for the year ending March 31, 1999. Accessed 16 March 2010. http://www.ic.gc.ca/eic/site/cb-bc.nsf/eng/01549.html.

Conacher, Duff. 1998. Bank Rhetoric or Customer Reality? Key Questions about the Competition Bureau's Analysis of the Proposed Bank Mergers. http://www.cancrc.org/english/comp-bur.html, accessed May 2007. Ottawa: Canadian Community Reinvestment Coalition.

– 2007. Priority Changes Needed to Federal Financial Institution Laws: Closing Key Gaps in Accountability and Consumer Protection, Brief on Bill C-37 to the House of Commons Standing Committee on Finance (February 19, 2007) and to the Senate Committee on Banking, Trade and Commerce (March 22, 2007). http://www.cancrc.org/english/recomm07.html, accessed May 2007. Ottawa: Canadian Community Reinvestment Coalition.

The Consultative Group to Assist the Poor. 2009. *Financial Access 2009: Measuring Access to Financial Services around the World.* Washington, DC: World Bank.

Consumer Measures Committee. 2009. Consumer Measures Committee: Links. Accessed 16 March 2010. http://cmcweb.ca/eic/site/cmc-cmc.nsf/eng/h_fe00018.html.

Consumer Protection BC. n.d. Payday Lenders. Accessed 16 March 2010. http://www.consumerprotectionbc.ca/index.php/businesses-payday-lenders-home

Cornell, Robert. 2003. *Asset Building and the Escape from Poverty: An Introduction to a New Welfare Policy Debate.* Paris: Organisation for Economic Co-operation and Development.

Corr, Caroline. 2007. *Alternative Financial Credit Providers in Europe.* Brussels: Directorate-General for Employment, Social Affairs and Equal Opportunity, European Commission.

Craig, David, and Doug Porter. 2006. *Neoliberalism: Governance, Poverty Reduction, and Political Economy,* Abingdon, UK: Routledge.

Credit Union Central of Canada. 2009. System Results, First Quarter 2009. Toronto: Credit Union Central of Canada.

Daly, Herman E. 1991. *Steady-State Economics.* Washington, DC: Island Press.

Daly, Herman E., and John B. Cobb Jr. 1989. *For the Common Good: Redirecting the Economy toward Community, the Environment, and a Sustainable Future.* Boston: Beacon Press.

Damar, H.E. 2009. Why Do Payday Lenders Enter Local Markets? Evidence from Oregon. *Review of Industrial Organization* 34, no. 2:173–91.

Dawson, William H. 1903. Municipal Pawnshops. *The Economic Journal* 13, no.50:248–51.

Dayson, Karl, and Pat Conaty. 2005. *Promoting Financial Inclusion: The Case for a Community Banking Partnership Approach.* Manchester, UK: Community Finance Solutions, University of Salford.

Department of Finance, Canada. 1999. *Reforming Canada's Financial Services Sector: A Framework for the Future.* Ottawa: Department of Finance.

– 2000. Canada's Credit Unions and Caisses Populaires. Accessed 19 June 2009. http://www.fin.gc.ca/toc/2000/ccu_-eng.asp#A%20brief%20history.

– 2002a. Canada's Banks. Accessed May 2007. http://www.fin.gc.ca/toc/2002/bank_-eng.asp.

– 2002b. The Canadian Financial Services Sector. Accessed 19 June 2009. http://www.fin.gc.ca/toc/2002/fact-cfss_-eng.asp.

– 2005. The Canadian Financial Services Sector. Accessed 18 June 2009. http://www.fin.gc.ca/toc/2005/fact-cfss-eng.asp.

Department of Justice, Canada. 2010. Tax Rebate Discounting Act. Accessed 12 February 2010. http://laws.justice.gc.ca/en/T-3/index.html.

Desmond, Tyler, and Charles Sprenger. 2007. *Estimating the Cost of Being Unbanked*. Boston: Federal Reserve Bank of Boston.

Devlin, James F. 2005. A Detailed Study of Financial Exclusion in the UK. *Journal of Consumer Policy* 28, 75–108.

Devlin, James F., and Milla Gregor. 2008. *From Access to Inclusion: An Evaluation of the Role of Basic Bank Accounts in Promoting Financial Inclusion*. London: Toynbee Hall.

Dollar Financial Corporation (DFC). 2008. *Dollar Financial Corporation 10-K Report*. Berwyn, IL: Dollar Financial Corporation.

– 2009. *Dollar Financial Corporation 10-K Report*. Berwyn, IL: Dollar Financial Corporation.

Dore, Ronald. 2008. Financialization of the Global Economy. *Industrial and Corporate Change* 17, no. 6:1097–112.

Dymski, Gary A. 2000. Access to Capital and Inner-City Revitalization: Urban Policy after Proposition 209. In *Back to Shared Prosperity: The Growing Inequality of Wealth and Income in America*, edited by Ray Marshall. New York: M.E. Sharpe.

– 2005. Financial Globalization, Social Exclusion and Financial Crisis. *International Review of Applied Economics* 19, no. 4:439–57.

– 2010. Why the Subprime Crisis Is Different: A Minskyian Approach. *Cambridge Journal of Economics* 34, 239–55.

Dymski, Gary A., and J. M. Veitch. 1996. Financial Transformation and the Metropolis: Booms, Busts, and Banking in Los Angeles. *Environment and Planning A* 28, no. 7:1233–260.

Edwards, Michael, and David Hulme. 1996. *Beyond the Magic Bullet: NGO Performance and Accountability in the Post-Cold War World*. West Hartford, CT: Kumarian Press.

EKOS Research Associates Inc. 2001. *Canadians' Knowledge and Awareness of Financial Products, Services and Institutions: FCAC Survey; Final Report*. Ottawa: Financial Consumer Agency of Canada.

Elliehausen, Gregory. 2006. *Consumers' Use of High-Price Credit Products: Do They Know What They Are Doing?* Vol. 2006-WP-02. Indianapolis: Networks Financial Institute at Indiana State University.

Elliehausen, Gregory, and Edward C. Lawrence. 2001. *Payday Advance Credit in America: An Analysis of Customer Demand*. Washington, DC: Credit Research Center, Georgetown University.

Environics Research Group. 2005. *Understanding Consumers of Canada's Payday Loans Industry*. Toronto: Canadian Association of Community Financial Service Providers.

Epstein, Gerald A., ed. 2005. *Financialization and the World Economy.* Cheltenham UK: Edward Elgar.

Ernst, Keith, John Farris, and Uriah King. 2004. *Quantifying the Economic Cost of Predatory Payday Lending.* Durham, NC: Center for Responsible Lending.

Ernst and Young LLP. 2004. *The Cost of Providing Payday Loans in Canada: A Report Prepared for the Canadian Association of Community Financial Service Providers.* Toronto: Ernst and Young LLP.

Erturk, Ismail, Julie Froud, and Sukhdev Johal, eds. 2008. *Financialization at Work: Key Texts and Commentary.* London: Routledge.

Les Études de Marché Createc. 2006. *General Survey on Consumers Financial Awareness, Attitudes and Behaviour.* Montreal: Les Études de Marché Createc.

Faruqui, Umar. 2008. *Indebtedness and the Household Financial Health: An Examination of the Canadian Debt Service Ratio Distribution.* Bank of Canada, Working Papers.

Federal Deposit Insurance Corporation (FDIC). 2007. FDIC's Supervisory Policy on Predatory Lending. In Federal Deposit Insurance Corporation's database online, Washington DC. Accessed 10 August 2007. http://www. fdic.gov/news/news/financial/2007/fil07006a.html.

– 2009a. Affordable Small-Dollar Loan Guidelines. In Federal Deposit Insurance Corporation's database online, Washington, DC. Accessed 10 September 2009. http://www.fdic.gov/SmallDollarLoans/.

– 2009b. Alternative Financial Services: A Primer. In Federal Deposit Insurance Corporation's database online, Washington. DC. Accessed 10 September 2009. http://www.fdic.gov/bank/analytical/quarterly/2009_vol3_1/ AltFinServicesprimer.html.

– 2009c. The FDIC's Small-Dollar Loan Pilot Program: A Case Study after One Year. In Federal Deposit Insurance Corporation's database online, Washington, DC. Accessed 10 September 2009. http://www.fdic.gov/bank/ analytical/quarterly/2009_vol3_2/smalldollar.html.

– 2009d. An Introduction to the FDIC's Small-Dollar Loan Pilot Program. In Federal Deposit Insurance Corporation's database online, Washington, DC. Accessed 10 September 2009. http://www.fdic.gov/bank/analytical/ quarterly/2009_vol3_2/smalldollar.html.

– 2010. Small-Dollar Loan Pilot Program. Accessed 24 March 2010. http:// www.fdic.gov/smalldollarloans/.

Ferguson, Niall. 2008. *The Ascent of Money: A Financial History of the World.* New York: Peguin.

Fernando, Nimal A. 2007. *Low-Income Households' Access to Financial Services: International Experience, Measures for Improvement, and the Future.* Philippines: Asian Development Bank.

Financial Consumer Agency of Canada (FCAC). 2003. *2003 FCAC Mystery Shopping Results.* Ottawa: FCAC.

– 2005. *2004–2005 FCAC Mystery-Shopping Results*. Ottawa: FCAC.
– 2008. Overview of Obligations: Banks and Federally Regulated Credit Unions. Accessed 16 March 2010. http://www.fcac-acfc.gc.ca/eng/industry/Obligations/Banks/Banks-eng.asp.
– 2009. Overview of Obligations: Voluntary Codes of Conduct and Public Commitments Monitored by FCAC. Accessed 19 March 2010. http://www.fcac-acfc.gc.ca/eng/industry/Obligations/CodesCommitment/default.asp.
– n.d., website. http://www.fcac-acfc.gc.ca/eng/about/index-eng.asp. Accessed 6 July 2011.
Financial Post. n.d. Financial Post Sector Analyzer. Accessed 7 December 2009. http://www.financialpost.com/news-sectors.
– n.d. FP500. Accessed 7 December 2009. http://www.financialpost.com/magazine.
Financial Services Authority. 2000. *In or Out? Financial Exclusion: A Literature and Research Review*. Consumer Research, no. 3. London: Financial Services Authority.
– 2001. *Women and Personal Finance: The Reality of the Gender Gap*. Vol. 7. London: Financial Services Authority.
– 2006a. *Financial Capability Baseline Survey: Methodological Report*. Vol. 47a. London: Financial Services Authority.
– 2006b. *Financial Capability in the UK: Establishing a Baseline*. London: Financial Services Authority.
– 2006c. *Levels of Financial Capability in the UK: Results of a Baseline Survey*. Vol.47. London: Financial Services Authority.
Fitzpatrick, Trevor, and Kieran McQuinn. 2005. *Measuring Bank Profit Efficiency*. Central Bank and Financial Services Authority of Ireland (CBFSAI), Research Technical Papers 3/RT/05.
– 2008. Measuring Bank Profit Efficiency. *Applied Financial Economics* 18, no. 1–3:1–8.
Flaherty, Jim. 2010. *Budget 2010: Leading the Way on Jobs and Growth*. Tabled in the House of Commons, 4 March. Ottawa: Public Works and Government Services Canada.
Flannery, Mark, and Katherine Samolyk. 2005. *Payday Lending: Do the Costs Justify the Price?* Vol. 2005–09. Arlington, VA: Center for Financial Research, Federal Deposit Insurance Corporation.
Frenette, Marc, David A. Green, and Garnett Picot. 2007. Rising Income Inequality in the 1990s: An Exploration of Three Data Sources. In *Dimensions of Inequality in Canada*, edited David A. Green and Jonathon R. Kesselman, Vancouver: UBC Press.

Gloukoviezoff, Georges. 2007. *France Country Study Stage II*. Brussels: Directorate-General for Employment, Social Affairs, and Equal Opportunities, European Commission.

Goetz, Anne Marie, and Rita Sen Gupta. 1996. Who Takes the Credit? Gender, Power, and Control over Loan Use in Rural Credit Programs in Bangladesh. *World Development* 24, no.1:45–63.

Government of Canada. 2002. Access to Basic Banking Services Regulations. *Canada Gazette* 136, no. 48 (30 November). Ottawa. Accessed 16 March 2010. http://www.gazette.gc.ca/archives/p1/2002/2002–11–30/html/reg-eng. html#i1.

Government of Manitoba. n.d. The Consumer Protection Amendment Act (Payday Loans), S.M. 2006, c. 31. Accessed 16 March 2010. http://web2.gov. mb.ca/laws/statutes/2006/c03106e.php.

Government of Ontario. n.d. Pawnbrokers Act, R.S.O. 1990, ch. P.6. Accessed 16 February 2010. http://www.e-laws.gov.on.ca/html/statutes/english/ elaws_statutes_90p06_e.htm.

Government of Saskatchewan. 2009. Government to Regulate Payday Loans. Accessed 16 March 2010. http://www.gov.sk.ca/news?news Id=c2d93ebd-7d00–427a-a822–284c05f8bb90.

– n.d. Bill 43 – Payday Loans Act. Accessed 16 March 2010. http://www. publications.gov.sk.ca/details.cfm?p=23076andcl=5.

Grant, Michael. 2001. *Alternative Financial Services in Canada: Findings from Focus Groups*. Toronto: Grant Insights.

Graves, Steven M. 2003. Landscapes of Predation, Landscapes of Neglect: A Location Analysis of Payday Lenders and Banks. *The Professional Geographer* 55, no. 3:303–17.

Green, David A., and Jonathon R. Kesselman, eds. 2006. *Dimensions of Inequality in Canada*. Vancouver: UBC Press.

Gueyie, Jean-Pierre, Klaus P. Fisher, and Martin Desrochers. 2004. Managing Contractual Risk through Organization: Strategic vs. Consensual Networks. In *Financial Services and Public Policy*, edited by Christopher Waddell. Montreal: McGill-Queen's University Press.

Hashemi, Syed M., Sidney R. Schuler, and Ann P. Riley. 1996. Rural Credit Programs and Women's Empowerment in Bangladesh. *World Development* 24, no. 4:635–53.

Hassan, M. Kabir, and Mervyn K. Lewis, eds. 2007. *Handbook of Islamic Banking*. Cheltenham UK: Edward Elgar Publishing.

Hilgert, Marianne A., Jeanne M. Hogarth, and Sandra G. Beverly. 2003. Household Financial Management: The Connection between Knowledge and Behavior. *Federal Reserve Bulletin*, July, 309–22.

Hillmer, Norman. 2011. Foreign Investment Review Agency. In *Canadian Ency-clopaedia*. Accessed May 2007, http://www.thecanadianencyclopedia.com/index.cfm?PgNm=TCEandParams=A1ARTA0002896.

Hogarth, Jeanne M., Christoslav E. Anguelov, and Jinkook Lee. 2003. Why Households Don't Have Checking Accounts. *Economic Development Quarterly* 17, no. 1:75–94.

– 2005. Who Has a Bank Account? Exploring Changes over Time, 1989–2001. *Journal of Family and Economic Issues* 26, no. 1:7.

Hogarth, Jeanne M., and Kevin H. O'Donnell. 1999. Banking Relationships of Lower-Income Families and the Governmental Trend toward Electronic Payment. *Federal Reserve Bulletin* 85, no. 7:459–73.

Holt, Richard P. F., and Steven Pressman. 2001. *A New Guide to Post Keynesian Economics*. London: Routledge.

Horn, Todd (Statistics Canada). 2009. Personal communication. 18 August.

Hulchanski, J. David. 2007. *The Three Cities within Toronto: Income Polarization among Toronto's Neighbourhoods, 1970–2000*. Research Bulletin 41, Toronto: Centre for Urban and Community Studies, University of Toronto.

Ipsos-Reid Corporation. 2005. *Public Experience with Financial Services and Awareness of FCAC*. Ottawa: Financial Consumer Agency of Canada.

Jacob, Katy, Malcolm Bush, and Dan Immergluck. 2002. *Rhetoric and Reality: An Analysis of Mainstream Credit Unions' Record of Serving Low-Income People*. Chicago: Woodstock Institute.

Jesson, Jill. 2004. Mystery Shopping Demystefied: Is it a Justifiable Research Method? *Pharmaceutical Journal* 272: 615–17.

– 2005. *A Typology of the Research Method: Mystery Customer; Putting Customer into a Methodological Context*. Vol. 5.01. Birmingham, UK: MEL Research.

Job Opportunities Task Force. 2007. *Overpriced and Underserved: How the Market Is Failing Low-Wage Baltimoreans*. Baltimore, MD: Job Opportunities Task Force.

Johnson, Robert W., and Dixie P. Johnson. 1998. *Pawnbroking in the U.S.: A Profile of Customers*. Washington, DC: Credit Research Center, McDonough School of Business, Georgetown University. http://www.msb.edu/.

Jones, Ken, Philip Bermingham, and Tansel Erguden. 2005. *Payday Lenders: A Location Analysis*. Toronto: Centre for the Study of Commercial Activity, Ryerson University.

Jones, Paul A. 2006. Giving Credit Where It's Due: Promoting Financial Inclusion through Quality Credit Unions. *Local Economy* 21, no. 1:36–48.

– 2008. From Tackling Poverty to Achieving Financial Inclusion: The Changing Role of British Credit Unions in Low-Income Communities. *Journal of Socio-Economics* 37, 2141–54.

Jones, Paul A., and Tina Barnes. n.d. *Would You Credit It? People Telling Stories about Credit.* Manchester, UK: The Co-operative Bank.

Kabeer, Naila. 2001. Conflicts over Credit: Re-evaluating the Empowerment Potential of Loans to Women in Rural Bangladesh. *World Development* 29, no. 1:63–84.

Karlan, Dean S. forthcoming. Using Experimental Economics to Measure Social Capital and Predict Financial Decisions. *American Economic Review* 95, no. 5:1688–99.

Karlan, Dean S., and Jonathan Zinman. 2005. *Observing Unobservables: Identifying Information Assymetries with a Consumer Credit Field Experiment.* New York: Federal Reserve Bank of New York.

Kazempiur, Abdolmohammad, and Shiva S. Halli. 2000. Neighbourhood Poverty in Canadian Cities. *Canadian Journal of Sociology / Cahiers canadiens de sociologie* 25, no. 3:369–81.

Kempson, Elaine, Adele Atkinson, and Odile Pilley. 2004. *Policy Level Response to Financial Exclusion in Developed Economies: Lessons for Developing Countries.* London: UK Department for International Development.

Kempson, Elaine, Stephen McKay, and Sharon Collard. 2003. *Evaluation of the CFLI and Saving Gateway Pilot Projects.* Bristol, UK: Personal Finance Research Centre, University of Bristol.

Kempson, Elaine, and Claire Whyley. 1999a. *Extortionate Credit in the UK: A Report to the DTI.* Bristol, UK: Personal Finance Research Centre, University of Bristol.

– 1999b. *Kept Out or Opted Out? Understanding and Combating Financial Exclusion.* Bristol, UK: Policy Press.

Kerton, Robert, and Anindya Sen. n.d. On Quality and Local Competition, Response to the Consultation: Merger Enforcement Guidelines as Applied to a Bank Merger. Ottawa: Competition Bureau. http://www.competitionbureau.gc.ca/eic/site/cb-bc.nsf/eng/01355.html. Accessed 6 July 2011.

Kingwell, Paul, Michael Dowie, Barbara Holler, and Liza Jimenez. 2004. *Helping People Help Themselves: An Early Look at Learn$ave.* Ottawa: Social Research and Demonstration Corporation.

Kingwell, Paul, Michael Dowie, Barbara Holler, and Carole Vincent. 2005. *Design and Implementation of a Program to Help Poor Save: The Learn$ave Project.* Ottawa: Social Research and Demonstration Corporation.

Kirby, Sandra L., Lorraine Greaves, and Colleen Reid. 2006. *Experience Research Social Change: Methods beyond the Mainstream.* 2nd ed. Peterborough, ON: Broadview Press.

Kitching, Andrew, and Sheena Starky. 2006. *Payday Loan Companies in Canada: Determining the Public Interest.* Vol. PRB 05–81E. Ottawa: Library of Parliament.

Langley, Paul. 2008. Financialization and the Consumer Credit Boom. *Competition and Change* 12, no. 2:133–47.

Law Commission of Ontario. 2008. *Fees for Cashing Government Cheques*. Toronto: Law Commission of Ontario.

– 2009. Fees for Cashing Government Cheques. Accessed 16 March 2010. http://www.lco-cdo.org/en/content/fees-cashing-government-cheques.

Lawford, John. 2003. *Pragmatic Solutions to Payday Lending: Regulating Fringe Lending and 'Alternative' Banking*. Ottawa: Public Interest Advocacy Centre.

Lawrence, Edward C., and Gregory Elliehausen. 2008. A Comparative Analysis of Payday Loan Customers. *Contemporary Economic Policy* 26, no. 2:299–316.

Leckie, Norm, Michael Dowie, and Chad Gyorfi-Dyke. 2008. *Learning to Save, Saving to Learn: Early Impacts of the Learn$ave Individual Development Accounts Project*. Ottawa: Social Research and Demonstration Corporation.

Leclerc, Andre, and Mario Fortin. 2004. Banking Production Measurement, Rationalization, and Efficiency of the Caisses Populaires Desjardins. In *Financial Services and Public Policy: Proceedings of a Conference Sponsored by the Schulich School of Business National Research Program in Financial Services and Public Policy*, edited by Christopher Waddell. Kingston, ON: Queen's University, John Deutsch Institute for the Study of Economic Policy, in cooperation with McGill-Queen's University Press.

Lee, Jinkook. 2002. The Poor in the Financial Market: Changes in the Use of Financial Products, Institutions, and Services from 1995 to 1998. *Journal of Consumer Policy* 25, no. 2:203–31.

Lees, Loretta, and David Ley. 2008. Introduction to Special Issue on Gentrification and Public Policy. *Urban Stud* 45, no. 12:2379–84.

Lees, Loretta, Tom Slater, and Elvin Wyly. 2007. *Gentrification*. New York: Routledge.

Ley, David, and Heather Frost. 2006. The Inner City. In *Canadian Cities in Transition*, edited by Trudi Bunting and Pierre Filion. Oxford: Oxford University Press.

Ley, David, and Heather Smith. 2000. Relations between Deprivation and Immigrant Groups in Large Canadian Cities. *Urban Stud* 37, no. 1:37–62.

Leyshon, Andrew. 2004. The Limits to Capital and Geographies of Money. *Antipode* 36, no. 3:461–9.

Leyshon, Andrew, Dawn Burton, David Knights, Catrina Alferoff, and Paola Signoretta. 2004. Towards an Ecology of Retail Financial Services: Understanding the Persistence of Door-to-Door Credit and Insurance Providers. *Environment and Planning A* 36, no. 4:625–45.

Leyshon, Andrew, Roger Lee, and Colin C. Williams. 2003. *Alternative Economic Spaces*. London: Sage Publications.

Leyshon, Andrew, and Jane Pollard. 2000. Geographies of Industrial Convergence: The Case of Retail Banking. *Transactions of the Institute of British Geographers* 25, no. 2:203–20.

Leyshon, Andrew, Paola Signoretta, and Shaun French. 2006. *The Changing Geography of British Bank and Building Society Branch Networks, 1995–2003.* Nottingham, UK: University of Nottingham.

Leyshon, Andrew, and N. Thrift. 1996. Financial Exclusion and the Shifting Boundaries of the Financial System. *Environment and Planning A* 28, no.7:1150–6.

– 1997. *Money/Space: Geographies of Monetary Transformation.* New York and London: Routledge.

Li, Wei, Alex Oberle, and Gary Dymski. 2007. Global Banking and Financial Services to Immigrants in Canada and the United States. *Journal of International Migration and Integration* 10, no. 1:1–29.

Lott, Sue, and Michael Grant. 2002. *Fringe Lending and 'Alternative' Banking: The Consumer Experience.* Ottawa: Public Interest Advocacy Centre.

Loxley, John, ed. 2007. *Transforming or Reforming Capitalism: Towards a Theory of Community Economic Development.* Halifax, NS: Fernwood Publishing.

Loxley, John, Jim Silver, and Kathleen Sexsmith. 2007. *Doing Community Economic Development.* Halifax, NS: Fernwood Publishing.

Lusardi, Annamaria, and Olivia S. Mitchell. 2007. Financial Literacy and Retirement Preparedness: Evidence and Implications for Financial Education. *Business Economics* 42, no. 1:35–44.

– 2008. Planning and Financial Literacy: How Do Women Fare? *American Economic Review* 98, no. 2:413–17.

Lyons, Angela C., and Erik Scherpf. 2004. Moving from Unbanked to Banked: Evidence from the Money Smart Program. *Financial Services Review* 13, no.3:215–31.

Maki, Dean M. 2002. The Growth of Consumer Credit and the Household Debt Service Burden. In *The Impact of Public Policy on Consumer Credit*, edited by Thomas A. Durkin and Michael E. Staten. Boston: Kluwer.

Mallett, Ted, and Anindya Sen. 2001. Does Local Competition Impact Interest Rates Charged on Small Business Loans? Empirical Evidence from Canada. *Review of Industrial Organization*, 19:437–52.

Manitoba Public Utilities Board. n.d. Miscellaneous Board Orders. Accessed 16 March 2010. http://www.pub.gov.mb.ca/misc07on.html.

Mann, Ronald J., and Jim Hawkins. 2007. Just Until Payday. *UCLA Law Review* 54, no. 4:855–912.

Mayer, Robert. 2003. Payday Loans and Exploitation. *Public Affairs Quarterly* 17, no. 3:197–217.

– 2004. Payday Lending and Personal Bankruptcy. *Consumer Interests Annual* 50: 76–82.

– n.d. *Payday Loans and Exploitation. Public Affairs Quarterly* 17, no. 3:197–217.

McArthur, Greg, and Jacquie McNish. 2009. Canada's Dirty Subprime Secret, *Globe and Mail*, 14 March.

McGuinness, Fred, and Sandra Young. 1976. *10 to 10: Canadian Credit Unions, from 10 Cents to 10 Billion Dollars in 75 Years*. Toronto: Southam Murray.

Meyer, Stephen P. 2007. Finance, Insurance and Real Estate Firms and The Nature of Agglomeration Advantage Across Canada and Within Metropolitan Toronto. *Canadian Journal of Urban Research* 16, no. 2:149–181.

Minkes, A.L. 1953. The Decline of Pawnbroking. *Economica* 20, no. 77:10–23.

Money Mart. 2006. Website. Accessed 22 March 2010. http://www.moneymart.ca/.

Montgomerie, Johnna. 2006a. The Financialization of the American Credit Card Industry. *Competition and Change* 10, no. 3:301–19.

– 2006b. Giving Credit Where It's Due: Public Policy and Household Debt in the United States, the United Kingdom, and Canada. *Policy and Society* 25, no. 3:109–41.

– 2007. The Logic of Neo-liberalism and the Political Economy of Consumer Debt-Led Growth. In *Neo-liberalism, State Power and Global Governance*, edited by Simon Lee and Stephen McBride. Dordrecht, Netherlands: Springer.

Montgomerie, Johnna, and Karel Williams. 2009. Financialised Capitalism: After the Crisis and beyond Neoliberalism. *Competition and Change* 13, no.2:99–107.

Mullainathan, Sendhil, and Eldar Shafir. 2009. Savings Policy and Decision-Making in Low-Income Households. In *Insufficient Funds: Savings, Assets, Credit, and Banking among Low-Income Households*, edited by R.M. Blank and Michael Barr. New York: Russell Sage.

Mullainathan, Sendhil, and Richard H. Thaler. 2000. *Behavioral Economics*. National Bureau of Economic Research, Working Papers 7948.

– 2001. Behavioral Economics. In *International Encyclopedia of the Social and Behavioral Sciences*, edited by Neil J. Smelser and Paul B. Baltes. Amsterdam: Elsevier.

Murray, John. 2010. Banking on a Better System: Lessons from Canada. Presentation by Deputy Governor of the Bank of Canada at the American University, Washington, DC, 7 April.

Nares, Peter, and Jennifer Robson-Haddow. 2003. Poverty Is About Assets as Well as Income. *Horizons* 6, no. 3:51–4.

National Australia Bank. n.d. NAB Small Loans Pilot Project. Accessed 24 March 2010. http://www.nab.com.au/wps/wcm/connect/nab/nab/home/about_us/4/3/6.

– n.d. No Interest Loan Schemes (NILS®). Accessed 24 March 2010. http://www.nab.com.au/wps/wcm/connect/nab/nab/home/about_us/4/3/3.

– n.d. StepUP Loans. Accessed 24 March 2010. http://www.nab.com.au/wps/wcm/connect/nab/nab/home/About_Us/4/3/4/.

National Bank of Canada. 2009. *Annual Report 2008.* Montreal: National Bank of Canada.

National Cash Advance. 2009. Website. Accessed 16 December 2009. http://www.nationalcashadvance.ca/findacenter.php.

National Council of Welfare. 1998. *Banking and Poor People: Talk Is Cheap.* Ottawa: Minister of Public Works and Government Services Canada.

– 2006. *Welfare Incomes 2005.* Ottawa: Minister of Public Works and Government Services Canada.

North, Douglas. 1990. *Institutions, Institutional Change, and Economic Performance.* Cambridge: Cambridge University Press.

Nova Scotia Utility and Review Board. 2010. Payday Loans Documents. Accessed 16 March 2010. http://www.nsuarb.ca/index.php?option=com_cont entandtask=viewandid=36andItemid=27.

Nussbaum, Martha C. 2006. *Frontiers of Justice: Disability, Nationality, Species Membership.* Boston: Harvard University Press.

OECD (Organisation for Economic Co-operation and Development). 2005. *Improving Financial Literacy: Analysis of Issues and Policies.* Paris and Washington, DC: OECD.

– 2006. *Economic Outlook,* November 2006, no. 80. Paris: OECD.

Office of the Superintendent of Financial Institutions Canada (OSFI). 2010a. Financial Data: Banks. Accessed 22 March 2010. http://www.osfi-bsif.gc.ca/osfi/index_e.aspx?ArticleID=554.

– 2010b. Table of OFSI Guidelines. Accessed 18 June 2009. http://www.osfi-bsif.gc.ca/osfi/index_e.aspx?DetailID=527.

– 2010c. Who We Regulate: Deposit-Taking Institutions. Accessed 22 March 2010. http://www.osfi-bsif.gc.ca/osfi/index_e.aspx?DetailID=568.

– n.d. Financial Data: Banks. Accessed 16 March 2010. http://www.osfi-bsif.gc.ca/osfi/index_e.aspx?ArticleID=554.

Ontario Ministry of Consumer Services. 2010. Payday Lending. Accessed 16 March 2010. http://www.sse.gov.on.ca/mcs/en/Pages/Payday_ Lending.aspx.

Osberg, Lars, 2009. Our Employment Insurance System Far Below OECD Average. *CCPA Monitor* 16, no. 4:1.

Ostrom, Elinor. 1990. *Governing the Commons: The Evolution of Institutions for Collective Action*. Cambridge: Cambridge University Press.

Pahl, Jan. 2008. Family Finances, Individualisation, Spending Patterns and Access to Credit. *Journal of Socio-economics* 37, no. 2:577–91.

Perkins, Dwight H., Steven Radelet, Donald R. Snodgrass, Malcolm Gillis, and Michael Roemer. 2001. *Economics of Development*. 5th ed. New York: W.W. Norton & Co.

Personal Finance Research Centre. 2005. *Measuring Financial Capability: An Exploratory Study*. Vol. 37. London: Financial Services Authority.

Phipps, Shelley, and Frances Wooley. 2008. Control over Money and the Savings Decisions of Canadian Households. *Journal of Socio-economics* 37, no.2:592–611.

Picot, Garnet. 2009. Personal Communication. 3 March.

Pierce, Nancy. 2008a. *Payday Lending: A REAL Solutions® Implementation Guide*. Washington, DC: National Credit Union Foundation.

– 2008b. *Payday Lending: The Credit Union Way*. Madison, WI: CUNA Lending Council.

Pollard, J.S. 1996. Banking at the Margins: A Geography of Financial Exclusion in Los Angeles. *Environment and Planning A* 28, 1209–32.

Public Interest Advocacy Centre. 2003. *Consumers and Financial Institutions: A Public Perspective on the Industry*. Ottawa: Public Interest Advocacy Centre.

Pyper, Wendy. 2007. Payday Loans. *Perspectives on Labour and Income*, April, 5.

Ramsay, Iain. 2000. *Access to Credit in the Alternative Consumer Credit Market*. Industry Canada Office of Consumer Affairs and British Columbia Ministry of the Attorney General.

– 2001. The Alternative Consumer Credit Market and Financial Sector: Regulatory Issues and Approaches. *Canadian Business Law Journal* 35, no. 3:325–401.

– 2003. Of Payday Loans and Usury. *Canadian Business Law Journal* 38, no. 3:386–93.

Robinson, Chris. 2006. *Regulation of Payday Lending in Canada: A Report to ACORN*. Toronto: ACORN Canada.

– 2007. An Introductory Guide to the Payday Lending Industry in Canada. A report to the Public Utilities Board of Manitoba. http://financial-exclusion.uwinnipeg.ca.

– 2009. Personal Communication. June.

Robson, Jennifer, and Peter Nares, eds. 2006. *Asset-Building in Canada*. Toronto: Social and Enterprise Development Innovations.

Rogaly, Ben. 1998. Combating Financial Exclusion through Co-operatives: Is There a Role for External Assistance? *Journal of International Development* 10, no. 6:823–36.

Rogaly, Ben, Thomas Fisher, and Ed Mayo. 1999. *Poverty, Social Exclusion and Microfinance in Britain*. London: Oxfam.

Royal Bank of Canada (RBC). 2009a. *2008 Annual Report*. Toronto: Royal Bank of Canada.

– 2009b. *2008 Corporate Responsibility Report*. Toronto: Royal Bank of Canada.

– 2010. *Annual Report 2009*. Toronto: Royal Bank of Canada.

Rutherford, Stuart. 2000. *The Poor and Their Money*. Oxford: Oxford University Press.

– 2002. *Money Talks: Conversations with Poor Households in Bangladesh about Managing Money*. Edited by Colin Kirkpatrick. Vol. 45. Manchester, UK: Institute for Development Policy and Management, University of Manchester.

Ruthven, Orlanda. 2002. Money Mosaics: Financial Choice and Strategy in a West Delhi Squatter Settlement. *Journal of International Development* 14, no. 2:249–71.

Ruthven, Orlanda, and Sushil Kumar. 2002. *Fine-Grain Finance: Financial Choice and Strategy among the Poor in Rural North India*. Manchester, UK: Institute for Development Policy and Management, University of Manchester.

Scotiabank. 2009a. *2008 Corporate Social Responsibility Report*. Toronto: Scotiabank.

– 2009b. *Annual Report 2008*. Toronto: Scotiabank.

Sen, Amartya. 1999. *Development as Freedom*. New York: Alfred A. Knopf.

Service Alberta. 2010. Payday Lending. Accessed 16 March 2010. http://www.servicealberta.gov.ab.ca/pdf/tipsheets/Payday_Lending.pdf.

Service Nova Scotia and Municipal Relations. 2010. Consumer Information: Payday Loans. Accessed 16 March 2010. http://www.gov.ns.ca/snsmr/consumer/paydayloans/default.asp.

Shafir, Eldar, and Richard H. Thaler. 2006. Invest Now, Drink Later, Spend Never: On the Mental Accounting of Delayed Consumption. *Journal of Economic Psychology* 27, no. 5:694–712.

Shaw, Martin. 2003. The Global Transformation of the Social Sciences. In *Global Civil Society 2003*, edited by Helmut Anheier, Marlies Glasius, and Mary Kaldor. Oxford: Oxford University.

Shefrin, Hersh M., and Richard H. Thaler. 1993. The Behavioral Life-Cycle Hypothesis. In *Economics and Psychology*, edited by Shlomo Maital and Sharone L. Maital. Cheltenham, UK: Edward Elgar.

Sherraden, Michael. 1991. *Assets and the Poor: A New American Welfare Policy*. Armonk, NY: M.E. Sharpe, Inc.

–, ed. 2005. *Inclusion in the American Dream: Assets, Poverty, and Public Policy*. Oxford and New York: Oxford University Press.

Sherraden, Michael, and Michael S. Barr. 2004. *Institutions and Inclusion in Saving Policy*. Boston: Joint Center for Housing Studies, Harvard University.
– 2005. Institutions and Inclusion in Saving Policy. In *Creating Wealth in Low-Income Communities*, edited by E. Belsky. Washington, DC: Brookings Press.
Sherraden, Michael, Mark Schreiner, and Sondra Beverly. 2003. Income, Institution, and Saving Performance in Individual Development Accounts. *Economic Development Quarterly* 14, 95–112.
Shragge, Eric. 1993. *Community Economic Development: In Search of Empowerment*, Montreal: Black Rose.
Siklos, Pierre L. 2004. *Money, Banking, and Financial Institutions: Canada in the Global Environment*. 4th ed. Toronto: McGraw-Hill Ryerson.
Silver, Jim, Parvin Ghorayshi, Joan Hay, and Darlene Klyne. 2006. *In a Voice of Their Own: Urban Aboriginal Community Development*.
Simpson, Wayne, and Jerry Buckland. 2009. Examining Evidence of Financial and Credit Exclusion in Canada from 1999 to 2005. *Journal of Socio-economics* 38, no. 6:966–76.
Skiba, Paige Marta, and Jeremy Bruce Tobacman. 2008. Uncertainty and Discounting: Explaining Patterns of Borrowing, Repayment, and Default (21 August). Vanderbilt Law and Economics Research Paper no. 08–33. http://ssrn.com/abstract=1319751.
Smith, Adam. 2001. The Theory of Moral Sentiments. Electronic Text Center, University of Virginia Library. http://etext.lib.virginia.edu/modeng/modengS.browse.html (accessed 5 July 2011).
Smyth, Sara. 2001. Criminalizing Usury: The Evoluation and Application of S.347 of the *Criminal Code. Review of Current Law and Law Reform*, 7, 24–31.
Social and Enterprise Development Innovations (SEDI). 2004. *Financial Capability and Poverty: Discussion Paper*. Ottawa: Policy Research Initiative.
– 2008a. *Delivery Models for Financial Literacy Interventions: A Case Study Approach*. Ottawa: Social and Enterprise Development Innovations.
– 2008b. *Financial Literacy: Resources for Newcomers to Canada*. Ottawa: Social and Enterprise Development Innovations.
Social and Enterprise Development Innovations (SEDI), and St Christopher House. 2006. *Financial Capability: Learning from Canadian Communities*. Toronto: Social and Economic Development Innovations.
Solo, Tova M., Clemente R. Duran, and John P. Caskey. 2006. *The Urban Unbanked in Mexico and the United States*. World Bank, Policy Research Working Paper Series 3835.
Sorenson's Loans Til Payday. n.d. Website. Accessed 16 December 2009. http://www.loanstilpayday.ca/index.html.

Squires, Gregory D. 2004a. The New Redlining. In *Why the Poor Pay More: How to Stop Predatory Lending*, edited by Gregory D. Squires. Westport, CT: Praeger.

–, ed. 2004b. *Why the Poor Pay More: How to Stop Predatory Lending*. Westport, CT: Praeger.

Squires, Gregory D., and Sally O'Connor. 1998. Fringe Banking in Milwaukee. *Urban Affairs Review* 34, 126–49.

– 2001. *Color and Money: Politics and Prospects for Community Reinvestment in Urban America*. Albany: State University of New York.

Statistics Canada. 1986. The General Social Survey of Canada. Accessed 16 March 2010. http://www.statcan.gc.ca/bsolc/olc-cel/olc-cel?catno=89F0115Xandlang=eng.

– 2005. General Social Survey of Canada. Accessed 16 March 2010. http://www.statcan.gc.ca/bsolc/olc-cel/olc-cel?catno=89F0115Xandlang=eng.

– 2006. Census Tract (CT) Profiles, 2006 Census. Accessed 19 March 2010. http://www12.statcan.gc.ca/census-recensement/2006/dp-pd/prof/92–597/index.cfm?Lang=E.

– 2007a. *Definitions and Concepts Used in Business Register*. Ottawa: Statistics Canada.

– 2007b. *North American Industry Classification System (NAICS) Canada*. Catalogue no. 12–501-XIE.

– 2009. Canadian Financial Capability Survey. Accessed 20 March 2009. http://www.statcan.gc.ca/cgi-bin/imdb/p2SV.pl?Function=getSurveyandSDDS=5159andlang=enanddb=imdbandadm=8anddis=2.

– 2011. Census Tract (CT) Profiles, 2006 Census, Catalogue no. 92–597-XWE.

– n.d. *Table 282, Labour Force Survey Estimates (LFS), by North American Industry Classification System (NAICS), Sex and Age Group, Unadjusted for Seasonality, Monthly (Persons Unless Otherwise Noted)*. CANSIM (database). Using E-STAT (distributor). Last updated 26 July 2007. Accessed 19 June 2009. http://estat.statcan.gc.ca/cgi-win/CNSMCGI.EXE?CANSIMFILE=EStat\English\CII_1_E.htm.

– n.d. *Table 384, Sources and Disposition of Personal Income, Provincial Economic Accounts, Annual (Dollars)*. CANSIM (database). Using E-STAT (distributor). Last updated 26 July 2007. Accessed 19 June 2009. http://estat.statcan.gc.ca/cgi-win/CNSMCGI.EXE?CANSIMFILE=EStat\English\CII_1_E.htm.

– n.d. *Table 2020705, Gini Coefficients of Market, Total and After-Tax Income, by Economic Family Type*. CANSIM (database). Using CHASS (distributor). Last updated 6 June 2008. Accessed 19 June 2009. http://dc2.chass.utoronto.ca/cgi-bin/cansimdim/c2_searchCansim.pl.

– n.d. *Table 2020706, Adjusted and Unadjusted Market, Total and After-Tax Income by Economic Family Type and Adjusted After-Tax Income Quintiles, 2007 Constant Dollars, Annually.* CANSIM (database). Using CHASS (distributor). Last updated 6 June 2008. Accessed 19 June 2009. http://dc2.chass.utoronto.ca/cgi-bin/cansimdim/c2_searchCansim.pl.

– n.d. *Table 2020803, Low Income Cut-Offs after Tax, 1992 Base; Number of Families; Total Families in Low Income.* CANSIM (database). Using CHASS (distributor). Last updated 6 June 2008. Accessed 19 June 2009. http://dc2.chass.utoronto.ca/cgi-bin/cansimdim/c2_searchCansim.pl.

– n.d. *Table 2030015, Survey of Household Spending (SHS), Household Spending on Miscellaneous Expenses (Legal, Financial), by Province and Territory.* CANSIM (database). Using CHASS (distributor). Last updated 6 June 2008. Accessed 19 June 2009. http://dc2.chass.utoronto.ca/cgi-bin/cansimdim/c2_search-Cansim.pl.

– n.d. *Table 3800009, Personal Expenditure on Goods and Services, Quarterly (Dollars).* CANSIM (database). Using CHASS (distributor). Last updated 6 June 2008. Accessed 19 June 2009. http://dc2.chass.utoronto.ca/cgi-bin/cansimdim/c2_searchCansim.pl.

Stegman, Michael A. 2001. The Public Policy Challenges of Payday Lending. *Popular Government* 66, no. 3:16–22.

– 2007. Payday Lending. *Journal of Economic Perspectives* 21, no. 1:169–90.

Stegman, Michael A., and Robert Farris. 2003. Payday Lending: A Business Model That Encourages Chronic Borrowing. *Economic Development Quarterly* 17, 8–32.

Stiglitz, Joseph E. 2002. *Globalization and Its Discontents.* New York: W.W. Norton.

– 2003. Information and the Change in the Paradigm of Economics, Part 2. *TheAmerican Economist* 48, no. 1:17–49.

– 2004a. Capital-Market Liberalization, Globalization, and the IMF. *Oxford Review of Economic Policy* 20, no. 1:57–71.

– 2004b. Information and the Change on the Paradigm in Economics, Part 2. *American Economist* 48, no. 1:17–49.

Stiglitz, Joseph, and Bruce Greenwood. 2003. *Towards a New Paradigm in Monetary Economics.* Cambridge: Cambridge University Press.

Stiglitz, Joseph, and Andrew Weiss. 1981. Credit Rationing in Markets with Imperfect Information. *American Economic Review* 71, no. 3:393–410.

Stoeker, Randy. 2005. *Research Methods for Community Change: A Project-Based Approach.* Thousand Oaks, CA: Sage Publications.

Stratcom Strategic Communications. 2005. *Survey of Payday Loan Users in Toronto and Vancouver.* Vancouver: ACORN Canada.

Sunstein, Cass R., and Richard H. Thaler. 2006. Preferences, Paternalism, and Liberty. *Royal Institute of Philosophy Supplement*, no. 59:233–64.

Tashakkori, Abbas, and Charles Teddle, eds. 2003. *Handbook of Mixed Methods in Social and Behavioral Research.* Thousand Oaks, CA: Sage Publications.

Task Force on Financial Literacy. n.d. *Executive Summary. Canadians and Their Money: Building a Brighter Financial Future.* Ottawa: Task Force on Financial Literacy.

Task Force on the Future of the Canadian Financial Services Sector. 1998a. Canadians' Expectations and Corporate Conduct. Background paper no. 4. Ottawa: Department of Finance.

– 1998b. *Task Force Report on the Future of the Canadian Financial Services Sector* (MacKay Report). Ottawa: Department of Finance, Canada.

TD Bank Financial Group. 2005. *From Welfare to Work in Ontario: Still the Road Less Travelled.* TD Economics Special Report. Toronto: TD Bank Financial Group.

–. 2009a. *2008 Corporate Responsibility Report.* Toronto: TD Bank Financial Group.

– 2009b. *Annual Report 2008.* Toronto: TD Bank Financial Group.

Tebbutt, Melaine. 1983. *Making Ends Meet: Pawnbroking and Working Class Credit.* New York: St Martin's Press.

Temkin, Kenneth, and Noah Sawyer. n.d. *Analysis of Alternative Financial Service Providers.* Washington, DC: Urban Institute Metropolitan Housing and Communities Policy Center.

Thaler, Richard H. 1992. How to Get People to Save. In *Personal Saving, Consumption, and Tax Policy,* edited by Marvin H. Kosters. Washington DC: American Enterprise Institute.

– 1999. The End of Behavioral Finance. *Financial Analysts Journal* 55, no. 6:12.

– 2000a. From Homo Economicus to Homo Sapiens. *Journal of Economic Perspectives* 14, no. 1:133–41.

– 2000b. Toward a Positive Theory of Consumer Choice. In *Choices, Values, and Frames,* edited by Daniel Kahneman and Amos Tversky. Cambridge: Cambridge University Press; New York: Russell Sage Foundation.

– 2004. Mental Accounting Matters. In *Advances in Behavioral Economics,* edited by Colin F. Camerer, George Loewenstein, and Matthew Rabin. Roundtable Series in Behavioral Economics. New York; Russell Sage Foundation; Princeton and Oxford: Princeton University Press.

–, ed. 2005. *Advances in Behavioral Finance, Volume 2.* Princeton and Oxford: Princeton University Press; New York: Russell Sage Foundation.

– 2008. Mental Accounting and Consumer Choice. *Markeing Science* 27, no. 1:15–25.

Thaler, Richard H., and Shlomo Benartzi. 2007. Save More Tomorrow: Using Behavioral Economics to Increase Employee Saving. In *Recent Developments in Behavioral Economics*, edited by Shlomo Maital. Elgar Reference Collection, International Library of Critical Writings in Economics, vol. 204. Cheltenham, UK, and Northampton, MA: Elgar.

Thaler, Richard H., and Cass R. Sunstein. 2003. Libertarian Paternalism. *American Economic Review* 93, no. 2:175–9.

– 2008. *Nudge: Improving Decisions about Health, Wealth, and Happiness*. New Haven, CT, and London: Yale University Press.

Todaro, Michael P., and Stephen C. Smith. 2006. *Economic Development*. 10th ed. Boston: Addison-Wesley.

United Kingdom. HM Treasury. 2004. *Promoting Financial Inclusion*. London: HM Treasury.

– n.d. Financial Inclusion. The National Archives. Accessed 12 January 2010. http://www.hm-treasury.gov.uk/fin_inclusion_index.htm.

United Kingdom. House of Commons Treasury Committee. 2006. *Financial Inclusion: The Roles of the Government and the FSA, and Financial Capability*. London: Stationary Office.

United Nations Development Program (UNDP). 2007–8. *Human Development Report*. New York: UNDP.

United States Federal Reserve Board. 2010. Federal Reserve Statistical Release. Accessed February 2010. http://www.federalreserve.gov/releases/h15/data.htm.

Vancity Credit Union. 2007. *Accountability Report 06–07*. Vancouver: Vancity Credit Union.

Vaziri, Mo. 2006. Islamic Finance, Rural Cooperative Financial Institutions (Credit Unions), and Micro Financing Strategies. *Investment Management and Financial Innovations* 3, no. 2:18–33.

Western Economic Diversification Canada. 2009. Funding for Business. Accessed 14 January 2010. http://www.wd.gc.ca/eng/259.asp.

Williams, Marva. 2007. *Cooperative Credit: How Community Development Credit Unions Are Meeting the Need for Affordable, Short-Term Credit*. Chicago: Woodstock Institute.

Williams, Marva, and Valjean McLenighan. 2004. *Building Community Assets: A Guide to Credit Union Partnerships*. Chicago: Woodstock Institute.

Williamson, Oliver E. 2000. The New Institutional Economics: Taking Stock, Looking Ahead. *Journal of Economic Literature* 38, no. 3:595–613.

Wilson, Alan M. 1998. The Use of Mystery Shopping in the Measurement of Service Delivery. In *Service Industries Marketing: New Approaches*, edited by Gillian Hogg and Mark Gabbott. London: Frank Cass.

Winnipeg Police Service. 2007. Pawn Unit. Accessed 16 March 2010. http://www.winnipeg.ca/police/Units_and_Divisions/pawn_unit.stm.

Woodstock Institute. 2003. Community Development Banks Substantially Outscore Other Banks in Serving Low-Income and Minority Communities: Implications for the Federal Budget and the Community Reinvestment Act. *Reinvestment Alert* 19, 1–4.

World Bank. 2009. *Banking the Poor: Measuring Banking Access in 54 Economies.* Washington, D C: World Bank.

World Council of Credit Unions. 2010. Website. Accessed 13 January 2010. http://woccu.org.

Yinger, John. 1998. Evidence on Discrimination in Consumer Markets. *Journal of Economic Perspectives* 12, no. 2:23–40.

Zelizer, Viviana. 1997. Poor People's Money. In *The Social Meaning of Money.* Princeton, NJ: Princeton University Press.

– 2000. Fine Tuning the Zelizer View. *Economy and Society* 29, no. 3:383–9.

Zinman, Jonathan. 2008. *Restricting Consumer Credit Access: Household Survey Evidence on Effects around the Oregon Rate Cap.* Federal Reserve Bank of Philadelphia, Working Papers 08–32.

Index

disclosure, 37, 167; financial challenges, 37–38; foreign investment in, 53–54; foreign outlets, 127; as fringe banks, 35, 37–38; geographic spatial analyses, 103–5, 104*t*; history of, 148*t*, 152; impact on consumers' lives, 99, 219*n*11; increase in, 168; information accessibility, 117; interest annual percentage rate (APR), 51, 107, 213*n*28; interest caps, 168; labour-intensive operations, 137–39; neoclassical economics and, 65–66; overview of, 37–38, 127–28, 145–48*t*; profitability and size, 127–30, 129*t*; regulations for, 37, 42, 142, 202; returns on equity, 37–38; scale and scope efficiencies, 38, 131–32, 135–36; trends in, 111; usury ceilings, 167–68; in Western Canada, 151. *See also* Cash Store Financial Inc.; National Money Mart

payday loans: behavioural economics and, 74; hearing on loan fee caps, 113–14, 215*n*5; information accessibility, 114–15; life cycle–permanent income theory, 67; overview of, 35; tied selling and, 50; trends in, 24, 111, 168

perfect competition. *See* competition

personal identification. *See* identification, personal

PHS Community Services Society, 186, 189, 195, 196, 208

Pigeon Park Savings (Vancouver): access by public to, 188; consumer survey, 118*t*; cross-cultural dialogue, 194–95; fees, 186; financial challenges, 190–94, 193*t*; innovation, 189–90; membership numbers, 192, 193*t*; overview of, 96, 186–87, 191–92; partnerships, 186–87, 191, 208–10; personal identification, 173, 189

political economy theory: methods, 61; overview of, 59–62, 79–81; poverty and community analyses, 83; power imbalances, 60–61; in rationality-institutions diagram, 62–63*t*; tiering of financial service markets, 81

Poor Pay More, The (Caplovitz), xiii, 5, 84, 88–89, 199–200

Portland Hotel Society, 186. *See also* PHS Community Services Society

postal banks, 54–55, 177

poverty: culture of poverty theories, 27, 73, 78; financial exclusion and, 7–8, 24, 199–201; gender and, 99; overview of theories, 59–62; poverty and community analyses, 83; poverty reduction, 154

poverty and community theory: overview of, 83; qualitative methods, 83; research studies, 88–92

Poverty, Social Exclusion, and Microfinance in Britain (Rogaly, Fisher, and Mayo), 90–91

PPS. *See* Pigeon Park Savings (Vancouver)

Prince Edward Island, payday lenders, 149*t*

product design: cheque holds, 108–10, 173; overview of, 108–10; personal identification, 108–10; reform proposals for mainstream banks, 118–19*t*